Lidia Zamenhof 1904–1942

LIDIA

The Life of Lidia Zamenhof
Daughter of Esperanto

by

Wendy Heller

GEORGE RONALD

OXFORD

WENDY HELLER was born in California and is a graduate of the University of California, Berkeley, where she studied languages. She has published articles and books on a wide variety of subjects. Four decades after Lidia Zamenhof's death, her story was all but lost until Wendy Heller reconstructed it piece by piece from personal interviews, archival files, documents and rare periodicals that escaped the destruction of World War II. *Lidia* is her fifth book.

Cover illustration by Marjan Nirou

GEORGE RONALD, Publisher
46 High Street, Kidlington, Oxford OX5 2DN

British Library Cataloguing in Publication Data

Heller, Wendy
    Lidia: life of Lidia Zamenhof, daughter of Esperanto.
    1. Zamenhof, Lidia   2. Bahais—Biography
    3. Esperanto—History
    I. Title
    297'.89'0924   BP395.Z3

    ISBN 0-85398-194-9
    ISBN 0-85398-195-7 Pbk

Printed and bound in Great Britain at
The Camelot Press Ltd, Southampton

Contents

CONTENTS

Illustrations

To
Dorothy J. Heller

If not now, when?

— Hillel

Preface

When in 1976 I first became interested in writing about Lidia Zamenhof, I knew very little about her and next to nothing about Esperanto, the language her father had created. I had read an article by Ugo and Angeline Giachery about Lidia, and it had evoked my immediate sympathy and interest, since, as a Bahá'í from a Russian and German Jewish background, I had some things in common with Lidia. I was curious to find out more about her. How, I wondered, had a young woman of her era made the decision to forgo marriage and, during the difficult days of the Great Depression, to devote her life to being an itinerant teacher of the language invented by her father? And, given her extraordinary devotion to the Esperanto movement, how and why had Lidia Zamenhof embraced the Bahá'í Faith?

There was no biography of Lidia available. I decided to write one; but it was not until 1980 that I was able to begin research for the project. Then I was faced by the question of where to begin. At first I despaired when I learned that the Zamenhof home, with all the family's papers, had been destroyed in the war. Nevertheless, I discovered, a significant amount of material had been preserved in archives in several countries as well as by individuals who had known Lidia and on whom she had made such an impression that they could not bear to throw away her letters, even after half a century had passed. In one case at least, much information was preserved intentionally with an eye to the future; during Lidia's visit to the United States, Mrs Della Quinlan persuaded her to leave behind the papers she had accumulated during her stay and donate them to the National Bahá'í Archives in Wilmette, Illinois, for future researchers. This researcher would like to acknowledge with gratitude the foresight of the late Mrs Quinlan.

The search for the answers to my questions about Lidia Zamenhof led me to explore paths I had not foreseen when I began my project; in fact, through research trips and correspondence, that search took me all over the world. I began with the one Esperantist I knew of: Mrs Roan Orloff Stone. This proved to be the best thing I could have done. Not only did Mrs Stone provide many leads which eventually led to further sources of information, but because she had been a close friend of

Lidia's she contributed invaluable personal glimpses, shared her letters with me, and granted me long interviews; later, she patiently reviewed my Esperanto translations and answered my many questions. For her kind and essential assistance I owe a great debt of gratitude.

I quickly realized that to do research about Lidia I would simply have to learn Esperanto. Although I had studied several other languages, I wasn't looking forward to the prospect of having to learn yet another language just in order to write a book. But I was surprised to find I could soon read Esperanto better than languages I had studied for years. Being used to associating other meanings with particular sound combinations, I found some of Esperanto's terms odd at first, but the strangeness soon wore off. I became impressed by the ideals underlying Esperanto as well as the tenacity of the language, now nearly a hundred years old, to endure – to withstand schism, war and persecution – to face the apathy and mockery of the general public, yet attract the praise of some of the most esteemed scientific, political, literary and religious figures of the age.

Esperantists often praise the practical usefulness of the language as a neutral medium of international communication, but the real meaning of this did not impress itself on me until I found myself in need of a certain piece of information about Lidia which could only be provided by a certain person in Sweden. Swedish was not one of my languages and my correspondent did not know English. But no matter; Esperanto gave us a bridge to communicate with one another. Time and again this occurred, and the instant collapse of the language barrier almost left an audible crash. Without Esperanto I would never have been able to communicate with many of the people, of various nationalities, whose reminiscences provided the information for this book.

Perhaps because the book is in English it is easy to overlook an important point which readers should be aware of: a great many of the primary and secondary sources I drew on were in Esperanto, including nearly all those regarding Lidia herself. For the most part, Lidia lived her life in Esperanto: she wrote, gave speeches, confided her deepest thoughts to friends, all in Esperanto. Those who leap to criticize the language of Dr Zamenhof as not being a living or a cultural tongue should note that Lidia Zamenhof not only lived and worked in Esperanto but expressed herself eloquently in the language, in images that have not lost their vividness, or in many cases, their relevance, after half a century.

Because one cannot understand a person without knowing something of the historical, cultural, social and spiritual environment within which that person lived her life, I found myself exploring Lidia's family history and the impressive figure of Ludwik Zamenhof, as well as the language he created and the ideals and beliefs Lidia shared with him and which played such an important role in her life. I discovered that Lidia and I had more in common than I had first thought. In 1980 I was astonished to discover a short story she had published in 1929 in *Pola Esperantisto* ('Polish Esperantist') called *'Birdo en kaĝo!'* ('Bird in a Cage!'). I knew at once the source of her inspiration for that story – a passage in *Some Answered Questions* by 'Abdu'l-Bahá – because my own, very similar tale inspired by the same statement had been published as a children's book in 1979 under the title *Clementine and the Cage*.

The story of the life of Lidia Zamenhof touches many other subjects – the history of the Jews in Poland, the life and thought of Ludwik Zamenhof, the Esperanto movement, the Bahá'í Faith, the two world wars, the Holocaust. Naturally, in this biography it was only possible and desirable to include just enough details about any of these as to provide a background for Lidia's own story. The necessity to compress history into a background for a portrait means that one must regretfully omit many events of the period covered which, however interesting and important in their own right, were not of crucial significance in the subject's own life. The story of Ludwik Zamenhof, as presented in this book, is merely a brief sketch and by no means complete. I hope that readers will finish the book with a curiosity to learn more about him, as well as other topics touched upon, and I encourage them to do so. Readers of English are fortunate to have available Marjorie Boulton's biography, *Zamenhof, Creator of Esperanto* (London: Routledge and Kegan Paul, 1960).

I hope that I will be forgiven for not providing bibliographical footnotes. As this is not intended as a scholarly or academic book, I felt that, for the majority of readers, such footnotes would be more of a hindrance than a help since many of the sources are not readily available to the general reader. For the benefit of those interested, a note on sources is appended.

For the most part, quoted passages originally in Esperanto were translated by me, with the exception of some excerpts from the speeches and writings of Ludwik Zamenhof, which were translated by Marjorie Boulton and are reprinted with the kind permission of Dr Boulton and her English publisher, Routledge and Kegan Paul. I would also like to thank Dr Boulton, who is a noted Esperanto poet, for translating the poem *'Lidia Zamenhof, kor fervora . . .'* by Kálmán Kalocsay, specially for this book.

Some readers may note that in other published works Lidia's name is often given as 'Lidja'. Until about 1936 she used that spelling, but after that date she spelled her name 'Lidia' in accord with official changes in Polish orthography introduced that year. Because this was her choice, I have followed it throughout this book and have taken the liberty of changing quoted material to conform to this style.

Place names have been given as in Webster's Dictionary, or, if not listed therein, as found in the New Oxford Atlas.

This book could never have been written without the assistance of a large number of people all over the world, who gave generously of their time, their hospitality and their memories. I would like to express my deep gratitude to Mrs Roan Orloff Stone and Mr Jim Stone for their hospitality in addition to the enormous help, mentioned above, which Mrs Stone has generously given me over the years.

I am greatly indebted to Dr Kent Beveridge of Vienna, Austria, for his patient and tireless efforts, including all the translations of material in German quoted in Chapter 5, arranging interviews for me in Vienna, uncovering and pursuing the story of Fritz Macco, obtaining documents and photographs and searching without complaint for the answers to my endless questions.

The assistance, over the years, of Dr André Védrine of Lyon, France, has been invaluable. Dr Védrine generously gave of his time and effort, gathering information about Lidia Zamenhof in France and locating people who had known her. It was largely through his efforts that I was able to find out so much about the period Lidia spent in France. The Esperantists of France were extremely helpful, sending me letters, reminiscences and photographs. I must mention in particular the Esperantists of Lyon and Villeurbanne, whose kindness, hospitality and enthusiasm showed me at once why Lidia came to feel that Lyon was a second home: Blanche Clavier, Pierre Dehan, Yvonne Gallon, Raymond Gonin and Mrs Gonin, Cécile Pral, René Lemaire, Gabriel and Marie Antoinette 'Olga' Eyssautier, Dr André Védrine and Ida Védrine. Others who, thanks to the efforts of Dr Védrine, contributed valuable information were Jean Amouroux, Félicien Baronnet, Giselle Baudry, Paule Raynaud Delafouilhouze, E. Caille, Georges Cau, Marcel Delcourt, Andrée Dessapt, Vidal Gaston, Jean Gibaux, André Gilles, Antoinette Guigues, Roland Jossinet and L. Robert.

I am also grateful to the many others, from many countries, who kindly allowed me access to their personal letters, photographs and reminiscences, and who made suggestions and provided other assistance, including Hans Bakker, Mies Bakker-Smith, Marc Bakker, Isaj Dratwer, Alice Dudley, Elcore Ebersole, Anna Grossmann, Dr Hartmut Grossmann, Gigi Harabagiu, Christian Haug, Marion Hofman, Adolf Holzhaus, Jan Jasion, Luise Lappinger, Christian Lauridsen, Anthony A. Lee, Helene and Martin Leonard, Doris Lohse, Irmgard Macco, Margot Miessler Malkin, Samuel E. Martin, Louise Baker Matthias, Ursula Mühlschlegel, Melinda Öjermark, Anna Pöllinger, Margaret Ruhe, Dr Charles E. Simon; Don Slocum, Lee D.

Stern, Ronald Taherzadeh, Henk Thien and Steve Tomlin. I would like to express my deep appreciation to Eugen Rytenberg for his invaluable contributions.

I was grateful for the opportunity to consult the collections of the British Library as well as the library of the British Esperanto Association, where the staff were very kind and helpful; and the libraries of the University of Geneva, Switzerland; Stanford University; the University of California, Los Angeles; the University of California, San Diego; the Simon Wiesenthal Library at Yeshiva University, Los Angeles; as well as the Los Angeles and San Francisco Bahá'í Libraries. The staff at the Stat- und Universitätsbibliothek of Bern, Switzerland, deserve special acknowledgement for their kindness and assistance beyond the call of duty.

My thanks are due to the staff of the International Esperanto Museum in Vienna, Dr Walter Hube and Herbert Maerz, for their assistance and for the opportunity to consult documents and periodicals in the Museum's collections, as well as for many of the photographs which appear in this book. I would also like to thank Catherine Schulze of the Esperanto League for North America, and Archivist Hal Dreyer for their help.

I would like to acknowledge the following Bahá'í National Spiritual Assemblies for the use of material from their Archives and for sending material to me: the United States, Hawaii, Japan, Austria, Germany, Switzerland; and the Spiritual Assembly of Urbana, Illinois. In particular I must mention the special assistance of Archivist Roger Dahl, as well as Elaine Schwartz, Dr Duane Troxel, Barbara Sims, Margot Zabih, Elizabeth Hackley and Eleanor Hutchens. To all those individuals who provided help though I didn't know their names, or may inadvertently have neglected to mention them, I am equally grateful.

I would like to express my special gratitude to the Universal House of Justice in Haifa, Israel, for its kind encouragement and assistance, and to the staff of the Audio-Visual Department and Research Department, Audrey Marcus and Ethna Archibald.

My warm appreciation goes to Russell and Ginnie Busey, Rose Lopez D'Amico, Anne-Marie Dupeyron, Mr and Mrs Sergei Blagoveschensky, and Charles and Hilda Pulley for their kindness, hospitality and help; and to Dr Ugo Giachery for his gracious attention, candid recollections and much tea and biscuits.

I am deeply thankful to Dr Marjorie Boulton for her personal assistance and warm hospitality; to Dr Celia Stopnicka Heller, for answering my questions; and to Dr Amin Banani, Dr David Ruhe and Mr Ian Semple for their encouragement: a kind word can go a very long way.

To those who read all or part of the manuscript and offered perceptive comments and valuable editorial and substantive suggestions, I am humbly appreciative: my editor May Ballerio, Gayle Morrison, Dr Amin Banani, Roan Orloff Stone, Jack Weinstein and Jan Jasion.

And finally I would like to acknowledge the members of the Zamenhof family including Dr Stephen Zamenhof and Dr Louis Zaleski-Zamenhof, who kindly gave of their time and recollections and reviewed the manuscript for accuracy; Dr Olga Zamenhof and Miss Mira Horne, for their contributions; and for permission to quote from the published and unpublished works of members of the Zamenhof family.

Above all, without the support, love and patient hard work of Dorothy J. Heller I could never have written, and certainly would never have completed, this book.

Clouds of the Future

By two in the afternoon people had begun to gather outside the Zamenhof home at 41 Królewska Street, on the edge of the Jewish quarter of Warsaw. It was 16 April 1917. The day was dark and rainy, but still they came, wearing solemn black, to the funeral of Dr Lazar Ludwik Zamenhof.

When the clock struck three, the procession began to make its way slowly toward the Jewish cemetery. The mourners followed the coffin, which was borne in an ornate black-canopied hearse. Even the two horses pulling the hearse were draped solemnly for the funeral. A sad-faced man with a white beard and a top-hat drove them.

Many of those who walked behind the coffin that day were poor Jews of Warsaw. They had known Dr Zamenhof as the good-hearted oculist who had treated them and their families for a few kopeks, or, when they could not afford that, for nothing at all. Most of those in the crowd were men, although a few women could be seen among the mourners, some wearing heavy black veils so thick one could not see the faces behind them. There were merchants and workers and young boys in student caps; middle-aged men in bowler hats, some even wearing silk top-hats and carrying canes; and bent old men with long white beards and the traditional long black caftan and cap of Eastern European Jews.

As the procession moved through the streets, more people joined it. Unlike traditional Polish Christian funerals there was no elaborate decoration, no band playing Chopin's funeral march. At Jewish funerals the size of the crowd indicated the importance of the one who had died. The crowd that day was immense.

Among the mourners in the procession was a slight, thirteen-year-old girl with long, blond braids. She would remember that day for the rest of her life. Many years later, she would recall: 'When, one gray, rainy day, the funeral procession turned slowly toward the cemetery, the streets in the quarter where he had lived so long were black with crowds of people. Those men, simple and poor, honored in the departed one a man who with great patience and devotion had cared for their eyes and for many had averted the terrible fate of blindness.' The departed one was her father.

Most of the mourners knew Zamenhof only as the kindly physician. Beyond the borders of his native land, however, he was known as the creator of Esperanto, the international language which was already spoken by thousands of people in countries from Mexico to Japan. Although Dr Zamenhof had admirers all over the world, they could not be there that day in 1917 to pay him their last respects. The world was at war, and Warsaw was occupied by German troops. The borders were closed. Not even all the Zamenhofs could be there. Several members of the family had been in Russia when Warsaw was invaded and were stranded behind the front lines of battle, unable to come home.

Among the solemn procession of Jews who trudged sadly to the cemetery that day, one man stood out conspicuously – a German military officer. Major Neubarth, the harbor commander, who was an Esperantist, and another German were the only foreign representatives at Dr Zamenhof's funeral.

As was typical for an April day in Warsaw, it was cold, although the ice had already melted on the River Vistula. The trees in the Jewish cemetery were still bare as the procession passed beneath them bearing the coffin and carrying armfuls of flowers.

The mourners gathered around the little hill where the grave had been dug. It was a good site, given by the Jewish community of Warsaw for the resting place of one of its most beloved sons. After the rabbi's eulogy, several eminent Warsaw Esperantists spoke emotionally about Dr Zamenhof, whom they revered as *Majstro*, which in Esperanto meant 'master' or 'maestro'. One was Leo Belmont, a well-known poet. Ludwik Zamenhof – the mortal man – had died, said Belmont, 'but Ludwik Zamenhof – brilliant soul, creator of a work that lovingly encompassed all the people of the earth, prophet guiding them on the way of brotherhood . . . did not die, because he is immortal!' The world did not yet appreciate the value of Zamenhof's life work, Belmont told them, but, he predicted, 'His glory will be extraordinary: because I see clearly, through the clouds of the future, a time when in all the capitals of the world his monument will stand!'

Later, the German officer Major Neubarth came forward and solemnly vowed in the name of the Esperantists of Germany that they would not cease to follow the example of Dr Zamenhof. They would be faithful in their Esperanto work, he promised, until the end.

The ancient, sorrowful tones of the Hebrew funeral prayers drifted on the air. Slowly the coffin was lowered into the ground and covered over with earth. Flower wreaths were piled high.

For many years, among the marble monuments in the Jewish

cemetery, only the simplest of tombstones would mark the grave of Ludwik Zamenhof. As the years passed, his daughter Lidia would return many times to this place, to the grave of her father. But now that he was gone, who would carry on his work? Who would strive to achieve his dreams?

ONE

The Doctor and the Dream

Although Lidia Zamenhof was only thirteen when her father died, his work and his dreams would deeply influence her entire life. Indeed, Ludwik Zamenhof had a profound effect on all who met him: his kindly ways, his lofty ideals, had endeared him to thousands who embraced the language he had created. Although his sometimes overzealous admirers showered adoration on him almost as if he were a religious leader, he was a very private and modest man, and such veneration for his person embarrassed and pained him.

Sometimes, children of famous parents find the responsibility of that relationship burdensome and wish to make their own way in the world, independent of the great, hovering shadow of one they can never hope to equal. Zamenhof's children, on the contrary, all chose to devote their lives to the same fields of endeavor as their renowned father had. His son, Adam, became a doctor and even surpassed the elder Zamenhof's fame in ophthalmology. His daughter Zofia also became a physician, specializing in internal medicine and pediatrics. But it was his youngest daughter Lidia who would dedicate her life to the work that had been most dear to Ludwik Zamenhof: the struggle for human unity. As Ludwik had, in his time, Lidia Zamenhof would find her chosen road difficult and would face opposition, frustration and disappointment. But the light of the ideal would always be before her, as it had been for her father, a beacon of hope that shone even in deepest darkness. Because one cannot understand Lidia without knowing something of Ludwik, her story properly begins with his story.

Ludwik Zamenhof was born in 1859 to Markus and Rozalia (Sofer) Zamenhof. He was the first of nine children including Sara (who died in childhood), Fania, Augusta, Feliks, Henryk, Leon, Aleksander and Ida. Ludwik's great-grandfather, Wolf Zamenhof, had come from the province of Kurland, in the southwest part of Latvia, but by the time of Ludwik's birth the Zamenhof family lived in Bialystok, in the district of Grodno, Lithuania, which at that time was part of the Russian Empire. Ludwik's childhood experiences in Bialystok, he later said, so profoundly affected him as to give the direction to all his future endeavors.

History had created in Bialystok a kind of crossroads where people from diverse cultures and nationalities came together, not in brotherhood but in hostility. Young Ludwik was most distressed by the fact that, often, they could not even speak to one another: the Russians, Poles, Germans and Jews of Bialystok spoke their own languages, and each group kept to itself, mistrustful and suspicious of the others. Ludwik learned quickly that he himself belonged to the group that, above all, was the target of suspicion and hatred: the Jews.

Although Jews had lived in the region of Poland since medieval times, when they had come from Germany at the invitation of Polish kings and nobles, they had always been treated as outsiders – accused of being economic exploiters, reviled from the pulpit as killers of Christ. Through the centuries, although there were periods during which the Jews of Poland were protected by royal charter, they were repeatedly subjected to discrimination, segregation and brutality. At times they were restricted to living apart from the Christian population in ghettos. On occasion they were expelled entirely.

The Christians among whom they lived never understood the inner world of the Jewish community. They saw only that the Jews dressed and acted differently, spoke a language that seemed strange to them, and followed religious rituals of an unknown nature. They eventually came to consider the Jews a separate race, an inferior foreign nation, living in their midst.

To the Jews, their own ways were the precious legacy of generations – their bond through the ages to Moses and the Hebrew prophets, back to the very Covenant God had made with Abraham. When they were tormented in the street, beaten and called 'mangy Jew' and 'onion-eaters', such cruelty only convinced the Jews that their own ways were best. They never fought back, but withstood the blows, trusting that God would send them the Messiah and lead them back to their ancient homeland, *Eretz Yisrael*, the Land of Israel. 'Next year', they always said at the close of the Passover service, 'in Jerusalem.'

The Jews saw their persecution as an inevitable part of the suffering they must endure during their exile. Those Jews who were martyred because of their faith, they believed, died for the 'sanctification of the name of God'. When, in the seventeenth century, a hundred thousand Jews were massacred during a decade of violence which had begun with a bloody Cossack uprising in the Ukraine, many Jews thought this unprecedented holocaust a sure sign that the coming of the Messiah must be near and their sufferings would soon end.

During the late 1700s, the Kingdom of Poland was abolished and its territory divided among Russia, Austria and Germany. The eastern territory became part of the Russian Empire. After 1815 the central part of Poland, which included Warsaw, became a semi-autonomous kingdom, subject to Russian rule. The Russian Empire now contained the largest population of Jews in the world, and the Jews would become a convenient scapegoat to divert the discontented masses from economic and political problems into mob violence against helpless men, women and children and the wanton destruction and plundering of their homes, shops and synagogues. The word for these savage attacks became a familiar and terrifying one to the Jews of Eastern Europe: *pogrom*.

As a young boy in Bialystok, Ludwik Zamenhof was not aware of all the complex reasons for the hatred and prejudice he saw around him, but he saw the suffering it caused, and this made a lasting impression on him. His sensitivity to the plight of his own Jewish people would eventually lead him to a concern for the plight of all mankind. 'Had I not been a Jew', he later said, 'the idea of a future cosmopolitanism would not have exercised such a fascination over me, and never should I have labored so strenuously and disinterestedly for the realization of my ideal.'

The most obvious barrier that young Ludwik saw between peoples was the difference of languages. He knew the biblical story of the Tower of Babel, which explained the confusion of tongues as God's punishment for the transgression of the descendants of Noah, who had attempted to build a tower that would reach heaven. As Zamenhof would later say, at that time the confusion of languages had been the result of sin; now it itself had become the cause of evildoing. Diversity of languages was, he felt, 'the only, or at least the chief cause that separates the human family and divides it into hostile factions. I was educated as an idealist: I was taught that all men are brothers, and meanwhile on the street and in the courtyards everything at every step caused me to feel that *men* did not exist: there were only Russians, Poles, Germans, Jews, etc. This always greatly tormented my young soul . . . I told myself that when I was older, I would not fail to do away with this evil.'

Ludwik Zamenhof vowed to give the world a language that all its peoples could use to communicate with one another, and thus, he hoped, to bridge their differences.

But what kind of language would serve as a tongue for all mankind? Of the thousands of languages and dialects in the world, which one to select? Quickly Ludwik abandoned the idea of choosing a living tongue for his 'human language'. No matter which one was chosen, there would be some people who would object. And those people whose native tongue it was would have an advantage over all the others. Choosing any one language could only imply that it was

1. *Markus and Rozalia Zamenhof, Lidia's grandparents, in 1878*

2. *Courtyard of the building where the Zamenhofs lived in the 1870s. Here the schoolboy Ludwik made his first attempts at creating a language*

3. *Ludwik and Klara Zamenhof, the year of their marriage, 1887*

superior in some way and others inferior.

Zamenhof became convinced that the only possible international language would be a neutral one, belonging to none of the living nations. After rejecting the idea of a classical language such as Greek or Latin, he began to dream of *creating* a new language for all mankind.

The problem sometimes seemed beyond him. How could one boy invent a language? 'Human language,' wrote Zamenhof, 'with its endless accumulation of grammatical forms, and its hundreds of thousands of words . . . seemed to me such a colossal and artificial machine that more than once I told myself: "enough of dreams! This enterprise is beyond human powers." And yet, I always came back to my dreams.'

Ludwik Zamenhof was not the first to think of creating a universal language. Proposals for constructing auxiliary languages had been circulated since the seventeenth century – Descartes mentioned the idea in a letter in 1629. In 1878, even before Zamenhof had completed his project, a proposal for a language called *Volapük* (Word Speech) was published by Johann Martin Schleyer, a German Catholic priest, who felt his work to be divinely revealed. But Volapük was arbitrary and difficult. Eventually it died out, its followers bitterly divided over Schleyer's authoritarian attitude and the issue of linguistic reforms.

At the age of fifteen Ludwik Zamenhof began to try to create his language. His first attempts were unsatisfactory, but as the years passed, he continued to work on his project.

By now the Zamenhof family had moved to Warsaw where Ludwik's father, Markus, taught languages. A strict disciplinarian, Markus Zamenhof had no formal education but was self-taught. However, he intended that his sons should go to university.

To earn the necessary money, the Zamenhof family took in boarders, and Markus took up the post of Jewish Censor. At home every night he scrutinized Jewish publications for any statement that might offend the Russian government or the tsar. With the money he earned, Markus was able to educate his sons. Four became doctors and one a pharmacist. As one would expect for that time, none of his daughters went to university.

In 1878 Ludwik was in the eighth class of the *gymnazium*, and his language was, as he wrote later, 'more or less ready'. There was still a great difference between his *Lingwe Uniwersala* (Universal Language) and what would eventually become Esperanto, but the idea, at least, had taken shape. He confided his creation to some of his friends and his brother Feliks. Attracted by Ludwik's idea and the simplicity of the language, they began to learn it.

On 5 December 1878 the small group of friends solemnly celebrated the birth of Lingwe Uniwersala, giving speeches in the new language and singing enthusiastically the anthem Ludwik had written. It began:

> *Malamikete de las nacjes*
> *Kadó, kadó, jam temp' está!*
> *La tot' homoze in familje*
> *Konunigare so debá.*

(Hatred of the nations,
Fall away, fall away, it is already time!
All mankind in one family
Must become united.)

In June, the young men finished school and went their separate ways. But when Ludwik's friends tried to tell others about the new language, they were scoffed at by 'mature' men and immediately repudiated the language. Ludwik found himself alone. He knew that he was still too young to display his creation publicly, and he decided to wait and continue improving the language. Ludwik received another blow when his father, who had tolerated Ludwik's project until now, abruptly became opposed to it. Someone had convinced him that his son's preoccupation with the language might be a sign of insanity. Markus made Ludwik promise to give it up until he had finished his university studies. He took away Ludwik's notebooks containing all his precious work – the entire grammar of the language and the translations he had made – and locked them up.

Soon Ludwik left for Moscow University, where he was to study medicine. In Moscow he was exposed to other intellectual currents, and his idealism took a new direction as he became involved in the early stirrings of what would eventually become the Zionist movement.

Like many young Jews of the time, Ludwik Zamenhof wanted to improve the intolerable situation of the Jewish people in Eastern Europe. His father and grandfather had been followers of the *Haskalah*, the Jewish Enlightenment, and the humanistic, rationalistic, and secularistic ideas which the Haskalah belatedly brought to Eastern European Jewry deeply influenced Ludwik.

Inspired by the Haskalah, and by what had appeared to be a shift toward liberalism on the part of the Russian government, some Jews like Markus Zamenhof had become convinced that if Jews abandoned their cultural isolation and became assimilated into the culture of the country in which they lived, retaining their own religion in a modernized form, they would be accepted as equal citizens. Markus Zamenhof was an admirer of Russian culture, however, not Polish. But Jews like the Zamenhofs, who favored modernizing Jewish religion and culture, were a minority in Eastern Europe. Most Jews clung to orthodox traditions and scorned the assimilationists.

In Ludwik's time, however, as anti-Semitism became more vicious and widespread, many assimilationists became disenchanted and doubted they would ever be accepted as equal citizens who happened to follow a different faith. When, following the assassination of Tsar Alexander II in 1881, pogroms broke out in two hundred towns and villages, the illusions of many were shattered. They turned their efforts in a new direction, convinced now that the Jews were not really just a religious group but a nation, and that their only salvation lay in the establishment of a Jewish state.

Ludwik Zamenhof was among those who rejected assimilation and embraced the idea of emigration. By his own account, in 1881 he organized some of his fellow students at Moscow University into the first Jewish political organization in Russia. At first, Ludwik had agreed with the faction that wanted to go to America, settle a territory, as the Mormons had done, and eventually form a state. But in order to avoid disunity in the movement, he soon gave his support to the majority, who held that Palestine was the only possible homeland for the Jews.

That same year, financial difficulties forced Ludwik to return to Warsaw, where on Christmas Day a pogrom broke out and the terrified family had to hide in the cellar. In Warsaw Ludwik continued his studies as well as his Zionist work, founding among the Jewish youth in Warsaw a society of *Khibat Zion* (Love of Zion), which aimed to form agricultural colonies in Palestine. Among religious Jews at that time, Zionism was still new and suspect. Most had not accepted the idea of a Jewish state, which was supposed to be established only after the coming of the Messiah. Zamenhof later recalled that when he spoke with passionate conviction of his belief in the reconstruction of the Jewish homeland, 'my fellow Jews mocked me severely'.

Ludwik longed to work on his language, which he felt would help the scattered communities of Jews all over the world communicate with one another and come out of their cultural isolation. Until now he had obeyed his father and had devoted himself to his studies. But when he asked to see his precious bundle of notebooks and papers, he learned Markus had burned them. Ludwik would have to begin constructing his language all over again, from memory. The break with his father would take many years to heal.

Ludwik continued to work on the language as he finished his medical studies and began to practice in a small village in Lithuania. 'The tranquil life of the place', he later explained, '. . . was conducive to thought and brought about a complete change in my ideas.' In the peaceful forests of Lithuania, Ludwik Zamenhof came to the conviction that nationalism of any kind, even Jewish nationalism, would 'never solve the eternal Jewish question' and bring his people equality and respect. 'You may imagine that it was with no little grief that I decided to abandon my nationalist labors,' he later recalled, 'but thenceforth I was to devote myself to realizing that non-national, neutral idea which had occupied the thoughts of my earliest youth – to the idea of an international language.'

The language was at last ready, but one problem troubled Ludwik. 'I knew', he wrote, 'that everyone would say to me: "Your language will be useful to me only when the whole world accepts it; thus I cannot accept it until everyone does." But because "everyone" is not possible without some individual "ones" first, the neutral language could have no future until its usefulness for each individual was independent of whether the language was already accepted by the world or not.' Zamenhof decided to devise a one-page 'key' which would include the grammar and vocabulary, translated into a national language. Anyone who received a letter written in the new language could readily translate it and compose a reply with the aid of a 'key' in his native tongue. Thus the auxiliary language could be used immediately for its crucial purpose – communication between people.

Ludwik Zamenhof returned to Warsaw, having decided that he was unsuited to general practice. The agony of seeing incurable patients die was more than he could bear. He took up ophthalmology, studying the specialty at the Jewish Hospital in Warsaw and in Vienna, then opening his practice in Muranowska Street in Warsaw.

At a *Khibat Zion* meeting he had met a young woman named Klara Zilbernik from Kaunas, Lithuania. Her father, the owner of a soap factory, was impressed by the serious young Dr Zamenhof. When Klara and Ludwik became engaged, Zilbernik told his daughter that Ludwik was 'a genius' and that Klara had 'a sacred task' before her. She believed so too, and would spend the rest of her life fulfilling it.

In 1887 Ludwik and Klara were married. Klara and her father agreed to use half the money from her dowry to enable Ludwik to present his language publicly, in the form of a small book. It appeared earlier that same year.

The forty-page document included translations in the new language, a model letter and original poems, as well as the complete grammar, a vocabulary of nine hundred words with their Russian translation, and promise forms to be filled out by those who agreed to learn the language, which Zamenhof had named *Lingvo Internacia* (International Language).

Ludwik Zamenhof faced the moment with excitement and some trepidation. 'From the day my book appeared,' he realized, 'I would no longer be able to go back; I knew what fate awaits a doctor who depends on the public, if this public sees him as a crank . . .' Zamenhof knew that pursuing his ideal openly might jeopardize his family's security and future happiness. 'But I could not forsake the idea that had possessed me body and soul,' he said, and he did not turn back.

TWO

One Who Hopes

Dr Zamenhof's little book soon brought so many letters asking questions and offering advice, that he published a second book as a way to answer them all. A circle of enthusiasts grew, as people began to learn the language and use it to correspond with each other and with Zamenhof. Ludwik hoped that the language would spread on its own so he could 'retire from the scene and be forgotten'. He had signed his first book with the pseudonym 'Dr Esperanto'. *Esperanto* meant 'he who hopes'. It quickly became the popular name of the language itself.

At first most of the Esperantists lived in the Russian Empire and included many Jewish intellectuals and followers of Tolstoy. But by 1889 the first *Adresaro*, or Directory of Esperantists, included people in Germany, Austria-Hungary, Britain, France, Sweden, the United States, Turkey, Spain, China, Romania and Italy; and soon there were Esperantists in South America, North Africa, South Africa and Australia.

The language was so simple that the entire grammar could be explained in sixteen rules. Words were formed by combining prefixes and suffixes with root words drawn mostly from German and Latin so as to be familiar to most speakers of European languages. Nouns were formed by adding -o; adjectives by adding -a (*vivo*, 'life'; *viva*, 'alive'). The plural was made by adding -j (pronounced as 'y' in 'boy'). The use of prefixes and suffixes had been a brilliant stroke. It greatly simplified the language. For example, the prefix *mal-* indicated the opposite meaning of the term to which it was added. Thus *bona* meant 'good', while *malbona* meant 'bad'. Not only did this do away with all separate negative terms, but it then became possible to create other words by using the prefix, such as: *dekstra*, 'right' / *maldekstra*, 'left'; *antaŭ*, 'before' / *malantaŭ*, 'behind'; *riĉa*, 'rich' / *malriĉa*, 'poor'. Instead of having to memorize a completely different word for each concept, one need only learn the roots and the prefix.

An example of the way Esperanto words were formed may be seen in *samideano*, a term that soon came to be widely used among the Esperantists. The root *sam-* meant 'same', the root *ide-* meant 'idea', and the suffix *-ano* meant 'member' or 'adherent'. Thus, *samideano* meant 'one who shares in the same idea', or 'fellow–idealist', in other words, Esperantist. The feminine form was created by adding the feminine -in-: *samideanino*.

The personal pronouns were *mi*, 'I'; *vi*, 'you'; *li*, 'he'; *ŝi*, 'she'; *ĝi*, 'it'; *ni*, 'we'; *ili*, 'they'; *oni*, 'one'. Verbs were completely regular and had only one form for each tense. The present ended in -as (*mi faras*, 'I do'), the past in -is (*mi faris*, 'I did'), the future in -os (*mi faros*, 'I will do'), the conditional in -us (*mi farus*, 'I should do'), the imperative in -u (*faru*, 'do!'; *ni faru*, 'let us do').

One case ending was used: the suffix -n served to indicate, among other things, the object of a verb – what would be called in Latin or Russian the accusative case. Thus 'I wrote the letter' would be rendered in Esperanto: '*Mi skribis la leteron.*'

Esperanto had been successfully launched into the world; Ludwik and Klara were further delighted when in 1888 their first child, Adam, was born. But soon troubles began to cloud their lives. Ludwik had difficulty establishing his medical practice in Warsaw. His fears had been justified – people saw him as an eccentric and were reluctant to go to him for medical treatment. Half of Klara's dowry had gone to publish the Esperanto books; the couple had only about five thousand rubles left. Then catastrophe struck.

Ludwik's father, Markus, had been accused by a personal enemy of letting an article critical of Tsar Alexander III pass censorship. The article was about wine; the offensive passage was: 'continual drinking of wine gradually destroys the intellectual and civilized abilities of a man's brain and sometimes it causes insanity and a loss of all reason.' The passage was interpreted as a comment on the tsar's drinking habits and a direct insult to his person.

Markus Zamenhof was removed from his post as censor and risked losing his teaching position as well, for his enemy's godfather was Minister of Education. The officials would have to be bribed, or Markus would face total ruin. Ludwik gave him the rest of Klara's dowry.

Markus kept his teaching post, but Ludwik was financially ruined. In the hope of establishing his medical practice in another city – where he would not be suspected of being a crank for his preoccupation with Esperanto – he traveled to several cities in Poland and as far away as Cherson in the Crimea. But there was not always enough work for an eye specialist. He returned to Warsaw in 1898, despairing and destitute, and reluctantly agreed to accept financial help from Klara's well-to-do father.

Ludwik decided to establish his practice among the poor Jews of Warsaw, and the family – a daughter named Zofia had been born in 1889 – moved into a flat in the poorest part of the Jewish quarter, at 9

Dzika Street, where Ludwik also had his consulting room. While other oculists in Warsaw charged high fees, Dr Zamenhof asked only a very modest amount, and when the patients could not afford that, he treated them without charge. Many poor people, who might otherwise have let their diseases go untreated, came under Dr Zamenhof's care. His practice grew, but in order to make a living he had to see many more patients than other doctors did. With assistance from Klara's father, the family was able to have some measure of financial security. On 29 January 1904 Ludwik and Klara's third child, a girl, was born. They named her Lidia.

By now Esperanto was spreading rapidly. The language had shown itself to be an easily learned, flexible vehicle for communication between speakers of different languages. Early on, Zamenhof had demonstrated its range of expression by translating Shakespeare and books of the Old Testament into Esperanto. By the time of Lidia's birth, there were Esperanto groups and magazines in many countries, and well-known literary and scientific figures had joined the ranks of the Esperantists. Count Leo Tolstoy had received a copy of the first Esperanto book and had learned to read the language, he said, 'after not more than two hours' study'. 'The learning of Esperanto and spreading it', he remarked, 'is undoubtedly a Christian work that helps in the creation of the Kingdom of God, which is the chief and sole purpose of human life.'

Plans were being made by French Esperantists to hold the first full-scale international congress of Esperantists in Boulogne-sur-Mer in 1905. Zamenhof, who was a shy and modest man, hesitated about going. Although as a student he had spoken to small, secret Zionist groups in Moscow and Warsaw, he had never given a speech before such a large, diverse audience. And he was already suffering from heart disease. The journey would be difficult for him, and costly. Zamenhof did not wish the Esperantists to treat him with any special honors at the gathering. He wished them to see in him 'not the author of Esperanto, but only a simple Esperantist'.

For a time it seemed Ludwik would not be able to attend the congress even if he wanted to. Russia was at war with Japan, and in January 1905 orders arrived commanding Zamenhof to serve as a doctor in the Russian army in Manchuria.

Klara was distraught at the news and even more upset at her husband's response to it. Although ill, Ludwik refused to ask to be excused from his duty. At last, family and friends persuaded him that his health could not bear the hard journey across Russia and China and the rigors of army medical service. The military doctors agreed. Instead of sending Dr Zamenhof to the front, they sent him into a hospital for a week.

The situation in Eastern Europe was unsettled as well. In the Russian Empire, there was uprising and revolution; terrible pogroms were carried out, one of the worst of which was in Bialystok.

Among the strikes and nationalist uprisings that occurred that year was a strike by students of a Polish grammar school in Warsaw. Ludwik and Klara were shocked when they learned that their son Adam had joined it. Ludwik took him out of school and sent him to stay with Klara's family in Kaunas, where he finished his preparatory studies.

In spite of all that had happened, as the year went on and the time of the Esperanto Congress approached, Zamenhof decided he would attend the meeting in France.

But more trouble awaited him in Boulogne-sur-Mer. The green flags with the five-pointed star, symbolic of hope and the emblem of Esperanto, were flying in the seaside town of Boulogne, but the leaders of the Esperanto movement in France were fighting among themselves. Several of the French leaders objected to the draft of the speech Zamenhof had sent to them, especially the poem 'Prayer under the Green Banner', which he intended to read at the end. They found particularly objectionable its last stanza, which contained the statement: 'Christians, Jews or Muslims, we are all children of God.' They did not think the audience would agree. Moreover, anti-Semitism was strong in France, which was still divided over the Dreyfus Affair, and the leaders did not want the audience to know Zamenhof was a Jew.

The creator of Esperanto was heartbroken to find that most of the French Esperantist leaders did not share his ideals. Although they warned him that the audience might even hiss at him if he read his 'Prayer', Zamenhof was determined to go through with it. He did agree to give up the last stanza of the poem, feeling that perhaps they knew more of the local climate of opinion, and he did not want to offend anyone, although the ideal was a lofty one. Otherwise, he determined to read the speech as he had written it.

The evening arrived. The small City Theater auditorium was filled with Esperantists. The room buzzed with the chatter of 688 people belonging to some twenty different nationalities. But instead of their own native languages, they were all speaking the International Language, Esperanto. A young Swiss, Edmond Privat, described the scene; 'Fervour was spreading under the lamps. A thrill of excitement surged through the waiting crowd. Suddenly there burst forth the music of the Esperanto hymn, *La Espero* ['Hope']:

> *En la mondon venis nova sento*
> *Tra la mondo iras forta voko . . .*

(Into the world has come a new feeling,
Through the world there goes a mighty summons . . .)

'With one accord, we all stood up. There was our beloved leader coming onto the stage with the chief officials of the congress. Short of stature, shy, touched to the heart, there he stood, with his broad forehead, round spectacles, and little grayish beard. Hands, hats, handkerchiefs waved in the air in half an hour's continuous applause. When he stood up after the Mayor's greeting, the enthusiasm thundered out again. But now he began to speak. The shouting ceased: we all sat down again.'

'I greet you, dear colleagues,' Zamenhof began, 'brothers and sisters from the great world family, who have come together from near and distant lands, from the most diverse states of the world, to clasp hands in the name of the great idea, which unites us all . . .

'This present day is sacred. Our meeting is humble; the outside world knows little about it and the words spoken here will not be telegraphed to all the towns and villages of the world; . . . this hall is not resplendent with luxurious clothes and impressive decorations; no cannon are firing salutes outside the modest building in which we are assembled; but through the air of our hall mysterious sounds are travelling, very low sounds, not perceptible by the ear, but audible to every sensitive soul: the sound of something great that is now being born. Mysterious phantoms are floating in the air; the eye does not see them, but the soul sees them; they are the images of a time to come, of a new era. The phantoms will fly into the world, will be made flesh, will assume power, and our sons and grandchildren will see them, will feel them and will have joy in them.'

Zamenhof spoke of how the human family had long been separated into warring, hostile groups who for many thousands of years had not understood one another.

'. . . Prophets and poets dreamed of some era, very misty and remote, when human beings would once again begin to understand one another and would again be united in one family; but this was only a dream. This was spoken of as some sweet fantasy, but not taken seriously; no-one believed in it.

'And now, for the first time, the dream of thousands of years begins to come true. In a small town on the coast of France people from the most diverse lands and nations have assembled . . . understanding one another, speaking to one another as brothers, like the members of one nation . . . We all stand on a neutral base, we all have truly equal rights; we all feel like members of one nation, like members of one family . . .'

His audience listened in respectful silence. Among the faces of young and old, men and women, there were shining expressions. His

15

voice grew more assured. 'We shall show the world that mutual understanding among people of different nations is perfectly possible . . . that the barrier between the peoples is not something inevitable and eternal, that understanding between creatures of the same species is no fantastic dream, but a perfectly natural phenomenon, which has only been long delayed by very sad and shameful circumstances, but which had to come sooner or later and which has now come . . .'

'Our literature is already very large', he went on, 'our magazines are very numerous, we now have Esperantist groups and clubs all over the world, and our name is now known to every educated person in the world. When I look at our present brilliant position, I remember with emotion the first pioneers, who worked for our cause in that unhappy time, when we met with nothing on every side but sneers and persecution.'

Some in the audience could see Zamenhof's hands begin to tremble as he neared the end of his speech.

'Soon the work of our Congress, dedicated to the true brotherhood of mankind, will begin,' he continued. 'In this solemn moment my heart is full of something not to be defined, something mysterious, and I feel I want to ease my heart with some prayer, to turn to some greater Power and invoke its aid and blessing. But just as in this moment I am not a member of any one nation, but a simple human being, even so I also feel that at this moment I do not belong to any national or sectarian religion, but am a simple human being. And at this moment all that is before the eyes of my soul is that high moral Power which every human being feels in his heart, and to this unknown Power I direct my prayer.

> To Thee, O mysterious, bodiless Force,
> O Power of the World, all-controlling,
> To Thee, source of Love and of Truth, and the source
> Of Life in its endless unrolling,
> Whom each may conceive in his way in his mind,
> But the same in his heart, in his feelings, shall find,
> To Thee, the Creator, To Thee, holding sway,
> To Thee, now, we pray.
>
> We turn to Thee now with no creed of a state,
> With no dogmas to keep us apart;
> Blind zeal now is hushed, and fanatical hate;
> Now our faith is the faith of the heart.
> With this truest faith, this unforced faith and free
> Which all feel alike, we are turning to Thee
> We stand now, the sons of the whole human race,
> In Thy holy place.

Thy creation was perfect and lovely, but men
Are divided, and war on each other;
Now peoples rend peoples like beasts in a den,
Now brother makes war on his brother;
Mysterious Power, whatever Thou art,
O hear now our prayer, our true prayer from the heart:
O grant us Thy peace, O give peace once again
To the children of men!

We are sworn to strive on, we are sworn to the fight
Till mankind is as one; O sustain us;
O let us not fall, but be with us, O Might,
Let no walls of division restrain us.
Mysterious Power, now bless our endeavour,
Now strengthen our ardour, and let us, for ever,
Whoever attacks us, however they rave,
Be steadfast and brave.

We will hold our green banner on high now, unfurled,
A symbol of goodness, and, blessed
In our task by the Mystery ruling the world,
We shall come to the end of our quest.
The walls that divide shall divide us no more;
They shall crack, they shall crash, they shall fall with a roar,
And love then and truth shall, all walls overthrown,
Come into their own.'

'When Zamenhof sat down,' Privat recalled, 'prolonged applause broke out again, and many eyes were wet.'

The leaders had been wrong. Zamenhof's sincerity and his message had touched the hearts of all.

THREE

The Inner Idea

Over the years, Ludwik Zamenhof had come to realize that there was another barrier that divided men even more severely than native language: religious prejudice and fanaticism. He had experienced firsthand the ugliness of anti-Semitism and the violence of pogroms. Until religious hatred was ended, Zamenhof now believed, the human family would not become united.

In the wake of the Revolution of 1905, anti-Jewish violence in Russian Poland became so bad that a prominent French Jewish Esperantist and noted oculist, Emile Javal, wrote Zamenhof suggesting that he take his family to Paris, where they would be safe. But Zamenhof would not leave Warsaw. Though he admitted life there was 'indeed terrible', he thanked him for the offer but refused.

Zamenhof longed to solve the problem of religious strife. Several years earlier, he had presented to the Jewish intellectuals of Warsaw a program he hoped would form the basis for a religious-moral movement among Jews. Zamenhof felt Judaism needed to be reformed, not to become assimilated to its Gentile surroundings, but to pare it down to its core: belief in one God and the law to love one's neighbor. All else in Judaism, he believed, was 'not laws, but customs and traditions'. 'The essence of the Hebrew people', he wrote, was the concept of 'one unknowable God for all mankind'. It was for this idea that the Jewish people had been created, and for which they had suffered in the course of millennia. 'The perfecting of this idea', he believed, 'is consequently the entirely natural mission of the Jewish people and their *raison d'être.*'

Zamenhof called his program Hillelism, after the first-century BC Hebrew sage Hillel, known as a tolerant man who interpreted the scriptures according to the spirit of the law. 'What is hateful to thee, do not unto thy fellow man', Hillel had said. 'This is the Torah: all the rest is commentary.' Zamenhof hoped that the principles of Hillelism would lead to breaking down the barriers of prejudice and would help the Jews to become accepted as equal citizens wherever they lived.

Although he found little support for his program – no Jew would support it openly – Zamenhof refused to give up the idea. He soon came to believe that such a movement should not be only for the Jews but for all mankind. He decided to offer his idea to peoples of all races and religions, and changed the name to *Homaranismo* to make it more universal. *Homarano* in Esperanto meant 'a member of the human family'.

The essence of Homaranismo was to be absolute equality, justice and mutual respect among peoples of all races and religions. Each Homaranist would be free to follow his own religion, but in dealing with members of other groups would be expected to act on the basis of neutral human religious principles. Each individual would be free to speak whatever language he wished at home, but when meeting people whose home language was different, should speak a neutral tongue. This language, for the present at least, was to be Esperanto. Modestly Zamenhof added that if, at some future time, the Homaranists wished to choose another language, they could do so.

The religious principles that would guide all Homaranists included recognition of God as the highest Power, unknowable to man, and the fundamental rule to 'act toward others as you would wish others to act toward you, and always listen to the voice of your conscience'.

'The essence of all religions is the same,' Zamenhof wrote, 'they are distinguished from one another only by legends and customs . . .' Zamenhof believed that these man-made customs and traditions, not the God-given teachings of love and brotherhood, were the source of religious dissension among people. The Homaranist, Zamenhof believed, ought to work toward a day when the diverse religious practices of all Homaranists would eventually give way to one set of neutral customs for all mankind. Zamenhof envisioned Homaranist temples where the words of the 'great teachers of mankind' would be read, and the young would be educated to struggle for truth, goodness, justice and brotherhood between all men, to value honest work, and to shun that which was ignoble. Zamenhof specified that the religious teachings to be promoted in the Homaranist temple must not conflict with science.

Zamenhof did not expect all the Esperantists to accept Homaranismo, but he expected that they, at least, would understand the convictions that had led him to develop it and would greet the idea with respect and tolerance. Not all those who were attracted to Esperanto, however, shared the tolerance or the ideals of Zamenhof. He did not anticipate the ferociousness with which some would attack Homaranismo – and its author as well.

Zamenhof had tried to clarify to all that his program of Homaranismo was completely separate from Esperanto, that one could be an Esperantist without accepting Homaranismo, and at first he published his Homaranist ideas under a pseudonym. Yet many guessed Zamenhof was the author.

One of those who attacked Zamenhof was a Lithuanian Catholic priest who was an Esperantist. He claimed Homaranismo was an attempt to replace Christ with Hillel, who, in fact, had been a contemporary of Jesus. To this Zamenhof replied that Homaranismo was not intended to be a new religion but a 'bridge which could peacefully link all the existing religions and later, little by little, fuse them together. That Christ dreamed of the brotherhood of mankind, none of us doubt; but also the founders of other religions dreamed of the same. If Christ and the other great teachers of mankind were now living together, surely they would easily agree among themselves, they certainly would place the "actual requirements of God" above differing forms, and we would now have not many religions but one religion for humanity.'

The most ferocious opponent of Homaranismo was Louis de Beaufront, a highly influential French Esperantist. Esperanto was only a language, de Beaufront claimed; connecting it to Homaranismo would only harm the cause. He published a letter mocking the author of Homaranismo and suggested sarcastically that while they were waiting for Homaranist temples to open, rituals could be performed in green forests, wearing green robes covered with gold stars.

Zamenhof had planned to present his proposal for Homaranismo at the Second Universal Congress of Esperanto in Geneva in 1906. But the storm of antagonism against the idea was so strong that some advised Zamenhof not to go to Geneva. Although he abandoned the idea of formally presenting Homaranismo, he resolved to speak openly of his beliefs at the congress. Zamenhof had been profoundly dismayed by the vicious opposition to what he felt were universal ethical ideals, and by claims that Esperanto was 'only a language'. To Zamenhof, Esperanto had never been only a language. He had created it for the unification of mankind.

On 28 August at 8 p.m., Geneva's Victoria Hall was filled. This year there were nearly twice as many in attendance as there had been in Boulogne. The Esperantists anxiously awaited Dr Zamenhof's speech. The trip had been hard on him. He was weakened by his heart condition and the bitter mental anguish of the attacks against him.

'Ladies and gentlemen!' he began. 'At the opening of our Congress you expect some kind of speech from me; perhaps you are expecting something official, indifferent, pale and without content, such as official speeches generally are. However, I cannot give you a speech like that. In general, I do not like such speeches, but especially now, this year, such a colourless official speech would be a great sin on my part. I come to you from a country where now many millions are having a difficult struggle for their freedom, for the most elementary human freedom, for the rights of man.' But Zamenhof would not speak of that: the congress could have nothing to do with politics. Another struggle was also going on, he said, 'a cruel struggle between the *races* . . . The state of things is fearful in the many-languaged Caucasus, fearful in West Russia. Accursed, a thousand times accursed, be racial hatred!

'When I was still a child in the town of Bialystok, I gazed with sorrow on the mutual hostility which divided the natural sons of the same land and the same town. And I dreamed then that after some years everything would be changed for the better. And the years have passed; but instead of my beautiful dream I have seen a terrible reality; in the streets of my unhappy native town savages with axes and iron stakes have flung themselves, like the fiercest wild beasts, against the quiet town-dwellers, whose sole crime was that they spoke another language and practiced another racial religion than that of the savage brutes . . . I do not want to tell you the dreadful details of the butchery in Bialystok; to you as Esperantists I want to say only that the walls between the peoples, the walls against which we fight, are still fearfully high and thick.'

If only the different peoples knew one another well, the stirring up of passions through lies and slander would not have such dreadful results, Zamenhof told them. If only they could communicate, they would come to realize their common humanity and the ethics and ideas they shared. 'Break down, break down the walls between the peoples,' he cried, 'give them the possibility of meeting and communicating on a neutral basis, and only then those atrocities which we now see in various places will come to an end . . .

'Now, when in various parts of the world the struggle between the races has become so cruel, we, the Esperantists, must work harder than ever. But in order that our work may be fruitful, we must first of all explain thoroughly to ourselves the *inner idea* of Esperantism . . .

'Unfortunately, of late there have been voices in the Esperanto Movement saying, "Esperanto is only a language; avoid even privately connecting it with any kind of idea, for otherwise people will think that we all have this idea, and we shall displease various people who do not have this idea." Oh, what words! From the fear that perhaps we may displease those people, who themselves wish to use Esperanto only for their practical purposes, we are all to tear out of our hearts that part of Esperantism which is the most important, the most sacred, that idea which is the chief aim of the Esperanto business, which is the star that has always guided all fighters for Esperanto! Oh, no, no, never! With vigorous protest we reject that demand. If we, the first fighters for Esperanto, are to be obliged to avoid in our activities everything idealistic, we shall indignantly tear up and burn everything we have written for the sake of Esperanto, with sorrow we shall obliterate the work and the sacrifices of our whole life, we shall throw the green star that we wear on our breasts far away, and we shall cry out in disgust, "With that Esperanto, which must serve only for commercial and practical purposes, we want nothing in common!"

'There will come a time when Esperanto, having become the property of all humanity, will lose its ideological character, then it will become only a language, one will no longer struggle for it; one will only derive profit from it. But now, when almost all Esperantists are not yet profiting but only struggling, we all are very conscious that it is not the thought of practical utility that causes us to work for Esperanto, but only the thought of the sacred, grand and important *idea* contained in the international language itself. This idea – you all feel it very well – is *brotherhood and justice among all peoples.*'

Zamenhof did not give up the matter even then. He still hoped the Esperantists would see that, as he told the next year's congress in Cambridge, England, the green banner, symbol of the language, was also as the flag of a country – Esperantoland – which had not only its own language, but its own laws, customs and principles:

'In the depths of your hearts', he told them, 'you all feel the green banner: you all feel that it is something more than the mere emblem of a language. And the more we take part in our yearly congresses, the more we shall become brothers, and the more the principles of the green banner will sink into our souls. Many people join Esperantism out of simple curiosity, or for amusement, or perhaps even hoped-for profit; but from the moment they first visit Esperantoland they become, in spite of their own will, more and more drawn into and subjected to the laws of that country. Gradually Esperantoland will become a school for the future brotherhood of mankind, and in that will lie the chief value of our congresses.'

Zamenhof had suffered much on the journey to England. After the congress he went to Bad Nauheim in Germany for six weeks' medical treatment. No doubt he hoped that upon his return home to Warsaw he would be able to recuperate, and once again devote himself to his medical practice and his Esperanto work. It was not to be so, for soon a sordid controversy exploded in Esperantoland.

During the first years of Esperanto's existence, various people had suggested changes they believed should be made in the language. Zamenhof hoped Esperanto would become a living language and would grow naturally in response to the needs of its speakers. But he was always cautious about introducing changes. Politely he considered all the 'reforms' that people offered, and he suggested that a Language Committee be created to deal with such matters. Many of the proposed changes were contradictory; one person might wish to change just the aspect that someone else liked best in the language.

Other changes Zamenhof himself had already considered and rejected. While they sounded good in theory, he felt they did not work in practice.

Some of those who suggested changes were well-intentioned Esperantists trying to help. Others, perhaps lured by the possibility of having some personal influence over the very form of a language, became obsessed with the idea of 'reforming' Esperanto. Zamenhof and others became alarmed at the prospect of Esperanto continually changing on the whim of anyone who felt the urge to make an 'improvement'. Zamenhof wished to preserve the integrity of his language, yet he was aware that conflict over reforms and the author's inflexibility had crippled Volapük.

Among those who had strongly opposed change was the Frenchman Louis de Beaufront. He was an enigmatic person and claimed to have given up his own international language project for Esperanto. De Beaufront had already become the center of controversy because of his desire to control the Esperanto movement in France. He was also one of the bitterest opponents of Homaranismo.

A Delegation for the Choice of an International Language had been formed in Paris largely through the efforts of a French Esperantist named Louis Couturat in an attempt to influence the International Association of Academies to endorse Esperanto. Zamenhof was asked to choose someone to represent Esperanto before the Delegation Committee. He chose Louis de Beaufront. In spite of de Beaufront's past behavior, Zamenhof wished to show his trust in him, and he was certain that de Beaufront, who had always opposed reforms, would defend Esperanto from its critics.

But de Beaufront and Couturat deceived Zamenhof; their real intention was to put forward a 'new' language Couturat had secretly 'created' called *Ido* (which meant 'offspring' in Esperanto). When Ido was presented, it proved to be Esperanto, changed to incorporate the demands of the reformists. Suddenly, de Beaufront abandoned his position as the defender of Esperanto and spoke in favor of Ido, leading everyone there to believe that the Esperantists approved of Ido. The committee voted to accept Esperanto as changed in accordance with Ido. When the Esperantists learned what had taken place, they were indignant. By the time it came to a final vote, most of the prestigious members of the committee abstained or had withdrawn, leaving only the Ido supporters, who of course voted to accept their own project.

Couturat now began a campaign of attacks against the Esperantists and Zamenhof himself. The mathematician and philosopher Bertrand Russell, an acquaintance of Couturat, wrote in his autobiography that Couturat's talk gave the impression that no people in the entire history of the human race had ever been 'quite so depraved as the Esperantist'.

When Couturat complained that the name of his language Ido did not lend itself to the formation of a term comparable to 'Esperantist', Russell suggested 'idiot' but Couturat 'was not quite pleased'.

The gentle Zamenhof endured the Idists' abuse patiently, though it grieved him deeply. But the behavior of de Beaufront was quite puzzling. He was an unhappy person who longed to be considered important, yet this was not enough to explain his treachery. He was already a popular and influential figure in the Esperanto movement and the president of an Esperantist society. Why did he, who for twenty years had worked for Esperanto, now renounce it and revile its founder? It has been suggested that de Beaufront's dramatic repudiation of Esperanto may have stemmed from his hostility toward Homaranismo. 'It is possible', Marjorie Boulton writes in *Zamenhof, Creator of Esperanto*, 'that de Beaufront, with his extravagantly intolerant nature came to hate Zamenhof over the question of Homaranismo and to want to hurt him.'

In 1908 at the Fourth Universal Congress in Dresden, Germany, Zamenhof did not spend his precious energy denouncing the traitors. Instead, he reminded the thirteen hundred Esperantists gathered there that only unity could lead them to their goal. Now, he said, let the episode be forgotten. 'Let us remember that our Congresses are a preliminary practice and education for this history of the future brotherhood of mankind. What are important for us are not some trivial external details of our language, but its essentials, its idea and its aim . . . perhaps the difference between the Esperanto of today and the evolved Esperanto of many centuries ahead will be great; but thanks to our careful protection the language will live vigorously, in spite of all attempts upon it, its spirit will grow strong, its aim will be achieved and our grandchildren will bless our patience.'

FOUR

Father and Daughter

When Lidia Zamenhof was born in 1904, her parents were already middle-aged: Klara was forty, Ludwik forty-four. Lidia's brother Adam and sister Zofia were grown up: when Lidia was two years old, Adam went to Switzerland to study medicine at the University of Lausanne, and Zofia followed a year later. Although Switzerland was far from home, it was practically their only choice if they wanted to become doctors. Only a small number of Jews were allowed to attend universities in the Russian Empire.

Except for occasional visits home, Adam and Zofia were away during most of Lidia's childhood. In later years the three of them would often be separated from each other, but the bond that linked them was a strong one and it endured in spite of long years apart.

As the only child left in the Zamenhof household, Lidia had her parents' attention to herself. She was their darling and their delight, but they did not spoil her. Dressed in a frilly, tiered dress, her shoes laced up above her ankles and a bow in her wispy blond hair, as she stood on a cushion to have her portrait taken, her round little face looked into the camera with a serious, almost solemn expression. Nearly all her photographs would show her with such a look. Her mouth tended to turn downward, so that her normal expression seemed one of secret sadness.

Lilka, as the family always called her, even when she grew up, had come at a time when her parents could enjoy her. Although the situation in Russian Poland was often insecure and sometimes dangerous, life was financially easier than it had been for the Zamenhof family in earlier years. Dr Zamenhof had a large practice, and he received additional income from his Esperanto books. The family was able to go on holidays to the country, and every year Ludwik and Klara traveled to the Universal Congresses, wherever they were held.

But Ludwik's health was getting worse: he was overworking himself, often keeping longer hours than he should, though from devotion to his patients, not for money. One day a week and sometimes two, he saw poor patients without charge. Although there had been no pogroms in Warsaw, conditions were terrible. Hundreds

25

of Jews were fleeing, seeking refuge and a new life outside Europe. Many poor emigrants, sometimes entire families, passed through the consulting room of Dr Zamenhof to be examined and treated for eye diseases so they could enter other countries. In 1908 Klara confided to her friend Mrs Moscheles in London, 'My husband's health would be better if he could rest even a little, but unfortunately he is always working very hard.' The mental anguish he had suffered made him nervous and agitated. 'He still cannot walk', wrote Klara, 'so he always sits home at his writing desk.'

Lidia received her first education at home, beginning at the age of six – she did not enter school until she was almost ten years old. Klara described Lidia at six as 'very able, bright and hard-working'.

Ludwik was not as strict with Lidia as he had been with Adam and Zofia. He never punished his children physically, although he sometimes made them stand in the corner. Lidia remembered her father's discipline as firm yet kind. 'When Lidia's cat caught its first mouse', Marjorie Boulton recounts, 'she ran eagerly to tell her father. No doubt she was disappointed by his gentle "Lidia, don't you think the mouse would like to live too?" but this was part of his training.'

Zamenhof taught his children always to be honest. Many years later Lidia recalled an incident which illustrated how much her father valued this virtue. Among the objects on her father's writing desk was a stone paperweight in the form of a dog. Once Lidia noticed that the base had been broken in two parts. 'Usually when I saw something broken, torn, I preferred not to ask how it had happened,' she recalled, 'because I was never completely sure whether I myself was not responsible for it. But as for the paperweight, I truly had a clear conscience. So I bravely asked my father: "Who broke it?"

'He answered, "I."

'I was almost speechless. Impossible! Papa broke it?! Could Papa actually break – ruin – something?'

Dr Zamenhof told his daughter that it had happened when he was a young boy.

'He had many brothers and sisters. Everyone knows that in a home where there are many children, it happens very easily that unexpectedly, for example, a window pane may shatter with a loud noise, or porcelain figures fall from their pedestals . . .'

Markus Zamenhof had been a strict father, Lidia wrote, 'who was not very forgiving if because of childish pranks some damage happened in the home.

'And then, one day . . . from my grandfather's writing desk a paperweight fell to the ground and broke. Terror gripped the little group of children, and undoubtedly their hearts pounded when they heard the stern question: "Who did that?"

'And then from among the trembling crowd bravely Ludwik stepped out and confessed: "I!"'

'The courageous confession touched my grandfather's heart. He forgave and did not punish the culprit.'

However, the children of Ludwik Zamenhof learned that there was one subject about which their father rarely revealed the truth: his own health. He did not wish to burden others on his account. In the same letter in which Klara confided to Mrs Moscheles that her husband could not walk, Ludwik had written to Mr Moscheles, 'I have indeed too much work and I feel rather tired . . . but I am not ill.'

Many years later, Lidia would remember her mother as 'loving, affectionate, maternal. I see you as you bent over my crib, to caress me and say good-night, to put your hand on my warm forehead before the thermometer told you I was really ill. I see how you bent over the household accounts, or how quickly your hand turned the wheel of the sewing machine, to make me a new simple cotton dress. And the cut-out scraps of material – oh, what joy! – would serve to dress my doll, my favorite one, who closed and opened her eyes.'

Though she was the only child at home, Lidia was not without companions of her own age. There were many young cousins who played together whenever their families visited each other. The children of the Zamenhof family had a special relationship with Uncle Feliks, Ludwik's brother. A pharmacist by profession, and something of a poet, Feliks Zamenhof often arranged entertainment evenings for the family and had a talent for writing little plays for the children. Whenever one of his children had a birthday or sometimes on other occasions, he wrote and directed little theater productions which Lidia and her young cousins performed.

Every week, all the Zamenhofs – brothers, sisters, aunts, uncles, cousins – would meet at one of their homes. This weekly Zamenhof family gathering was a tradition that lasted long after the children had grown up, although, as Lidia's cousin Stephen Zamenhof has recalled, 'later on, the younger people had better things to do and just the old ladies attended'. While the children played, he remembered, 'the adults discussed what was going on during the week – mostly food prices and servants not being what they should be, and so on'. When the family met at Ludwik's home, all looked forward to Klara's strawberry tarts with cream. Many years later, cousin Julian Zamenhof recalled that 'an atmosphere of enthusiasm and reverence' surrounded Dr Zamenhof. Stephen remembered that the children called him 'Wujaszek Ludwik' – 'little uncle Ludwik'. At those weekly gatherings, Julian remembered, his uncle sat 'cigarette in hand, talking quietly without flourish or emphasis, never gesticulating; and yet whatever he said seemed important: one had to listen to him.

'He was also a great listener himself; he would readily listen to a child, a patient, a tram conductor or royalty; he would always speak, behave and listen in the same way, with respect and attention.'

While the young cousins were permitted to roam through the house in their play, one room was strictly forbidden to them: Uncle Ludwik's consulting room. The children resented this, for the room was full of books and interesting objects, and had great possibilities for exploring. Once, the eleven-year-old Julian spoke up, giving vent to the bitterness the children felt because they were not allowed to go into the wonderful room.

'". . . all these Esperantists, whoever they happen to be,"' he argued as spokesman for the rebellious crowd, '"may enter his study whenever they like and yet we, his family, would be admitted only in the case of a sore eye . . . They are strangers whilst we are family!"'

'Uncle Ludwik listened patiently with a kindness yet without a trace of a smile.

'"They are not strangers; they are also my family; they share my greatest belief in the need of mutual understanding, and help me to propagate this idea amongst those who most need it but do not yet realise their need."'

From an early age Lidia knew that there were many other people who were important in her father's life. She knew she must wait until all the patients had left his office before she might play a game of ball with him, although sometimes, when she thought he had been working long enough, she would bravely enter and ask him to play ball with her. And he would cheerfully give in for a few minutes.

'From my childhood,' Lidia later wrote, 'I remember the patients' waiting-room, where some came with flaming red eyes, others would cover their painful eye with a piece of cotton wool, sometimes stained, and still others, the saddest ones of all, did not come alone; relatives or friends accompanied them, because in their own eyes all sight was gone.

'After the visit of those patients, I often saw grief on the face of my father – it was the deep, heartfelt compassion for those from whom fate had robbed their sight.'

Lidia learned that although her father cared deeply for his patients, he was even more dedicated to his Esperanto work. Long after the last patient had left, he would work on, answering the many letters he received from Esperantists all over the world, writing articles, and translating books into Esperanto.

To Lidia, his closest companion seemed to be his typewriter. 'It stood on a little oak table near the window in our dining room,' she later wrote. 'In the evenings it was pushed toward the light of the lamp that hung over the table. In the daytime it worked only a few hours, but its real life began in the evenings. The clatter of its little keys was almost a lullaby for me; something seemed missing when it was silent.

'I became used to its monotonous melody, in which the rapping of the keys was interrupted by a lovely ring announcing the end of a line, and the grating noise of the carriage return; my dolls always found its wooden cover a very convenient pram.

'I hardly remember the time when it took up its place in our house. Years flowed by – it always worked on tirelessly, being not only a machine but almost a friend to my father. A never-impatient, never-despairing friend, but always faithful, always hopeful.

'At first I regarded it as an old, serious friend of the family. I would stand nearby and, with interest, gaze at the working of its mechanism. At last I became brave enough to sit on the stool and hit the keys, rejoicing that the letters were much more beautiful than those my awkward hand wrote in a notebook. But my first real joy was when I typed an exercise and proudly showed it to my teacher. I am sure that was the only reason she did not scold me much about mistakes which on another occasion might have elicited her severe criticism.'

The Zamenhof house was often full of Esperantists. Many came from other countries to visit Dr Zamenhof, almost as an act of pilgrimage. Lidia could not help observing the deep respect these strangers showed to her father, although it must have seemed rather mysterious to her at first. On one occasion in 1909 Lidia amused the guests attending a celebration for her father's fiftieth birthday. Klara had brought her into the room to introduce her to the gathering, which included many eminent Esperantists. Then they sat down to listen to a succession of speeches in Esperanto complimenting the Majstro and his family. Suddenly Lidia jumped up, indignant, exclaimed in Polish, 'What are they jabbering about? I *don't* understand a word!' and marched out of the room.

On the shelves in Zamenhof's excellent library were Esperanto books sent by their authors from all over the world. Once Lidia heard a visitor say that those books, more than any statue of marble or granite, would be a lasting monument to her father's greatness. She never forgot those words.

But her main interest in Esperanto at that time was as a source for her stamp collection, as she rescued from the wastebin the many colorful foreign postage stamps on letters sent to her father.

Though Lidia's family were Jews, they were not religiously observant. While orthodox Jews did no work on the Sabbath, not even cooking, at the Zamenhof home Saturdays were little different from the rest of the week. In fact, Saturday had always been the day when great armloads of packages were taken to the post office – the books ordered by Esperantists all over the world. Pious Jews followed the dietary laws carefully, but the Zamenhofs did not separate dairy products from meat in their home, and, Lidia's cousin Stephen recalled, on occasion they ate ham.

Very early Lidia learned the values her father cherished, especially: to regard each human being as a member of the family of mankind, whatever his race, religion, language or class. Though this was the way of things in the Zamenhof home, Lidia soon learned that in the world beyond their courtyard on Dzika Street not everyone shared those ideals of brotherhood and tolerance.

Secularized Jews like the Zamenhofs, who did not follow orthodox ways, were a people apart. Although they might live in the Jewish quarter, they did not participate in traditional Jewish society. In appearance and speech they were more like Poles, yet Poles did not accept them. Although Ludwik Zamenhof knew Yiddish and had spoken Russian at home, by the time Lidia was born the home language of the Zamenhofs was Polish – though the older Zamenhofs often used Esperanto. Lidia was enrolled as a Jew at birth, but by her own account she never took part in Jewish religious activities or community life. To most Poles, however, people like the Zamenhofs were little different from the other Jews.

In his 1920 biography, *The Life of Zamenhof*, the Swiss professor Edmond Privat evoked the anguish it must have caused young Lidia to be different – neither orthodox Jew nor Polish Catholic:

'She . . . very early showed herself to be thoughtful and of independent will. Her father respected her character. The little girl noticed everything with clear-seeing eyes. For the evening meal at home there was tea, with slices of ham. By the Jewish faith this was a sin against God. Religion forbade the use of pig's flesh. With Catholics it was the same about eating meat on Friday. But father was a free-thinker. Why?

'In the Polish churches there sounded the music of the organ under brilliantly coloured paintings. Eloquent priests who preached there spoke of the eternal glory of the martyrs, crucified both for fatherland and Christ. Why not become a Pole and a Christian?

'Yet at school the Christians turned their backs on the little Hebrew girls. Some of the chauvinistic parents told them to. Simple hearted friendships were broken. Words of mockery were heard. Was there anywhere any love and nobility? Zamenhof's little daughter threw her arms in silence around his neck. The child had begun to understand the deep pain at his heart . . .'

At the same time as Lidia was beginning to experience the cruel reality of racial and religious hatred, her father was refining his own theories about religion. In a new book about Homaranismo published in 1913, when Lidia was nine, it was clear that he had changed some of

4. *Number 9 Dzika Street, in the Jewish quarter of Warsaw, Russian Poland*

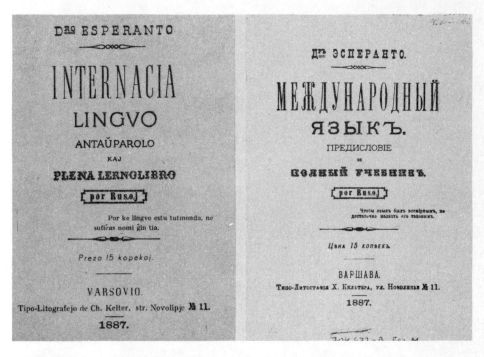

5. *Title pages of the 'First Book' in Esperanto and Russian: 'Dr Esperanto /
International Language / Introduction / and / Complete Textbook/for Russians / In
order that a language may be worldwide, it is not / enough to call it so. / Price 15
kopeks. / Warsaw. / Printing House of Ch. Kelter, Nowolipje Street No. 11. /
1887'*

6. *The first international Esperanto congress in Boulogne-sur-Mer, August 1905. Ludwik Zamenhof is number 1, Klara Zamenhof is number 2*

7. *Lidia, aged 3*

8. *Lidia aged 5, in 1909. From an Esperantist magazine of the time*

9. *Adam and Zofia Zamenhof, taken around 1908*

10. Dr Ludwik Lazar Zamenhof in 1909

his ideas. Previously he had accepted the fact that people belonged to a religion not because they believed in it but because they were born into it. Now, however, he asserted that 'religion should only be a matter of sincere belief, and not play the part of a hereditary tool of racial disunity'.

The Homaranist, he wrote, should be able to say, 'I call my religion only that religion . . . in which I actually believe . . . If I believe in none of the existing revealed religions, I must not remain in one of them only for racial motives and by so doing mislead people about my beliefs and contribute to endless generations of racial disunity, but I must – if the laws of my country permit – openly and officially call myself a "free-thinker", not, however, identifying free-thought especially with atheism, but reserving for my belief full freedom.'

Yet to have no religion at all was not satisfactory either. Zamenhof recognized that belonging to a religious community filled a social, if not a spiritual need; sharing customs, traditions and festivals gave richness to life. A person without religion lived a pale and prosaic existence. This could especially be seen among those secularized Jews of Poland who had completely withdrawn from Jewish tradition. In *On the Edge of Destruction: Jews of Poland Between the Two Wars*, sociologist Celia S. Heller has noted that the lives of these people, who were neither practicing Jews nor Christians, often had a 'spiritual emptiness' which 'seems to have resulted in a mystic yearning in some of their young'.

Zamenhof was clearly aware of the void which lack of religion left in the life of a child. Perhaps he saw it in his own little Lidia. 'A child', he later wrote, 'cannot be fed on abstract theories and rules; it needs impressions and a tangible environment. The child of a formally declared non-religionist can never have in its heart that joy, that warmth, which is given to other children by the church, traditional customs, the possession of "God" in the heart. How cruelly does the child of a non-religionist often suffer when he sees another child, perhaps very poor, but with a happy heart, going to church while he himself has no guiding rules, no festivals, no traditions!'

Zamenhof still hoped that Homaranismo would spread and attract followers so that people of any race or religion – especially those with no religion at all – could come together and share warmth and fellowship and traditions of their own, even as they affirmed their ethical ideals. Once Zamenhof might have hoped that by the time Lidia was old enough to learn about such things, a congregation of Homaranists would exist so that she could have such experiences. But in his revised edition of the *Declaration on Homaranismo*, Zamenhof deleted all references to the Homaranist temples he had once dreamed of. He concluded the *Declaration*, however, adding that those who were 'free-thinkers', having ceased to believe in their religion of birth, should form a community of their own. Once there was such a community, which the individual could 'join with full satisfaction for my conscience and for the needs of my heart', he must declare that community to be his official religion and must pass it on to his children. Until such a community was established, the free-thinker must 'remain officially enrolled in the religion into which I was born, but I must always add to its name the word "free-thinker" to show that I include myself in it only temporarily . . .' It must have been with some grief that Zamenhof wrote those lines, for they opened up the possibility, even the inevitability, of severing his last ties to Judaism.

FIVE

Green Stars and Gingerbread Hearts

The Ninth Universal Congress of Esperanto was to be held in Bern, Switzerland, in August 1913. As usual, Ludwik and Klara would attend. Adam and Zofia were in Lausanne, Adam working in the university eye clinic, Zofia finishing her medical studies. They planned to travel to Bern and meet their parents there. Lidia was now nine, and old enough to go along on the journey. But Klara wrote Zofia confiding she did not know what to do about Lilka. The determined little daughter of 'Dr Esperanto' had stubbornly refused to learn his language, although she did understand the meaning of *bonan nokton* (good-night) and *ĉokolado* (chocolate).

Klara knew Lidia would be bored at the congress if she could not understand what was going on. And it would be embarrassing that Dr Zamenhof's daughter did not know Esperanto. Klara did not want to take Lidia along, but she did not want to leave her at home either. Zofia and Adam conferred and decided to advise their mother to leave their young sister with a relative. But when Zofia and Adam met their parents in Bern they were astonished to see Lidia there too – speaking Esperanto.

Klara had found her own solution. She explained to Lidia that if she did not learn Esperanto, she could not go with her parents to Switzerland. Of course Lidia wanted to go on the journey so, with the same strong will with which she had resisted learning the language, she began to try to learn all she could. After six weeks, she had learned enough to satisfy her mother and obtain her permission to go.

As the train carried them toward Bern, Lidia must have watched in wonder the landscape that sped by outside the window. She had lived all her life in the crowded and grimy Jewish quarter of Warsaw, but here was a fairy-tale land of red-roofed chalets, milk-chocolate-colored cows grazing on slopes below the dark forest, and jagged snow-topped Alps. And then, at last, there was Bern, with its old towers and spires and fountains, and its whimsical sixteenth-century *Zytglogge*, the clock tower whose mechanical figures went through their antics to announce each hour. Under the arcades of its streets were inviting tea-rooms and the tempting window displays of pastries and

33

candies and, of course, chocolate in every shape and variety.

The Zamenhofs, guests of the congress, stayed in a modest *pension* called Beau-Site across the Kornhaus Bridge and quite a long walk from the Casino, where the congress would be held. A journalist wrote of seeing some of them one day, on their way to their lodgings: Mrs Zamenhof, Zofia, Adam and 'Oh, I was about to forget – her nine-year-old ladyship, Miss Lidia Zamenhof, a very charming and (I beg pardon!) amusing little person'.

Although that last week of August 1913, the Bern newspapers were full of unrest in the Balkans, revolution in China and Mexico and other disturbing events in the world, they printed many articles about the Esperanto congress. 'Welcome!' cried *Der Bund*. 'From all parts of the world, by ship and by train, hundreds of people are traveling at this hour to the capital of Switzerland to the ninth Esperanto World Congress.

'They wear a little green star in their buttonholes, the sign of hope (*espero*), and they all speak the same lovely language . . . Origin or extraction, language and religion, do not form an obstacle for any of them during these days, as the common language and the peaceful attitude make all equal and remove all the difficulties that are common to other international conventions.

'All public and hidden enemies of the international auxiliary language should cast a glance at this mixed meeting . . . Many of them would then suddenly have a different opinion about the utopia they enjoy condemning with a superior smile.'

The Casino, a stately building of sandstone, overlooked the green ribbon of the Aare River and commanded a splendid view of the Bernese Alps. On Monday Lidia was with the congress-goers who crowded into its Grand Hall. Attending the yearly Esperanto congresses would be an important part of her life as an adult, and this first experience made a strong impression on her, as she observed the Esperantists' great respect and adoration for her father. Lidia watched and listened as applause and cheers broke out when Dr Zamenhof stepped up to the podium, followed by the Esperanto dignitaries and congress delegates. In the midst of the cheering, the notes of the Esperanto anthem *La Espero* rang out in the deep tones of the organ, and a thousand voices sang the words of Ludwik Zamenhof:

> Into the world has come a new feeling,
> Through the world goes a mighty call;
> On light wind-wings
> Now may it fly from place to place.
>
> Not to the sword thirsting for blood
> Does it draw the human family:

To the world eternally at war
It promises holy harmony.

Beneath the holy banner of hope
Throng the soldiers of peace,
And swiftly spreads the Cause
Through the labor of the hopeful.

Strong stand the walls of a thousand years
Between the sundered peoples;
But the stubborn bars shall leap apart,
Battered to pieces by holy love.

On the neutral foundation of common speech,
Understanding one another,
The peoples in concord shall make up
One great family circle.

Our busy band of comrades
Shall never weary in the work of peace,
Till humanity's grand dream
Shall become the truth of eternal blessing.

After the welcoming speeches were given, a gold medal was presented to Dr Zamenhof in gratitude for his years of labor, and a girl in Swiss folk costume offered a bouquet of red roses and white edelweiss to Klara. Applause exploded like a hurricane, one observer noted, the audience 'sparing neither its palms nor its throats'.

Later, in the street outside, several hundred Esperantists assembled to parade through Bern, green banners and national flags flying above their heads. With a crowd of curious Bernese watching, the diverse collection of mostly foreigners marched to the square in front of the Federal Palace to sing the Swiss National Anthem – in Esperanto. Afterward they marched back to the Casino, where the Zamenhof family was sitting on the balcony. As they stood before Dr Zamenhof they cheered and sang *La Espero*.

The newspaper *Der Bund* reported that the official banquet held Wednesday at noon 'again filled the Grand Hall of the Casino . . . A well-made statue of the father of Esperanto, Dr Zamenhof, encircled with a laurel wreath, was placed on the podium which was decorated with the Esperanto star on a white field in a beautiful flower arrangement. The appearance of Dr Zamenhof – he came with his wife and a lovely blond little daughter – was greeted with a lively cry of celebration.' There were so many dinner speeches, the reporter commented wryly, that 'you really knew you were at a *language* conference!'

This was Zamenhof's first congress as an 'ordinary Esperantist'. The year before, he had formally renounced his position of leadership in the Esperanto movement so that he could devote his time to Homaranismo. 'Esperanto is now so firmly established,' he told an interviewer in Bern, 'that I wish that Esperantists would no longer regard me as "chief" and "master". I have transmitted the language to the Esperantists themselves . . . I have always thought that it is not fitting that the name of any one person should be identified with our movement. Someone may not like my political or religious ideas, or my personal character, and he might thus conceive objections to Esperanto. Everything which I do or say he would link with the new language; and it is better for the success of the movement that henceforth I stand not before the Esperantists but among them.'

Nevertheless, the Esperantists did not conceal their reverence – almost worship – for the creator of their 'beloved language'. As Marjorie Boulton writes, 'the sun itself encouraged the hero-worshippers, for during the official banquet a spectator from the gallery saw how a sunbeam through a high circular window was making a halo round Zamenhof's head'.

During the week there were many meetings, as well as a garden party, theater evenings and a costume ball where one could buy gingerbread hearts with ILOVEYOU spelled out on them in Esperanto.

The Esperantists' cherished symbol, the green star, seemed to show up everywhere, to the amusement of the cynical reporter from the *Berner Tagblatt*. 'Of course the star had to be on the cake,' he remarked. 'Even shoestrings don't seem to be an improper place [for the star], and we cannot rule out the possibility that somewhere the green star decorates soft flesh in the form of a tattoo.'

Some time during the week a British correspondent for a progressive religious magazine, the *Christian Commonwealth*, interviewed Dr Zamenhof. Zamenhof told the interviewer that he felt there was an increasing understanding of the inner meaning of the movement. 'Its aim is to promote the real brotherhood of man,' he explained, 'and that internal idea is now very much better understood. We may not live to see its realisation, but I feel certain that our children or grandchildren will reap its benefits.'

Then the interviewer asked: 'Do you consider that the command which 'Abdu'l-Bahá recently gave his followers to learn Esperanto will have much effect in spreading the language in the East?'

'Abdu'l-Bahá, son of Bahá'u'lláh, the founder of the Bahá'í Faith, had often encouraged the Bahá'ís to learn Esperanto. The week of the congress, the *Christian Commonwealth* had published one of a series of articles about 'Abdu'l-Bahá's experiences in the prison city of 'Akká. His father, Bahá'u'lláh, had been exiled from His native Persia and finally incarcerated with His family and companions in 'Akká, where Bahá'u'lláh died in 1892. After revolution toppled the Ottoman sultan 'Abdu'l-Bahá was set free. In 1911 he began a journey through Europe and North America speaking about the religion established by his father. 'Abdu'l-Bahá and Ludwik Zamenhof never met, although they came close to crossing paths: in 1913 'Abdu'l-Bahá was in Europe en route to Haifa, but by June he had already left for the Middle East. In any case, Ludwik Zamenhof was evidently acquainted with some of the teachings of the Bahá'í Faith, which included the principle of a universal auxiliary language.

As early as 1863, when Ludwik Zamenhof was still a child, Bahá'u'lláh, then in Constantinople, had expressed the principle of a universal language and mentioned the possibility of using a created language for that purpose. In His last book, written in 1891, Bahá'u'lláh described the Constantinople incident. Addressed to Shaykh Muḥammad Taqí, son of a notorious Shiite clergyman of Isfahan, the volume is known in English as *Epistle to the Son of the Wolf.* In it Bahá'u'lláh recounts:

'One day, while in Constantinople, Kamál Páshá visited this Wronged One. Our conversation turned upon topics profitable unto man. He said that he had learned several languages. In reply We observed: "You have wasted your life. It beseemeth you and the other officials of the Government to convene a gathering and choose one of the divers languages, and likewise one of the existing scripts, or else to create a new language and a new script to be taught children in schools throughout the world. They would, in this way, be acquiring only two languages, one their own native tongue, the other the language in which all the peoples of the world would converse . . ." When in Our presence, he acquiesced, and even evinced great joy and complete satisfaction. We then told him to lay this matter before the officials and ministers of the Government, in order that it might be put into effect throughout the different countries. However, although he often returned to see Us after this, he never again referred to this subject . . .

'. . . At present', Bahá'u'lláh continued, addressing Shaykh Muḥammad Taqí, 'a new language and a new script have been devised. If thou desirest, We will communicate them to thee . . .'

In the interval between Bahá'u'lláh's conversation with Kamál Páshá in 1863 and his Epistle to Shaykh Muḥammad Taqí in 1891, two international languages had been created and were in use: Volapük, which was already in decline and which later died out; and Esperanto. But neither the shaykh nor anyone else ever asked Bahá'u'lláh the name of the language to which He was referring.

Bahá'u'lláh wrote of the concept of a universal language on other occasions and explicitly included the possibility of using a created language for the international tongue. The importance He ascribed to the principle of a universal language is evident in His specifying it in the *Kitáb-i-Aqdas*, His Book of Laws. The achievement of this principle, He affirmed, would be a sign of the 'coming of age of the human race'.

Early on, some Bahá'ís had been attracted to Esperanto and had seen it as the fulfillment of Bahá'u'lláh's words. Among those who learned Esperanto during Zamenhof's lifetime were Agnes Alexander, who came from a Christian missionary family in the Hawaiian Islands and lived in Japan; J. E. Esslemont, a Scot; and Lutfu'lláh Ḥakím and Mírzá Muḥammad Labíb, Persians. Martha Root, the well-known American Bahá'í who would play an important role in Lidia's life, apparently began to study Esperanto in 1912 although she did not master it until many years later.

As to the 'command' to learn Esperanto, which the interviewer mentioned to Dr Zamenhof in Bern, although 'Abdu'l-Bahá had strongly and repeatedly encouraged Bahá'ís to study Esperanto, most of the Bahá'ís never took this as a binding requirement. However, according to the published translations of remarks made in two addresses in 1913, 'Abdu'l-Bahá seems to have expressed his wishes very clearly. In February 1913 'Abdu'l-Bahá had addressed an Esperanto meeting in Paris, and his words were reported in the Bahá'í magazine *Star of the West* thus:

'In the world of existence an international auxiliary language is the greatest bond to unite the people. Today the causes of differences in Europe are the diversities of language. We say, this man is a German, the other is an Italian, then we meet an Englishman and then again a Frenchman. Although they belong to the same race, yet language is the greatest barrier between them. Were a universal auxiliary language now in operation they would all be considered as one . . .

'Now, praise be to God, that Dr Zamenhof has invented the Esperanto language. It has all the potential qualities of becoming the international means of communication. All of us must be grateful and thankful to him for this noble effort, for in this way he has served his fellow-men well. He has invented a language which will bestow the greatest benefits on all people. With untiring effort and self sacrifice on the part of its devotees it will become universal. Therefore every one of us must study this language and spread it as far as possible so that day by day it may receive a broader recognition, be accepted by all nations and governments of the world and become a part of the curriculum in all the public schools. I hope that the language of all the future international conferences and congresses will become Esperanto, so that all people may acquire only two languages – one their own tongue and the other the international auxiliary language. Then perfect union will be established between the people of the world.

'. . . I hope that you will make the utmost effort, so that this language of Esperanto may be widely spread. Send some teachers to Persia if you can, so that they may teach it to the young people, and I have written to Persia to tell some of the Persians to come here and study it.'

And in an address given in January in Edinburgh, Scotland, under the auspices of the Edinburgh Esperanto Association, 'Abdu'l-Bahá was reported in *Star of the West* to have said: 'We . . . have commanded all Bahá'ís in the East to study this language very carefully, and ere long it will be spread through the entire East.'

Dr Zamenhof answered the interviewer's question: 'I feel greatly interested in the Bahá'í movement, as it is one of the great world-movements which, like our own, is insisting upon the brotherhood of mankind, and is calling on men to understand one another and to learn to love each other. The Bahá'ís will understand the internal idea of Esperanto better than most people. That idea is, "on the basis of a neutral language to break down the walls which divide men and accustom them to see in their neighbour a man and a brother". I, therefore, think that, when the Bahá'ís learn Esperanto, its internal idea will be a great moral force that will compel them to propagate it . . . I have always found that the most zealous workers for Esperanto are those who appreciate its internal idea, and not those who see in it merely an instrument for material profit . . . Many people have doubted whether Esperanto would be accepted by Eastern peoples; I have never done so, and I feel certain that the Bahá'ís will carry the language into many places where ordinary European propagandists would never have gone.'

This quickly proved to be true: Bahá'ís such as Mírzá Muḥammad Labíb were soon teaching Esperanto classes in Persia. Martha Root would use Esperanto extensively in her world travels and would be instrumental in introducing the language into China, while Agnes Alexander would be one of its proponents in Japan. Many years later, an Esperanto historian commented: 'The active sympathy of the Bahá'ís greatly helped the spread [of Esperanto] in the Oriental countries. Often a traveling Esperantist is asked if he is a Bahá'í.'

The connection between the two movements, Bahá'í and Esperanto, would have great meaning to Lidia in years to come. But that day in Bern, while her father was discussing the matter with the interviewer, she was surely more interested in watching the whimsical *Zytglogge* and the big brown bears, the city's mascots, in their Bear Pit.

On Thursday morning, the streets of Bern were wet with a light rain that had fallen during the night, and light fog hung in the Aare valley. But as two special railway carriages left Bern for an excursion to Interlaken, the fog slowly dissolved and the sun came out.

They went by train to the shore of the Thunersee and from there by steamer to Interlaken. There were so many Esperantists – about 650 – that luncheon had to be held in sixteen different hotels. In the afternoon, in an open air theater, they watched a performance of Schiller's *William Tell* and in the evening enjoyed a concert and fireworks display. 'The color green formed – coincidentally or not,' a correspondent reported, 'a large part of the fireworks, and every time that it could be seen, a cry was wrenched from the throats of the crowd.' The sprays of rockets lit up the soft Alpine night as if it were day, and 'Bengal lights' filled the garden with changing colors. The Esperantists arrived back in Bern around midnight.

At the Esperanto oratory contest that week, a French Esperantist's speech on 'Fatherland' won first prize. Other orators spoke on heroism, courage, universal brotherhood and capital punishment. The Esperantists went home cherishing memories of Bern and wishing each other 'Till the Tenth!' But much would happen before the Esperantists gathered in a congress again. Fatherland, courage, brotherhood and death would soon be more than topics for speech contests, and the Bengal lights and rockets that lit up the sky all over Europe would not be a mere fireworks display.

SIX

Something Is Guiding Us

Soon after the Zamenhofs returned home from Bern, Lidia entered the first class of the eight-year Modern School for Girls, in the center of Warsaw. She had had to pass an examination in order to be accepted. For the next eight years, Lidia would attend school there six days a week, studying science, mathematics, history, geography, languages, literature and drawing. As a Jew, she was excused from religion classes.

A contemporary remembered Lidia at ten as a bright student, obedient and neat, and lovely 'as an angel', with long blond braids and a big blue silk ribbon tied in a bow, which 'accented her angelic nature even more'. As a child Lidia was apparently interested in art and painting, and seems to have continued to paint and dabble in applied art until her college years, when other activities claimed her interest.

The year 1914 came, and Dr Zamenhof was finishing his Esperanto translation of the Old Testament. The worn old typewriter clacked out its monotonous melody. Of those days Lidia later wrote, 'I grew, passed from dolls to fairy tales, from fairy tales to ever more realistic stories, it – the machine – working on unceasingly, recounted in its monotone voice the same old story.

'One wintry night, when after seven years' patient effort, my father finished some important work, gay laughter rang out in our house, congratulations, chatter. The machine stood quietly, silently, in its little corner. And in my childish brain came the thought that if I were the machine I should feel offended by such neglect during that ceremonious evening which I myself had helped to bring about. But the lifeless machine was above human anger and jealousy, and the next day it sang, in its usual melody, a new song of work.

'Thus it worked tirelessly for many years – but the happy time passed. Ever more often it stood silent, motionless against its will and against the will of the man whose heart was pained by the occurrences of the outside world.'

The Tenth Universal Congress of Esperanto was to take place in Paris in August 1914. It promised to be the largest gathering of Esperantists yet: 3,739 people had registered. But this year only Dr and

Mrs Zamenhof intended to go. Adam and Zofia had come home from Switzerland at last so Lidia would stay in Warsaw with her brother and sister.

A Worldwide Jewish Esperanto Association had been formed and intended to hold its first meeting during the 1914 congress in Paris. The leaders invited Dr Zamenhof to attend. He replied that he would gladly attend the meeting, but he declined to join the association. His convictions as a Homaranist prevented him from participating in any nationalist organization. 'I am profoundly convinced', he explained, 'that all nationalism offers mankind only the greatest unhappiness, and that the aim of all men should be to create a harmonious humanity.' He expressed his belief that the nationalism of oppressed races, as a natural self-defensive reaction, was more pardonable than the nationalism of the oppressive races, but if the nationalism of the strong was ignoble, that of the weak was imprudent; for each gave birth to and supported the other. The end result was 'a vicious circle of misery from which mankind will never escape unless each of us sacrifices his group selfishness and tries to stand upon completely neutral ground'.

Around 28 July Lidia's parents left for Paris, although the newspapers were full of the threat of war, and talk of war was on everyone's lips. The fuse that would ignite the powder keg of Europe had been lit in Sarajevo on 28 June when Serbian nationalists assassinated Archduke Franz Ferdinand and his wife. A month had passed while diplomats issued ultimatums and armies mobilized. In spite of the clear signs that war was imminent, Adam later recalled that in Warsaw 'generally it was not believed very much that the war actually could happen, and certainly no one supposed that it would be so serious and so long'.

The Zamenhofs traveled through Germany and had reached Cologne on the first of August when Germany declared war on Russia. Suddenly, as subjects of the Russian Empire, the Zamenhofs found themselves in a hostile land.

In Warsaw the family immediately began to worry when they heard nothing from Ludwik and Klara. The children had gone on holiday in the country but returned home as soon as they learned of the outbreak of war.

On the advice of some German Esperantist friends, the Zamenhofs had abandoned plans to continue on toward Paris and had decided to return home. But the borders were shut. At last, after a harrowing two-week journey, traveling by way of Sweden and Finland, crowded into trains without enough food, they managed to reach Warsaw. Many other people from the Russian Empire, some of whom had been taking the cure at German spas, found themselves, like the Zamenhofs, suddenly among enemies. But while most of Europe was in the grip of nationalistic hatred, Esperantists often helped other *samideanoj* who had been stranded in hostile countries.

Because of Dr Zamenhof's fragile health, the difficult journey was very fatiguing and unpleasant, Adam recalled, but more so because of 'the mighty moral blow he received, as it were, seeing the sudden appearance of hate between people to whom he had preached brotherhood'.

'He came home', Lidia's brother wrote, 'with heart broken not only in a symbolic sense. The serious heart disease in fact began during this unhappy period. Dejected, he resumed his daily work in Warsaw, always more sadly, when he saw that the war became ever more cruel and hope for its early end was more and more uncertain.'

Zofia and Adam both received their licenses to practice medicine within the Russian Empire. At the beginning of the war, Zofia went to spend a few months working under the guidance of her uncle Dr Zilbernik in Lebedin, a town in the administrative district of Kharkov, in the Ukraine. Adam worked as his father's assistant in Warsaw.

Lidia was in her second year of school. For her, life went on as usual. Every day her mother braided her hair, fried her an egg and sent her off to school. When Lidia came home in the afternoon, she could expect Klara's loving inquiries about her day, whether she had been called on to answer a question, whether there had been the dreaded classwork during the arithmetic lesson. But her father, who had always helped her with her homework, especially arithmetic, was more ill than he had ever been.

Dr Zamenhof's heart was failing. After an especially bad attack of angina which frightened the entire family one night, Adam took over most of his father's work, caring for the poor patients who streamed in for advice and treatment. From then on, Adam did not allow his father to do that fatiguing, daily work in his consulting room.

Now, Zamenhof had his mornings free to work on the project dearest to him, Homaranismo, for he saw patients only two hours in the afternoon. Although he no longer had to sit at his desk long into the night, to his family's chagrin he still worked the whole day without rest, and often without leaving the house. In vain Klara tried to get him to go outside and breathe some fresh air. But there was no suitable place to walk in the neighborhood of Dzika Street in the noisy and crowded Jewish quarter. To find some greenery and clean air, one had to travel a long distance by tram or droshki. The family thought it would be good for Ludwik if he lived somewhere near a garden.

In July 1915 the Zamenhofs moved to flat number 7 at 41 Królewska Street, in a fashionable section of Warsaw, just outside the Jewish quarter and opposite the Saxon Gardens and the Warsaw Stock Exchange. Królewska Street was a rather nice wide boulevard for

Warsaw, and lined with trees, cousin Stephen Zamenhof recalled. The Saxon Gardens were a good-sized park with flowerbeds, benches to sit on in the shade of horse-chestnut trees, fountains, a small lake, summer theater, coffeehouses, a little *orangerie* with tropical plants, and lots of space for children to play. Vendors of sweets sold their wares in the park, while horse-drawn droshkis ran along the thoroughfare.

The new Zamenhof flat was quite comfortable, cousin Stephen remembered. It was 'a rather expensive apartment at that time, with an outside, glass elevator which didn't always work. There were several rooms, with a huge consultation room which had all kinds of dark cubicles to look in the eyes.'

Here Dr Zamenhof could work more tranquilly and might be able to forget the fact that he could no longer accomplish as much as he once had. Adam made sure that his father saw only a few patients.

Although some Esperantist friends came to visit, the enforced isolation was difficult for Zamenhof to bear. Still, Adam remembered, 'never did my father cease to be an optimist and till the last moment of his life strongly believed that soon the terrible war would give way to the strong and brotherly cooperation of all peoples'.

At the beginning of the war Zamenhof began work on an essay he hoped would help make this happen. It was called 'After the Great War – Appeal to the Diplomats'. He was able to send it abroad and it was published in England, Hungary and Switzerland in 1915. In the essay Zamenhof appealed to the statesmen who would remake the map of Europe after the war. Zamenhof saw clearly the importance of the task before them and warned: 'It will depend on you whether the world is to have . . . an established peace for a very long time and perhaps for ever, or whether we shall have only a short period of quiet which will soon be interrupted again by the breaking out of fresh racial conflicts or even new wars.'

Zamenhof called on the diplomats to ensure that each country belonged equally to all of its citizens, and to see that each race had equal rights. He added that it would be better if instead of the diverse small and large nations, there were a 'United States of Europe' and that a pan-European tribunal should be established to settle disputes.

He concluded: 'Gentlemen, diplomats! After the terrible war of extermination which has set mankind lower than the most brutish beasts, Europe looks to you for peace. It looks not for a brief interval of pacification, but a permanent peace, such as is alone fitting for a civilized human race. But remember, remember, remember, that the only means by which such a peace can be attained is to abolish for ever the *chief cause* of wars, the barbarous survival from the most remote pre-civilized antiquity, *the dominance of one race over other races.*'

More and more frequently Dr Zamenhof's heart disease interrupted his work at the typewriter, and he would be forced to rest in bed for several days. 'But', Adam wrote, 'he could not rest even one day without work . . . Even ill, he made notes in a small pocket calendar which was always found on the nightstand. And if sometimes we discreetly wanted to enter his room to see whether he was sleeping or perhaps needed something (he himself never called on anyone) we almost always saw him with a pencil in his hand.'

On days when Zamenhof was too ill to work and was forced to lie and rest, Lidia and Adam might play music for him, Adam playing the cello while Lidia accompanied him on the piano. When he was well enough to leave the house, Lidia might go for a droshki ride with him in the park.

Although conditions were difficult in Warsaw during the early years of the war, life went on. Lidia worked at her studies and played with her dolls, and the war raging in Europe was little more than a topic of conversation for the adults at the weekly family meetings. But now, when she went to the wastebin in her father's study to retrieve the colorful stamps from foreign countries, there were none.

It was Lidia's father who explained to her the meaning of the war. 'I was a ten-year-old child when the cataclysm happened,' she wrote many years later. 'I did not think much about [the war] although it had already shaken the world, uprooted many lives, destroyed many homes. I played gaily and amused myself, free of care. Then my father, whose eyes, since the beginning of those black days, were always sad, pointed out to me how much blood and tears now flowed in the world, how many children cried for their papas.'

Years later, Lidia reflected on why her father had talked to her about the war, and why he had made her aware of the suffering so many others endured, among them children like herself. Would it not have been better to allow her the corner of sunshine she had found in a world in which the light had gone out? She realized that her father had not made her think about the war to cloud her happiness, but to instill in her 'sympathy for the suffering of human beings, for the torn, wrenched humanity'. Those feelings, Lidia wrote, 'planted in the soul of a child, grow until at last they bear fruit in the soul of the mature person. This fruit is the sense of human solidarity, of the brotherhood of all men from whatever nation or race, of the unity of mankind.'

The painful realizations that once shattered the gaiety of a child's play would become the guiding force behind her life's work, just as it had been for her father. This work would be, as she later described it: 'to construct a bridge between the peoples, to help them to unite beneath the banner of humanity.'

In 1915 the German army's plan was to hold off the Allies on the Western Front while sending its main forces east, against Russia. The German lines advanced across Poland. In August Warsaw fell.

The Russian government, giving ground to the German armies, had blamed the Jews for its military defeats and accused them of being spies for the Germans. Thousands of Jews were deported farther east into Russia. When early in the war Russian troops overran cities in Austrian Poland, bloody pogroms were carried out against the Jews there. In Warsaw, under the German occupation, things were not easy but in some ways they were better than they had been under the tsar, for the Germans wanted to have the population of Poland on their side, against the Russians, from whom they promised to liberate them.

When Warsaw was occupied by the German army, Lidia's sister Zofia found herself separated from her family by the Eastern Front. She had been assigned a post as a village doctor in Shtepovka, a village between Kiev and Kharkov, and was unable to return home. Nor could she write letters directly to her family, who were in enemy-occupied territory. However, through an Esperantist in Denmark, Margarethe Noll, Zofia and her family were able to exchange a few messages.

Usually Zofia had to confine her messages home to a postcard, which might arrive in Denmark months later, stamped with the post offices it had passed through and, of course, the stamp of the imperial censor. In October 1916 a worried Zofia wrote Miss Noll that she had learned from a French Esperantist that her father had been gravely ill. She asked Miss Noll to find out about his health, 'But don't write that I know something,' she said, 'because then father will not write the truth. Ask in your name about his health and write to me the truth, I beg you.'

Two months later, Edmond Privat, as a citizen of neutral Switzerland, was able to visit Ludwik Zamenhof. It would be Privat's last interview with his mentor, who was very ill and 'could only speak softly'.

Zamenhof confided to Privat his wish to convene a congress to create a universal society for people of various races and religions who felt themselves united by common ethics and tolerance – the Homaranist community he had always longed for. The thought that he would never complete the task chagrined him. 'It was the goal of my whole life,' he repeated. 'For it, I would sacrifice everything.'

According to Marjorie Boulton, 'Zamenhof warned Privat not to put too much hope in the coming liberation of many subject peoples: set free, they would refuse to others the rights they wanted for themselves; there would never be real harmony in the human family until all its members were free and there was some kind of sovereign world government.'

11. *Dr Zamenhof (center) and dignitaries at the formal opening of the Bern congress, 1913*

12. *Part of the audience at the Bern congress*

13. *Klara, Ludwik and Zofia (standing) in 1912*

14. *From left: Lidia, Klara, Adam and Ludwik. Taken in 1916 during the war, while Zofia was in the Ukraine*

15. *Dr Zamenhof in his consulting room at Dzika Street*

16. *The funeral procession through the streets of Warsaw, 17 April 1917*

17. *Lidia, the schoolgirl*

In January 1917 Zofia wrote Miss Noll of the tragic news that Ludwik Zamenhof's youngest brother Aleksander was dead. Miss Noll's letter relaying this sad information reached Warsaw in April. It had a shattering effect.

Aleksander Zamenhof had been an army doctor during the Russo-Japanese War. He had viewed such suffering among the casualties he treated that he vowed never to take part in another war. When Aleksander was again ordered into the Russian Army, rather than serve in the war he had taken his own life.

The news of Aleksander's death, unexpected and terrible, was a great blow to Ludwik Zamenhof. 'Though he never complained, because he did not wish anyone else to suffer when he suffered,' Adam recalled, 'he looked more wretched and pitiful than we had ever seen him. But it seems that till death he did not think about himself so much as about his beloved idea, through which he wanted to bring happiness to mankind, and he felt truly unhappy that because of illness he no longer could complete his daily task, which would lead to victory.'

On the fourteenth of April, Dr Zamenhof seemed somewhat improved, and the prospect of beginning his work again put him into a good humor. At five in the afternoon, the doctor came to call and they had a friendly conversation. Feeling tired, Zamenhof asked the doctor if he could rest on the divan. When Klara approached to help her husband, she found him dead.

Later, the family discovered on Zamenhof's writing desk some notes for a manuscript he had been working on when he died. As weakness and pain had overcome him at last, Ludwik Zamenhof had struggled to set down his thoughts about a subject he had never mentioned publicly before: God and immortality. He acknowledged that many people who had been uninterested in religion often became 'believers' at the end of life. Atheists would explain this, he said, as insincerity or senile deterioration of the brain, or as a last self-deception in the face of inevitable death. Zamenhof foresaw that people would want to apply those explanations to him. He knew that, just as he had faced suspicions of being a crank when he had first put forward Esperanto, once again he risked being considered demented if on his deathbed he began to speak of religion. But as always, Zamenhof resolved to express his beliefs honestly although it would bring him no sympathy from anyone. 'While in the scientific and free-thinking world I shall lose all respect,' he wrote, 'at the same time, in the world of believers I will find no compensating sympathy, but probably only attack, because *my* faith is completely different from *their* faith! . . .

'My mother was a religious believer,' he wrote, 'my father was an atheist. In my childhood I believed in God and immortality of the soul, in the form in which my religion of birth instructed. I do not remember exactly in which year of my life I lost my religious faith, but I remember that I reached the highest degree of my unbelief at around the age of fifteen or sixteen. That was also the most tormented period of my life. In my eyes, life lost all meaning and value . . . All seemed so senseless, useless, aimless, so absurd!

'I came to feel that perhaps [death is] not disappearance, perhaps death is a miracle . . . that something is guiding us for a high purpose . . .'

He never finished the essay.

The sixteenth of April was dark and rainy. The streets were black with crowds of people as the funeral procession slowly moved toward the Jewish cemetery. The cantor chanted the ancient Hebrew prayers, the men wept, the women behind their black veils wailed with grief. The coffin was lowered into the ground.

In the empty flat on Królewska Street, the typewriter stood in its little corner, covered with a black cover. 'It stood quiet,' Lidia wrote years later, 'indifferent, without feeling – the machine.'

As a child Ludwik Zamenhof had once vowed that when he grew up he would do away with the evils of the adult world which afflicted his native Bialystok. He had created Esperanto, had seen it spread around the world and bring together peoples of different races, religions and nationalities under the green banner of brotherhood. Now, on his death, Ludwik Zamenhof's thirteen-year-old daughter determined to carry on his sacred work. Lidia had learned Esperanto well by now, and some time during the war she began to make her first, unsure attempts at translating Polish literature into Esperanto.

That old typewriter, shrouded by its black cover, seemed almost a symbol of Ludwik Zamenhof's spiritual bequest. 'Months passed,' Lidia later wrote. 'On the little oak table the machine stood – closed. I hesitated a long time before I dared lift the cover again. And it seemed to me then that I was lifting the cover of the coffin . . .

'I began to type – the keys reverberated. Slowly, fearfully, as with wonder, like someone who awakens after a long sleep and asks where he is, who are those around him. And its wordless sounds seemed perhaps the most touching words of consolation . . .'

SEVEN

Pictures on the Canvas

The Zamenhof family was plunged into grief after Ludwik's death, but Klara took it hardest. To those around her she seemed like a person who had lost her purpose in life. Lidia watched as her widowed mother aged 'suddenly, incredibly suddenly'. The mother's grief made a deep impression on her daughter, whose 'child's eyes', Lidia later recalled, 'could not help but see how your thoughts and memories flew back to the past, to happier days'. For the rest of her life Lidia would remember her mother's sorrowful Sunday pilgrimages to the cemetery and how she would come back from those walks 'aching and broken'.

Eventually, left with the care of the thirteen-year-old Lidia, Klara recovered from her grief. She plunged herself into Esperanto work, still fulfilling her 'sacred task' to carry out her husband's dream. Now her goal in life was to see a suitable monument raised upon his tomb.

In 1918 the war ended, and Poland became an independent nation for the first time in over a hundred years. The three empires that once ruled it had not survived the war: the emperors of Germany and Austria-Hungary were defeated, the tsar of Russia overthrown by revolution.

But independence only brought fresh turmoil to Poland. The nation had been under foreign domination for so long that it had no experience governing itself, and its new government faced grave problems. Although the nation was now free, it was also poor and overpopulated. In the rural areas its peasant population was much larger than the land could support. Cities were crowded as well: there was nowhere for the landless peasants to go, and few industries to provide jobs. After the borders of Poland were finally fixed, the country contained a population that was only two-thirds Polish. The rest included Ukrainians, Jews, Byelorussians, Germans, Lithuanians, Russians and Czechs. The presence of so many people who considered themselves of a different nationality from the rest of the population was a problem Poland was never able to solve.

Once again, the Jews suffered. The war had hardly ended when the pogroms began. The winter of 1918–19 saw ferocious outbreaks of anti-Semitic violence in 130 towns and villages, carried out with the support and participation of soldiers in the new Polish Army. Jewish shops were boycotted; homes were looted; synagogues were desecrated; hundreds of men, women and children were tortured and beaten; and untold numbers of people were killed. In several towns, large amounts of money were extorted from the Jewish communities as fines for alleged disloyalty and as the price for providing protection against the violence, protection later refused them.

As a result of reports about the pogroms, which the Poles denied, the Allies decided that, as a condition of independence, Poland must sign a treaty guaranteeing full civil rights and religious freedom to its national minorities. Many Poles, however, resented this as an insult to the national honor. Poland's government never enforced the Minorities Treaty and in 1934 renounced it entirely.

After the war, great empires had fallen and millions of people lay dead, but the 'war to end all wars' and its aftermath merely laid the groundwork for new conflict. The territorial divisions made at Versailles and the break-up of the Austro-Hungarian Empire into republics released a wave of nationalism. Germany itself was left nearly intact, but the allocation of territory to Poland – even though that same land had been taken from Poland long ago – and of the Rhineland to France, was deeply resented.

France and Britain were determined to have revenge on Germany, to squeeze it 'till the pips squeaked'. But the humiliating conditions of peace and the impossible war reparations demanded of the defeated Germans, as well as economic crises and the political unrest sweeping the demoralized country were more than the weak new Weimar government could bear. In the chaotic years that followed, Germany's bitter resentment found its expression in rabid nationalism and virulent anti-Semitism, and the stage was set for the rise of Adolf Hitler.

In Poland fighting did not end with the armistice that brought the Great War to a close. Though the nation had been declared independent, its borders were not immediately decided. A state of war existed with Poland's neighbor, the new communist state of the Soviet Union, and Polish troops clashed with the Red Army.

In 1919 Adam Zamenhof was called up to serve as a military doctor in the Polish Army. The next year Zofia, still in the Ukraine, was mobilized into the Red Army as a regimental doctor. In a tragically ironic twist of fate, the children of Dr Zamenhof found themselves serving in armies at war with each other.

In the spring of 1920 the Polish Army advanced east into the Ukraine to Kiev. Soviet troops began to push back the Poles and counter-attacked until by June Warsaw itself was in danger of invasion. But in August the Red Army was stopped on the banks of the Vistula River and forced back.

It was not until two years later that Adam and Zofia were both released from military service and allowed to go home. Adam soon took up his practice again. His father's patients accepted him in place of their beloved doctor, and Adam was able to provide for his mother and younger sister Lidia.

Zofia returned to Warsaw exhausted and weak. The terrible conditions she had lived under for years had drained her strength: she had had typhus three times. When she regained her health she began to practice internal medicine and pediatrics in a hospital. At last the Zamenhof family were together again, and Lidia, Zofia and Adam were living under the same roof with their mother.

Many years later, cousin Stephen Zamenhof, who was also Klara's godson, recalled Lidia, Adam and Zofia as they were at that time. Zofia was, he said, 'the official physician of the family. Whenever anybody in the family was sick, Zofia would come, especially for the children.' She had 'short hair and a rather deep voice. She looked like a typical Bolshevik doctor – energetic, masculine, and she had such a manner with children; so we were kind of afraid of her. But she was a very good-natured person.'

Adam was tall and thin, and, Stephen Zamenhof remembered, 'very kind and intelligent'. In 1923 Adam married Dr Wanda Frenkel, also an ophthalmologist, whom he had known since childhood. She had been inspired by Ludwik Zamenhof to study ophthalmology. Adam became absorbed in his medical field, writing books and scientific articles on eye diseases. He was one of the first European surgeons to perform operations on the retina and became highly respected for his research, eventually becoming a *docent* (associate professor) at the University of Warsaw – a remarkable achievement at a time when Jews were being excluded from Polish universities.

Lidia, as a teenager, was of slight build and 'not handsome at all', Stephen recalled, 'but she had an interesting face'. Stephen remembered that his cousin Lilka was 'always busy translating literature into Esperanto . . . She believed that she had a mission in life, from her father, to propagate Esperanto.'

It was expected, Stephen recalled, that Zamenhof children would study to become doctors – or at least dentists or pharmacists. 'It was so ingrained that everyone had to be a doctor – everybody *was* a doctor – that the bones and books were passed from one member of the family to another, depending on what he or she was studying in medical school,' he said. In Lidia's generation of Zamenhofs, Adam, Zofia, and cousins Julian and Mieczyslaw, Stephen's brother, became doctors. Several other cousins became dentists. Stephen recalled feeling like an outcast because he was in polytechnical school, not studying medicine. Eventually, however, he became a professor of microbiology and immunology in America.

Unlike her brother, sister and cousins, Lidia showed no inclination to become a doctor, and the treasured bones and worn medical books were never passed to her. If she ever wanted to follow the family tradition of medicine, or if she, like her cousin, felt an outcast because she was not doing so, she did not say. It would be some years yet until Lidia found what she really wanted to do – a profession that would allow her to carry out her mission of spreading Esperanto.

Lidia's mother, however, had definite ideas about what she wanted for her daughter's future. Klara wished her to study law and perhaps become a lawyer. No Zamenhof had yet done that. Surely Klara also wished for her daughter to have long life and a family of her own. But none of those would be Lidia's lot. In a reminiscence about her mother which Lidia wrote years later, she alluded in a melancholy way to Klara's dreams for her, dreams that would never come true. 'Your wishes were not fulfilled,' she wrote, 'and you painted on the canvas of hope pictures to which destiny did not add its signature.' What those pictures were, Lidia never revealed.

In 1921, at the age of seventeen, Lidia had finished the eighth year of the Modern School for Girls. She received good – but not excellent – marks in chemistry, physics, astronomy, natural sciences, Latin, German, history and drawing; and satisfactory marks in Polish, French, geography and the dreaded mathematics. She was accepted into the University of Warsaw and began her studies there. One of her mother's wishes, at least, was fulfilled, for she studied law. But Lidia could not give her heart to the subject; years later she revealed to a friend that she did not like law.

Lidia's university years were a period of political and social unrest in Poland. The first democratically elected president of the nation was assassinated two days after taking office in November 1922, because he had been elected by the vote of the National Minorities Bloc, which was led by a Jew. Some churches held masses of thanksgiving that the 'President of the Jews' had been killed.

At the University of Warsaw Lidia had to face the ugly reality of anti-Semitism, which was at a peak in the early 1920s. Because Jews traditionally valued education, they worked hard to get into university. Thus, there was a larger number of Jews in the universities than their proportion in the population. Angered by this, anti-Semitic Polish students and nationalist political parties called for restrictions on the number of Jewish students. The same year Lidia entered college, quotas limiting Jews were introduced at one Polish university in the Schools of Law and Medicine. Although this quota was struck down, anti-Jewish agitation continued in the universities, and unofficial quotas were introduced a few years later. 'At all times and at all universities', Celia S. Heller has stated, 'Jewish students were heckled, humiliated, and attacked by some of their Polish fellow students and helpers from anti-Jewish terrorist groups outside the university.'

Seven years had passed since Ludwik Zamenhof's death, and new graves now surrounded his humble resting place in the Jewish cemetery. Among all the grand tombstones, his was the only simple marker. The Esperantists had organized an international committee to collect funds to raise a monument, and a local committee in Warsaw was to arrange for its construction. They chose a simple design created by Warsaw sculptor M. Lubelski: blocks of granite surmounted by a globe of the world. The monument was to be carved in Aberdeen, Scotland, of gray Scottish granite. Klara was distressed when by the summer of 1924 it was still not completed.

Klara Zamenhof had tried to carry on her husband's Esperanto work as best she could. For many years she kept up his correspondence with the Esperantists, but at last she became too ill to answer the mountain of letters that continued to arrive from all over the world. Every year she attended the Esperanto congresses, and it became a tradition to greet her formally in the opening ceremony. In August 1924 Lidia accompanied her mother, who was by now very ill, suffering from liver cancer, to the Sixteenth Universal Congress of Esperanto in Vienna. Over three thousand Esperantists were there. On Sunday, the tenth of August, the congress opened in the Konzerthaus. One of the speakers was Edmond Privat.

He spoke of Vienna's past, when centuries ago medieval knights going off to battle had gathered in the Cathedral of Saint Stephen. 'In those days knights waged war by force. But times have changed,' he said. The world war had killed not only millions of youths, it had also put an end to ancient knighthood, to the old era. 'A new time, a new epoch for mankind has begun,' said Privat. 'Also a new knighthood.

'The knighthood of the new era is no longer the heroes of force and arms. They are no longer covered by shining silver or gold armor. Their hands no longer hold iron weapons. The new heroes are the knights of the *ideal* and of love for mankind. Their strength, the spirit; their arms, convictions and example.

'The mysterious force, of which Zamenhof sang, unites them and sends them throughout the entire world to fulfill their task and bring humanity toward more light, more peace, more justice. Our task is very clear: we must slay the dark dragon of misunderstanding among peoples, we must spread that language in which dwells the youthful spirit of the new humanity.'

No doubt Lidia was moved by the words of Esperanto's chief orator, her father's disciple. One may imagine she felt, as the Esperantists always did, re-inspired by his exhortations to go forth and fulfill their sacred task. Perhaps, as he spoke, she even thought: she would be one of those knights of the new era, armed with the spirit and the language of Zamenhof; she would go forth to slay the dark dragon and bring humanity toward the light of understanding. In any case, it was there in Vienna that Lidia began to take up a public role in the Esperanto movement. She attended many of the specialist meetings at the congress and took part in the meeting of the Esperanto students, where she was chosen to serve as secretary of the International Student Esperantist Association. But it was at the final working session of the congress that she really made her presence, and her convictions, known.

A proposal had been presented to the congress asking that all should accept the opinions of the Academy of Esperanto and the Language Committee concerning changes in the language. Ever since Zamenhof's death, it had been crucial that the authority of the linguistic institutions be respected in order to guard the integrity of the language. Vasily Eroshenko, a blind expatriate Russian who taught at the University of Peking, expressed his opinion that while the Academy must control the evolution of the language, it must allow that evolution to occur. The Academy was too conservative, he felt, and did not sufficiently respect the usage and preferences of the people.

The discussion went on, various persons offering their views on the subject. Then, probably to the astonishment of many in the audience, a slight, pale young woman rose to speak. It was Lidia. She asserted that several of the speakers were confusing evolution with anarchy. The evolution of the language could succeed, she said, only if it were limited by a certain amount of discipline.

It is not hard to imagine that there were indulgent smiles in the Konzerthaus at the impassioned words of the young university student, Miss Zamenhof. But Edmond Privat, at least, might have been reminded poignantly of the idealism of another Zamenhof as a student: Lidia's father.

The Esperantists would soon learn that here was another Zamenhof who would speak her mind and express her convictions openly and fearlessly. As she did that day in Vienna, Lidia would always urge unity and warn against anything that might lead to division or schism in the Esperanto movement.

Klara had struggled bravely through the congress, although it was evident that she was in great pain. On the way home, she spent some weeks at a spa in Czechoslovakia. The treatment did her no good; she returned home seriously ill and was confined to bed. The doctors decided to operate but soon found it was futile; the cancer had spread too far. Lidia watched her mother's agony helplessly. 'Death began to cover you with the veil of unconsciousness before your heart stopped

. . .' Lidia later recalled. 'Treacherous illness – which revealed its malevolent face when escape was no longer possible. And nailed to your bed of suffering, you waited for death because, yes, you were aware at the end that it was your last illness.' At the beginning of December word reached Klara that the goal she had worked toward would finally be achieved: the monument for Ludwik Zamenhof's grave had been completed and was on its way to Warsaw. Klara did not live to see it set in place: on December 6, 1924 she died. Her last wish was to be buried beside her husband.

'You went away,' mourned Lidia, 'you left that wasting body, which we committed to the earth. May the earth be light upon you . . . and may you be happy in the world where there is no more pain. That is what your daughter, in the hour of remembrance, wishes for you.'

Once again a funeral procession wound its way through the streets of the Jewish quarter of Warsaw, down Dzika Street then toward the cemetery. Once again the mourners listened to the oratory of Leo Belmont, followed by nine others. The prayers were intoned; the coffin glided downward. The verses of *La Espero*, sung with sadness, drifted up to the winter sky. Once again the earth was piled up and heaped with flower wreaths.

EIGHT

Geneva

The Esperanto movement had rapidly rebuilt itself after the devastation of the Great War. As a wave of renewed hope for peace and an awareness of internationalism spread, Esperanto gained recognition, respect and acceptance for its usefulness. But the road was still rocky. In some countries, nationalism continued to hinder Esperanto's progress, while within the movement disagreement over the question of neutrality divided the Esperantists.

As a result of highly successful courses in various countries, Esperanto had spread in socialist circles. But leaders among them disagreed with the traditional political neutrality of the Esperanto movement and felt Esperanto ought to be used openly as a tool of class struggle. In 1921 they broke away from the 'neutral' movement, forming a radical workers' Esperanto movement. The schism dealt Esperanto a serious blow within and without. Rightist extremists outside the movement, suspicious of anything 'international' in character, and frightened by the strong, openly leftist workers' movement, accused the entire Esperanto movement of dangerous revolutionary tendencies.

After the war, when the League of Nations was created, many Esperantists hoped that this new international body, which shared Esperanto's aims of international cooperation and peace, would recognize the benefits of the language Dr Zamenhof had created, and perhaps even adopt it. The Esperantists had just the person to present their case – the distinguished Edmond Privat, who eventually served as a member of the Persian delegation. The matter was brought before the League as a resolution expressing the hope that Esperanto might be taught more widely in the schools 'in order that children of all nations from now on should know at least two languages, their native tongue and an easy means for international communication'. But the delegate from France angrily opposed even considering the matter, claiming 'there already is an international language – French'.

Eventually a favorable report on 'Esperanto as an International Auxiliary Language' was prepared by the Secretary-General of the

League. The report found the language to be widely used internationally and asserted that Esperanto was much easier to learn than any other language. Its use was encouraged in the schools. But again the French delegate objected, acting on orders from his government to oppose any language other than French. In the end the matter was referred to the League's Committee on Intellectual Cooperation, which refused to recommend Esperanto because it feared that the learning of an auxiliary language would discourage people from studying national languages. Largely under the pressure of French nationalism, the League of Nations let the matter drop.

Zamenhof would not have been surprised. In 1891 he had cautioned the Esperantists not to wait for the help of important persons or governments in the belief that the success of Esperanto depended on such assistance. On the contrary, Zamenhof had said, they would take notice only after the movement became successful on its own.

Although the League of Nations would not recognize it as an official international auxiliary language, Esperanto gained recognition and support in other quarters. In 1924 Persia (no doubt through Edmond Privat) introduced a resolution that Esperanto be recognized as a 'clear language' for telegraphy, which was unanimously accepted by the League of Nations as well as the Universal Telegraph Union. The International Labor Office, which was supported by the League, began to use Esperanto, as did various commercial and scientific organizations. Later, when the French government reversed its hostile attitude, the French Academy of Sciences passed a resolution supporting Esperanto.

Although the fundamental structure and grammar of Esperanto remained unchanged from the form in which Zamenhof had first stated them, as the language was increasingly used, it grew in vocabulary. Zamenhof's first word list had contained about 900 roots; by 1930 an Esperanto dictionary contained 3,800 roots, from which about 40,000 words could be formed.* But Esperanto had become much more than a language. It was a cultural movement complete with local, national and international institutions, its own history and cherished traditions. The 'practical and commercial utility' of Esperanto was given a new twist as 'Esperanto' cigarettes, made in Scotland, came on the market (*'La internacia fumajo!'* the advertisement cried – 'The international smoke!'), and in Britain one could purchase Cadbury's 'Esperanto' chocolates at the local confectioner's.

More important, and far more lasting, Esperanto also had its own literature. In the first few decades of Esperanto's life, a great amount of literature had been translated into the international language, not just

---

* The *Plena illustrita vortaro de Esperanto* ('Complete Illustrated Dictionary of Esperanto'), published in 1970, contained 16,000 roots, of which at least 160,000 words could be formed.

from Western European languages, which shared linguistic roots with Esperanto, but from Chinese, Japanese, Armenian, Hungarian, Russian and Polish, among others. The work of translators had shown Esperanto's potential for literary expression, as well as its ability to make a diversity of national literatures accessible to a wide international audience through a single translation.

After World War I, original Esperanto literature began to flourish. Several literary 'schools' sprang up, the most important of which was the Budapest School, whose major figures were two Hungarians: the poet Kálmán Kalocsay, a medical doctor by profession; and Julio Baghy, a poet, novelist and actor. The literary journal of the Budapest School was *Literatura Mondo* (Literary World), which published some of Lidia's short stories during the 1930s.

After Klara's death, the Esperantists hoped that members of the Zamenhof family would continue to take part in the Esperanto movement personally. While no one could replace Ludwik Zamenhof in their hearts, some hoped that Adam would carry on his father's work for Esperanto as he had followed in his father's footsteps in medicine. Adam knew the language well and had been active in the movement during his school years, translating works of Pushkin and helping his father with correspondence and the Directory of Esperantists. But now Adam's medical practice left him no time for Esperanto activities.

Zofia also knew Esperanto fluently. Like her brother, while she was growing up she had helped her father, especially with his library. Although she kept informed about the movement and went to the yearly congresses, she too was busy with her medical practice.

Shortly after Klara's death a Warsaw Esperantist, Edward Wiesenfeld, published a collection of biographical sketches of the Zamenhof family called *Galerio de Zamenhofoj* (Gallery of Zamenhofs). Beginning in January 1925, it ran in installments in the international Esperanto newspaper *Heroldo de Esperanto* (Herald of Esperanto). In it Wiesenfeld gently chided the young Dr Adam Zamenhof for not taking over his father's role in Esperanto. He also lamented that Zofia 'does not actively take part in Esperanto life'.

In the edition of *Heroldo* for February 14, the chapter about Lidia appeared. Wiesenfeld, who had been present when Lidia spoke up at the Vienna congress, described the twenty-one-year-old 'Miss Lili' as 'in character and temperament . . . typical Zamenhof, only somewhat unrefined, which is explained by her youth . . .' 'Esperanto interests her,' Wiesenfeld wrote, 'and she is the only Zamenhof child active in the international language . . . After returning from Vienna, her fervor for Esperanto grew even more, and we hope to have in her one

of the most fervent pioneers of the Esperanto cause on Polish soil.'
Wiesenfeld's perceptive conclusion was: 'The youngest, but the most
promising.'

One wonders what might have made him call Lidia 'unrefined'.
Perhaps that independence of spirit which had made her a determined
and sometimes stubborn child now seemed too forthright and
assertive for a young lady. Though Wiesenfeld excused her rough
edges as a sign of immaturity, Lidia seems to have been a serious young
woman who was deeply concerned with the gravest issues of the time,
and who had little use for frivolous pursuits.

By the summer of 1925 the blond braids of childhood were gone.
And the youthful, tousled curls she had worn, with a defiant
expression, in the photograph that appeared in *Gallery of Zamenhofs*
had been replaced by the short, bobbed style of the 1920s. She had
inherited much of her father's looks, unlike her sister Zofia, who
resembled their mother. Lidia was quite short – about five feet – and
petite, with her father's thoughtful blue eyes. In later years, people
would say she was 'exactly his image'. She had a prominent, jutting
chin which accentuated her air of determination.

Lidia had finished her course work at the University of Warsaw. In
the autumn, she would take her exams and receive the degree of
Magister Juris – Master of Law. But in Poland a degree in law did not
lead as directly to a profession as a degree in medicine. The Polish bar
association was strict about admitting Jews – very few were accepted.
If she wanted to pursue a career as a lawyer, she would have to work in
a law office for several years before she could begin to practice. Because
studying law had been her mother's idea, and she did not want to
become a lawyer, she probably did not give the idea much thought.
Perhaps that summer, as she worried about her final examinations and
anticipated graduation, she wondered what she should do afterward.

Lidia seems never to have considered simply getting married and
having children. At that time, of course, it was quite unusual for a
woman to have any goal other than becoming a wife and mother. If a
woman did choose to work in a profession, that choice usually
required foregoing marriage, as it was generally believed that a woman
could not have both a family and a career. In the Zamenhof home,
however, it seems to have been expected that each person would do
some kind of work which was of service to humanity, and in the
extended Zamenhof family there were several two-career families –
often both spouses were doctors. Yet, neither Zofia nor Lidia ever
married. This also was not unusual in the Zamenhof clan. Many years
later Julian's wife, Dr Olga Zamenhof, recalled that there were at least
six Zamenhof women who did not want to marry at all.

Homemaking did not interest Lidia, who never learned to cook – she described herself as 'completely unsuited' to it. The life of the intellect and working for the Zamenhof ideals was far more important to her. But unlike Zofia, who with her brusque manner and masculine appearance was, as her cousin Stephen described her, 'a bit discouraging, probably, to men', Lidia was not at all unfeminine. She had a great tenderness, and a great sympathy for the plight of women.

Although she was not beautiful in the usual sense, Lidia had an inner beauty that attracted those who met her; surely many of the young Esperantist men would have been honored to marry the daughter of Zamenhof. Yet perhaps the very fact that she was the daughter of the Majstro made people afraid to approach her. Throughout her life, although many admired and respected her, few people ever truly became close to her. On one occasion Lidia did confide to a friend that once she had 'lost her heart', but that was all she ever revealed of it. Isaj Dratwer later recalled that 'we Esperantists – then young men – used to say Lidia Zamenhof has only one lover, which is the Esperanto language!'

Over the years Esperanto had indeed become Lidia's great love. She had become an active member of *Konkordo* (Concord), a Warsaw Esperanto society, and some remembered her as its 'guiding spirit'. Ever since the Vienna congress she had served as secretary of the International Student Esperantist Association, helping to draw up its by-laws.

During the war, Lidia had begun translating Polish literature into Esperanto. Until now she had not tried to publish her translations, thinking them not good enough. She had not given up, but had kept improving her translating skills. At last she had something she was ready to publish: a collection of five short stories by the Polish author Henryk Sienkiewicz. It came out the year she finished university, published in a slim octavo volume by Hirt & Sohn in Leipzig, Germany. The reviewer from *Literatura Mondo* was enthusiastic, calling Lidia's translation 'distinguished and remarkable'. He added that 'it would not be surprising if the first edition quickly ran out, because the little work merits the attention of every literature-lover'.

The child who once had stubbornly refused to learn Esperanto had grown up to see in the language more than just a family legacy. Through her father's example, and his careful and gentle instruction, his ideas and beliefs – the inner idea of Esperanto – had taken root in Lidia's heart. As a child she had seen the result of pogroms, war and the occupation of her country. As a young woman in her teenage years and as a university student, she had observed the war's aftermath of suffering, further injustice and revenge – the very things her father had warned of – and she believed that peace would not come until there was brotherhood and justice among all the peoples of the world. But this could not occur until they could communicate with each other. Esperanto, she believed, provided the ideal means for that.

Although Ludwik Zamenhof had become convinced that the unification of mankind would only come about through a world religion, Lidia at twenty-one was not interested in religion. By her own account she had believed in God as a child, but had lost this faith. By 1925 Lidia Zamenhof was, as she described herself, 'an atheist'.

As a sensitive young woman, Lidia must have felt deeply the conflict of national identity that troubled many young Polish Jews from non-religious families. She identified herself as a Jew, though a secular one. Although Lidia described herself officially by the Polish term *wyznania mojżeszowego* (of Mosaic Faith), which was preferred to the literal *Żyd* (Jew) by those who wished to distance themselves culturally from orthodox Polish Jewry, she disdained those Jews who denied their Jewish affiliation and who tried to 'pass' as Gentiles, sometimes even converting to Catholicism in an attempt to further their careers. Yet Lidia loved Poland too, and felt a great affinity for Polish literature.

Among the Esperantists in Poland between the wars, the majority were Jews. There were some notable exceptions, though these were few. Most Poles were cold toward Esperanto. Fiercely patriotic, they still remembered a time under foreign domination when the languages of other nations had been imposed on them. One might have expected them to understand the need for a neutral auxiliary language, but the general attitude at that time in Poland was 'unfriendly', recalled Eugen Rytenberg, who taught Esperanto in Warsaw during the 1930s. Most Poles considered Esperanto 'a Jewish affair', Lidia later said, and they wanted to have nothing to do with it.

But in the international Esperanto movement, Lidia met people from all over the world, some from countries that had only a short time ago fought a bitter war against each other. To most of the Esperantists, differences of nationality or religion meant little. Even if they did not all share a fervent belief in the 'inner idea', at least they considered themselves brothers and sisters in *nia kara lingvo* (our dear language). Among the Esperantists Lidia was at home.

The Seventeenth Universal Congress of Esperanto was to be held in Geneva, Switzerland. Lidia went with her sister Zofia. Years later she reminisced: 'When in the summer of 1925 I took a train to go from Warsaw to Vienna and from Vienna to Geneva in order to attend the Esperanto congress held that year in the City of Nations, I did not imagine that each turn of the wheels was bringing me nearer to a contact which was to mean Life for me.'

After two sleepless nights Lidia arrived in Geneva. The city was just recovering from a heat wave, and Saturday, the first of August, was beautiful. As it was the Swiss national holiday, that evening the tree-lined quais along Lake Leman were festooned with lights, music played, and fireworks boomed out over the lake, reflected their colors on its surface. At eight o'clock the night vibrated as all the churchbells in Geneva pealed in celebration. The Esperantists, enjoying their 'Get-Together Evening', strolled in the university's Promenade des Bastions, the gardens decorated with lights, while musicians entertained them.

In Geneva, newspaper articles had been appearing about the congress for two weeks before it began, and just before the meeting opened the *Tribune de Genève* had printed a long article sympathetic to Esperanto. 'It is no longer the time for facile jests and anti-Esperantist nonsense,' wrote the reporter. 'Today that is left to the ignorant, because it is in serious circles, whether practical people . . . or academics and scholars . . . that Esperanto counts its most earnest champions.'

A number of Geneva's postal employees and gendarmes had been studying Esperanto so they could assist the thousand participants expected to attend the congress. The Esperanto-speaking gendarmes could be recognized – how else? – by a green star embroidered on the sleeve of their tunics.

On Sunday, the day the congress was to begin, Geneva was shrouded in gray skies that poured rain all day. But just in time for the opening ceremony the rain stopped.

At eight o'clock the crowd filled opulent Victoria Hall. After the welcoming speeches, Edmond Privat rose to speak. He reminded the audience how in the same hall, nineteen years earlier, Ludwik Zamenhof had spoken to them of the pogroms in Bialystok. That evening Zamenhof had told them not to blame any nation or people, but rather the *darkness* which causes men to act toward each other in such a beastly and savage manner. 'Give forth the light of mutual understanding, show forth the light of mutual knowledge and friendship,' said Privat, 'those were the words of Zamenhof at the Geneva congress. And when I remember that, I think also about all those geniuses who, as he did, always strove to bring this world some light . . . great men in this world have always worked for the light . . .'

But Ludwik Zamenhof was gone. And, Privat said, 'that charming person, whom we all loved to see at the congress' – Klara – would not be with them again. Privat asked them to stand in her honor. 'With pleasure we welcome the two daughters of our Majstro: Zofia and Lidia Zamenhof, who do us the honor of attending the congress. *Ili vivu!* Long may they live!' he cried, and applause filled the hall.

'The memory of their noble parents', Privat went on, 'remains engraved in all our hearts. They are indeed brave, courageous young women working for noble and beautiful goals. Let us thank them warmly for that, as well as for coming to Geneva.' Once more the congress audience applauded.

One afternoon Lidia and some friends strolled in the gardens near the Palace of the League of Nations, laughing and chatting and admiring the magnificent landscape. Lake Leman blindingly reflected the last golden rays of the sun. 'A rare enthusiasm of joy,' Lidia later recalled, 'some enchantment impelled us, as if carefree children, from flower bed to flower bed, from group of trees to group of trees. At last we stopped at a small square, in the middle of which was an object. We approached and regarded it curiously.

'On two poles hung a piece of bronze, whose surface was decorated with dragons, serpents and strange hieroglyphs . . . It drew us, attracted us. "What is it? What could it be?" someone asked. One of us struck the bronze lightly with a finger. A lovely hum, like a soft, distant echo of a sound, could be heard. We struck it again. The mysterious, wistful sound reverberated. "A bell! Let's ring it!" someone cried.

'"Yes, a bell –" a voice intruded, "a bell sent as a gift from China to the League of Nations so that it might be rung when peace reigns in the world."

'The sense of playfulness left us. Respectfully we stepped away from the mysterious bronze. To call up its sound now, when the odor of blood still rises on the air, when serpents of hate still hiss in the swamps of chauvinism, would be to profane the bell.'

Lidia mused: 'Bell of peace! You, an enigma fashioned of bronze beside the yellow rivers of the Celestial Land! You emigrated from the heart of your homeland and have been set upon the shore of the most beautiful lake, between mountains that touch the clouds. And patient, like eternity – inscrutable, like eternity – you await the promised hour. That hour will come . . . you will ring, and winds will carry your echo far, to the snows of the North and to the deserts of the South, through green valleys and to snowy peaks. You will peal out and then swords will clang no more, nor will cannons roar, but the bells of all the temples of the world will repeat your song announcing to mankind the beginning of the new era!'

Thursday, August 6, promised clear weather, but a new storm was on its way, bringing back the clouds and rain. Earlier that week someone had invited Lidia to one of the *fakkunvenoj*, or specialist meetings, planned for Thursday. The congress program listed it simply as 'Bahá'í Meeting'. The name did not mean anything to her, Lidia later recalled. 'I looked at the congress schedule. Another meeting, in which I had more interest, was to take place about the same time. I decided quickly: I shall not go to that Bahá'í meeting.' But when the day came, the other meeting ended sooner than she expected. Lidia saw no reason to refuse the Bahá'í invitation. She went, but, as she described it, 'out of politeness'.

The meeting had begun at three o'clock in the office of the International Bahá'í Bureau. The Bureau office was near Victoria Hall, on the Boulevard Georges-Favon, a busy, wide, tree-lined street. Lidia approached the door of the brown-gray building. Above the door was the building number carved in stone: 19.

For some time, the Bahá'ís had been working on preparations for the two meetings held there that week. They hoped to attract Esperantists to come and learn more about the Bahá'í Faith. If they did not attract the Esperantists to their religion, at least they drew them in to enjoy their hospitality. 'Whoever wanted to drink good tea (for free!) surely went to the Bahá'í office to listen to the talks by Bahá'ís,' reported *Heroldo de Esperanto*. '. . . With joy we learned that everywhere the Bahá'ís are learning our language . . . We admired also the fervor and devotion of one of the great apostles . . . Martha Root.' Miss Martha Root, an American freelance journalist, had come to Switzerland from Haifa, Palestine, specially to help open the International Bahá'í Bureau and arrange the Bahá'í meetings at the congress.

A small, plain-looking woman of fifty-three who dressed somewhat eccentrically, Martha Root often impressed people at first as 'a little mouse'. But her dynamic spirit and sincerity drew people to her. In 1914 she had resigned her position as society editor of a Pittsburgh newspaper in order to travel as a freelance foreign correspondent, and for some years she had dedicated her life to traveling the world, most often alone, lecturing and writing about the Bahá'í Faith. Although she was often ill, she traveled and gave speeches until exhaustion overtook her. She kept up a seemingly inhuman pace in a race against the disease which was inexorably consuming her body: since 1912 she had known that she had cancer.

Unconcerned with personal comfort, Martha Root traveled third class and often dined on such simple fare as a bit of cheese and an egg she boiled in her hotel room. Yet in every country she visited, she approached eminent people in many fields and met with royalty and presidents to whom she gave her message.

Martha Root had been studying Esperanto over the years, knowing it would help in her travels. Indeed, as she went from country to country, she found that Esperanto opened many doors for her. Although her original interest in Esperanto had been as a means of attracting people to the Bahá'í teachings, she became a fervent Esperantist. Martha sympathized wholeheartedly with the principles of Esperantism, believing that the international auxiliary language ought to be a neutral one. 'To people who have traveled and met the statesmen and the masses in different lands,' she wrote, 'it is evident that any national tongue is not only not acceptable as a universal help-language, but it is unsuitable to the international thought content of a new universal cycle.' Although her native language was English, she did not wish to see English forced 'upon a world that does not want it'.

In June Martha Root had written to the congress organizers asking that the Bahá'ís be allowed to hold a meeting at the Geneva congress. 'Our aim is the same as yours,' she wrote, 'the Bahá'í Movement is the "Esperanto" of religions.'

That Thursday afternoon, Lidia arrived late; the meeting had already begun. 'The hall was decorated in cool evergreens', Martha Root described her handiwork in a report, 'and mingled with the greens were filmy white flowers and clusters of violet blooms native to Switzerland. The portraits of 'Abdu'l-Bahá and Dr Zamenhof were decorated with green boughs and Esperanto flags.'

The main room of the Bureau had space for sixty people. For the meeting, the doors to the adjoining rooms had been thrown open to allow another forty people to sit and hear the discussion comfortably.

In her report about the event Martha Root noted that both Zofia and Lidia were there and that Zofia read from a paper of her father's on the need of a universal religion. Martha Root quoted Dr Zamenhof's remarks on the Bahá'í Faith to the interviewer at the 1913 Bern congress as well as a statement Zamenhof had made earlier that 'The person of 'Abdu'l-Bahá and his work I very highly esteem; I see in him one of the greatest benefactors of mankind.' A Russian lady, Mrs Umanski, read the laudatory statements 'Abdu'l-Bahá had made to various Esperanto groups, and Dr Adelbert Mühlschlegel, a physician from Stuttgart, Germany, gave a short talk in Esperanto about the Bahá'í Faith.

'The Bahá'í Movement is not merely a new oriental religion among other religions or spiritual movements, it is simply the renewal of religion,' he said, 'because there exists only one God, one love, one truth, one religion.' It was only the forms of the Divine Manifestation that changed, Dr Mühlschlegel explained. 'The great prophets are the reflections, the manifestations of the one divine light . . . They show forth the Divine light according to the capacity of the people of that time and place, which change. Consequently, the external forms of religion also change,' he went on, 'that is, after some time they are given a different form by a new prophet. We humans then say this or that prophet founded a new religion. In truth, he founded only a new, more modern form of the human religion.'

Moses and Christ had taught the people according to their needs and capacity, he said. 'Now Bahá'u'lláh has come. He speaks to the whole of humanity today even more complicated, more diverse than then

. . . Through Bahá'u'lláh Christians will understand Christ better, as through Christ we better understand Moses. Bahá'u'lláh fulfills and carries out the words of Christ just as Christ fulfilled the words of Moses . . .'

He went on to explain that one of the Bahá'í principles was the use of an international auxiliary language, either to be chosen from among the existing languages or created. This language, he explained, was to be taught to children in all the schools of the world, '"so that the whole world may be considered as one country and one home".

'"The best-beloved fruit of the tree of knowledge is this majestic word:"' he said, paraphrasing Bahá'u'lláh, '"Ye are all the fruits of one tree and the leaves of one branch. Glory is not his who loves only his country, glory is his who loves the whole world." Let us think about it, *samideanoj!*

'This was ordained many decades ago by a prophet in an uncivilized oriental land. Dr L. L. Zamenhof during his blessed life carried out that Esperanto inner idea, the spirit of the future new humanity, the spirit of Bahá'u'lláh. Because of that, Dr Zamenhof was a true Bahá'í. And all Bahá'ís in the whole world honor him as an ideal model, love him as *majstro* and brother.'

At last the meeting was thrown open for discussion, and tea was served. During the open forum, Martha Root later reported with delight, 'the President of one of Europe's best known Peace Societies and a noted Esperantist' said, '"Let us work that all Bahá'ís may become Esperantists and all Esperantists become Bahá'ís!"'

Almost fifty years later, in 1974, Dr Mühlschlegel recalled seeing Lidia at that meeting, and that during the discussion Lidia spoke with Martha Root. But Lidia remembered only 'some speeches, some readings . . . as I came only out of politeness, I did not pay any special attention to what was going on. The words were going into one ear and out of the other. Soon after I left Geneva I forgot about it all.'

Martha Root, however, remembered the two daughters of Dr Zamenhof and, with her usual determination, looked for ways to make contact with them again. After the Geneva meeting she wrote to Ella Cooper, an American Bahá'í, about an idea that had come to her. Martha planned to go to Warsaw, where she hoped Lidia and Zofia would let her board with them for a time. 'If I could stay with them for a month,' she wrote, 'I would learn so much, not only in speaking out in the spirit of Dr Zamenhof's idea – and also, I could tell them so much about the Bahá'í Cause.' If some of the Zamenhofs became Bahá'ís, Martha believed, 'it would be a great impetus to the Bahá'í Cause in all the Esperanto circles of the world . . .'

Martha was drawn specially to Lidia, who 'seemed so *sad*. I always wished that she could know the joy of 'Abdu'l-Bahá's life. It comes to

me very strongly that this would be a very wise plan, to try to go there
. . .'

When the congress closed, Lidia went home to Warsaw, never thinking she would see that American lady again.

While the peaceful Esperanto congress, dedicated to bringing down barriers between people, had been meeting in neutral Switzerland, elsewhere in the world others were busy building those barriers higher than ever.

Even as Lidia had been traveling from Warsaw to Geneva on her way to the congress, some fifty thousand people were also leaving Poland, but against their will. They were ethnic Germans who had lived in what was once German Poland. Five years before a plebiscite had been held and these people, mostly small farmers and artisans, had voted to keep their German citizenship. Now the Polish government – upheld by the Hague Court of Arbitration – was deporting them. Forced to leave their homes, carrying whatever of their possessions they could, once they got to Germany they would have nowhere to go. In retaliation Germany expelled twenty thousand Poles from its territory.

After the Great War Poland had been given a strip of German, but once Polish, land that separated East Prussia from the rest of Germany. That first week of August 1925 the German newspapers were complaining bitterly about this 'Polish corridor', insisting that because of it two million Germans in East Prussia were cut off from the fatherland. The widow of American President Wilson, traveling through Germany, was being greeted with hostility and insults; while in the United States the Italian representative to the League of Nations was denouncing 'utopian schemes' for world peace, claiming that war was the natural way of things, and speaking out for the movement that had swept Italy, called fascism.

And in Los Angeles, California, the executive committee of the American Chemical Society had just adopted a resolution denouncing the League of Nations' ban on poisonous gases in warfare. The League, said the chemists, showed 'a lamentable lack of understanding of chemical warfare', which, the scientists felt, was more humane than ancient forms of butchery.

NINE

Spiritual Mother and Daughter

At last, the monument for the grave of Dr Zamenhof had been shipped from Scotland to the Free City of Danzig (now the Polish port city of Gdansk) on the Baltic Sea. From there it was transported by train to Warsaw. But when the stone was examined on arrival, it was discovered to have some errors in the lettering. Correcting them would be costly, but the sculptor, Lubelski, insisted the errors be corrected or he would not allow his name on the monument. At last, everything in order, the monument was set in place over the tomb. Although it would mean postponing the unveiling for several months, the committee decided to hold the public dedication ceremonies on the ninth anniversary of Zamenhof's death, in April 1926.

Shortly before this date Lidia received a telegram signed 'Martha Root' asking for an opportunity to speak at the unveiling ceremonies on the relation of Zamenhof's life work to the principles of Bahá'u'lláh. 'After a few moments of pondering and musing,' Lidia later recalled, 'I connected this somehow with the meeting in Geneva and with one of the persons I met there.' She reported the telegram to the committee, which consented to Miss Root's request.

On April 18 – the date had been put ahead to the nearest Sunday – the weather was mild and clear. An hour before the ceremony, several hundred people were already gathered, silent and respectful, near the entrance gate to the area where the tomb was located, near the front of the cemetery. Esperanto flags waved in the air above the monument, which was shrouded by a black cloth. The slope in front of the grave was landscaped with greenery in the shape of a five-pointed Esperanto star. Around the monument, holding Esperanto flags, stood an honor guard of students.

By eleven o'clock five hundred people had gathered, including representatives of the Jewish community, Esperanto societies and educational institutions, as well as reporters, photographers and some government officials. Several people had come from the provinces, and some, including Martha Root, from other countries.

The family and speakers arrived, and the crowd made room for them on the terrace beside the monument. At eleven o'clock the

68

ceremony began. Professor Odo Bujwid of Krakow cut the ribbon and unveiled the stone, as the choir sang *La Espero*. After several speeches, Adam Zamenhof came forward in the name of the Zamenhof family to place the first immense flower wreath at the foot of the monument. Then, one by one, others approached, offering their flower wreaths and speaking a few words of homage to Dr Zamenhof.

Martha Root had come as the delegate of the Bahá'í movement. She stepped up to the tomb and placed white roses at the foot of the stone. Then, as she later reported, she 'spoke to the people the message of love and esteem from Shoghi Effendi, Guardian of the Bahá'í Cause and the greeting of the Bahá'ís of the World. It was significant,' she noted, 'that all speeches extolled the spirit of Esperantism, its power to make the world "one great family gathering".'

At five o'clock that evening, the Warsaw Esperantists and the delegates who had come from other cities and lands gathered at a reception at the Zamenhof home. Martha Root was among them and described her feelings as she entered Dr Zamenhof's study, which the family had kept intact as a kind of shrine: 'All felt a thrill to walk up those steps where he had so often walked and visit the room where he had done much of his life work,' she wrote (apparently unaware that Zamenhof had lived in the apartment on Królewska Street for only the last few years of his life).

'. . . His office contains, besides all the instruments and paraphernalia, a set of Esperanto books from the first leaflets to the last volumes, certainly it is the most interesting Esperanto library in the world. Here, there, everywhere in the office are gifts, Esperanto flags and banners, pictures of world Esperanto congresses. Mr Joseph Gabowicz, one of the best sculptors of Poland has made a bust of Dr Zamenhof which is so like him, that as it stood on the piano and the friends filling the room sang the "La Espero" it seemed as if the figure moved and lived; Dr Zamenhof's spirit was in their midst.'

After Leo Belmont's speech, Martha Root stood up. This was the moment she had come for, to talk about 'The Bahá'í Movement as One Form of Homaranismo'. She quoted 'Abdu'l-Bahá's words praising Zamenhof and Esperanto, and Dr Zamenhof's statements about the Bahá'í Faith, as well as remarks he had made expressing his interest in the Bahá'í movement as 'one of the great world movements which, like Esperanto, insist on the brotherhood of mankind'. If the words sounded familiar to Lidia they well should have; Martha had read the same quotations a year before in Geneva at the Bahá'í meeting. After more speeches, one of the ladies sang songs of Beethoven and Schubert in Esperanto.

Lidia became intrigued by Martha Root, who spoke about her religion so fervently, in Esperanto tinged with an American accent.

'Very soon I started wondering', Lidia later recalled, 'what made this woman, neither wealthy nor strong, wander about the world.'

Martha Root stayed in Warsaw for two more weeks. As she had hoped, she arranged to stay with the Zamenhof family. Zofia and Adam were at the hospital during the day, but Lidia, who had begun studying English, was at home. Lidia agreed to help Martha with her Esperanto, and Martha was to help Lidia with her English. 'I feel we shall have a wonderful time together,' Martha wrote to friends in America, 'and that we shall learn more than "languages". It will bring Esperanto and the Bahá'í Movement closer together.' Martha moved into the Zamenhof flat, sharing Lidia's room. She intended to pay the Zamenhofs for her room and board 'and I hope pay generously, because their father gave his all to found Esperanto and they are working hard'.

Martha Root felt she had been guided to Lidia. 'Bahá'u'lláh and 'Abdu'l-Bahá have planned it', she wrote Ella Cooper. 'For months have been praying for this . . . I feel that 'Abdu'l-Bahá and Dr Zamenhof are wishing this closer coming together of the two movements.'

But when Martha spoke to Lidia about the religion, Dr Zamenhof's daughter was skeptical. 'Soon she told me what was the Cause to which she was sacrificing her life', Lidia later wrote. 'I can't say I accepted it at once. Too long was I indifferent to matters of faith. I remember asking her whether an atheist (myself!) can be a Bahá'í. And when she told me that the Bahá'ís do believe in the existence of God, I decided within myself: well, I am not going to be a Bahá'í. But Martha could not be discouraged easily. She knew how to be patient, to be faithful – and to pray. It was her pure and spiritual personality which appealed to me at that time more than any written statements.'

Having grown up with the atmosphere of veneration that surrounded her father, Lidia was perhaps specially susceptible to a personality like Martha's, sincerely and wholly devoted to the life of the ideal. Martha also had, Marzieh Gail has recalled, 'an understated, maternal tenderness about her', which was probably comforting and alluring to Lidia, who had only recently lost her own mother. Martha and Lidia did form a deep, enduring bond of love that was as that between mother and daughter. Martha referred to Lidia in letters as her 'spiritual child' and Lidia thought of Martha as her 'spiritual mother', but to them the expression was more than simply a figure of speech.

Although, as Lidia has remarked, it was Martha's 'pure and spiritual personality' which attracted her at first, Martha's message, the Bahá'í teachings, struck a chord in Lidia. She had grown up with, if not a personal belief, at least a family loyalty to her father's philosophy as the most advanced teachings on the subject of mankind as 'one great

18. Lidia's matura, or certificate of graduation and grades from the eight-year Modern School for Girls of the Association of the Cooperative School (formerly of A. Warecka) in Warsaw. The first subject, religion, is blank; as a Jew, she was excused from it

19. Lidia: the blond braids of childhood gone

21. Sketch of Lidia at the Geneva congress, by
O. Lazar.

20. A group of Esperantists gathered at the Jewish cemetery on the anniversary
of Zamenhof's death in 1923. Lidia stands to the right of the grave; Klara, to the
left.

22. *Martha Root*

23. *A group of eminent Esperantists at the Geneva congress in 1925. Front row: Zofia at left, Lidia at right. Second row, third from left: Edmond Privat; sixth from left, Professor Paul Christaller*

family circle'. Now, suddenly, she saw his concepts in another perspective. 'It seems to me,' she told Martha, 'that Esperanto is only a school in which future Bahá'ís educate themselves. The Bahá'í Movement is a step forward. It is larger.'

On the face of it, this was quite a startling statement. For Zamenhof's own daughter to say that something else was larger than Esperanto, that the cause to which her father had devoted his life was 'only a school' no doubt deeply shocked many Esperantists and may even have seemed treasonous.

Yet the creator of Esperanto had never regarded the Esperanto movement as an end in itself, but rather as a means to educate people about unity. Zamenhof himself had believed that the idea of a neutral language could never succeed without a world religion. Lidia's words to Martha Root seemed to echo what Ludwik Zamenhof had told the Universal Congress of Esperanto in 1907: 'Gradually Esperantoland will become a school for the future brotherhood of mankind.'

The Esperantists learned of Lidia's remark almost immediately, for Martha Root quoted it in an article she wrote about the unveiling ceremony. The newspaper *Heroldo de Esperanto* published an excerpt in its 4 June edition, calling attention to the statement as remarkable but removing the word 'only' – perhaps to soften the effect on the Esperantists.

Ludwik Zamenhof's daughter saw no contradiction or conflict of loyalties in accepting the Bahá'í Faith. Its essential teachings were not in conflict with Zamenhof's ideas, but seemed to confirm them and expand them. Here were the concepts of Zamenhof's Homaranismo – one God as the unknowable Creator of all, one mankind to live in peace as one great human family, the agreement of the essential teachings of the Great Teachers of the past, accord between science and religion, a universal auxiliary language.

But if the principles were the same, why accept the Bahá'í Faith over Homaranismo? Lidia's personal admiration for or attraction to Martha Root was not enough to explain it. Ludwik Zamenhof had never claimed to found a religion, but the Bahá'í teachings, Lidia came to believe, carried the power of divine inspiration. 'In the Teaching of Bahá'u'lláh', Lidia explained many years later, 'I found the universality which only the truly God-given teaching can give to searching mankind. That is why it attracted me at the beginning.' And between Esperanto and her new-found Faith, Lidia perceived a fundamental spiritual bond. She became, in her own words, 'profoundly convinced' that 'Esperanto was created directly under the influence of Bahá'u'lláh, although the author of the language did not know it'.

Lidia did not feel that becoming a Bahá'í affected her Jewishness, for, to her, being a Jew was a racial or ethnic matter, not a religious one.

The idea of accepting any *religion* proved more of an obstacle for Lidia. 'I myself was as if in darkness', she recalled of this early period, in a letter written many years later, 'and only now do I see how shadowy and unhappy was that darkness and how bright are the rays of the Light, the source of all life and truth.'

'After Martha's departure I was left alone', Lidia wrote. 'From time to time her letters, full of love, stimulated me again. Besides this, however, there was no one by my side to remind me of God when I was forgetting Him and to uphold my spirit when it was sinking into indifference. But there was also no one to become a test to me and to let me see a face which the Spirit did not yet brighten with the same light I saw in my spiritual mother. My spiritual interest was as a sea-tide – coming and going, coming and going. Sometimes it would be so low that as far as I can recount, even under the surgeon's knife I did not turn to God. But when the tide was coming on, each time its waves covered a larger surface of my soul. I began to try to pray to God, in Whom I had not believed for many years.

'One desire finally crystallized in me: I wanted to go to Haifa.'

No doubt during Martha's stay in Warsaw she told Lidia about her pilgrimage to the Bahá'í holy shrines in Haifa, Palestine, and encouraged her to make a pilgrimage herself. Lidia had become a Bahá'í too late to meet 'Abdu'l-Bahá, who had died in 1921. The leadership of the Bahá'í community had passed to his grandson Shoghi Rabbani, known as Shoghi Effendi, whom 'Abdu'l-Bahá had named in his will as Guardian of the Bahá'í Faith. Because of the unstable and often dangerous conditions in Palestine, it was necessary to get Shoghi Effendi's approval before making the journey of pilgrimage, so, Lidia later wrote, 'my spiritual mother wrote to the Guardian asking for permission'.

To Lidia's disappointment, Shoghi Effendi answered that she should wait.

Lidia saw Martha Root again in August at the Eighteenth Universal Esperanto Congress in Edinburgh, Scotland. For this 'Congress of Joy' the weather in Scotland was warm and pleasant; the *Scotsman* reported that Edinburgh had never seen so much sunshine in one week. The most crowded place in the city was the railway station: it was August Bank Holiday, and people streamed out of town for the long weekend. The city gave the Esperantists free use of the streetcars and the conductors greeted the visitors in Esperanto.

Two Bahá'í meetings were held at the congress, which took place in the halls of the United Free Church of Scotland, where in 1913 'Abdu'l-Bahá had once given a public talk. Dr Immanuel Olsvanger, a Polish Jew who was a leader of the Zionist movement in Britain, chaired the first Bahá'í session on August 2 and introduced Martha Root, who spoke on 'The Positive Power of Universal Religion'.

Afterward there was a talk about the progress of the Bahá'í Faith in different lands, with stereopticon slides of 'Akká and Haifa, music and readings from the words of Bahá'u'lláh. Lidia brought her sister Zofia to the meeting. The Swiss scientist and Esperantist Dr August Forel sent the gathering a telegram: 'Long live the universal religion of Bahá'u'lláh! Long live the universal auxiliary language, Esperanto!'

But the reaction was not universally approving. At the congress, Martha reported, 'two people attacked the Cause!' Philosophically she added, 'But one has to expect some criticism.'

The next year's congress, in the Free City of Danzig in 1927, marked the fortieth anniversary of the birth of Esperanto. Lidia, Adam and Zofia all attended. At the opening ceremony, Martha Root had arranged to read a message of greeting from Shoghi Effendi, the Guardian of the Bahá'í Faith. 'My dear fellow-workers in the service of humanity,' he had written the congress, 'I take great pleasure in addressing you . . . and in wishing you from all my heart the fullest success in the great work you are doing for the promotion of the good of humanity.

'It will interest you, I am sure, to learn, that as the result of the repeated and emphatic admonitions of 'Abdu'l-Bahá, His many followers even in the distant villages and hamlets of Persia, where the light of Western civilization has hardly penetrated as yet, as well as in other lands throughout the East, are strenuously and enthusiastically engaged in the study and teaching of Esperanto, for whose future they cherish the highest hopes.

'I am voicing the sentiments of the unnumbered followers of the Faith throughout the world, when I offer you through this letter, the cordial expression of sincere best wishes and fervent prayers for the success of your noble end.'

Martha spoke again at one of the Bahá'í meetings, on 'Bahá'í Proofs of Life after Death'. 'The reason for our birth into this world is not only to acquire material happiness or these external conditions which seem to us so important,' she said. 'On the contrary . . . the real reason for our birth is to awaken the spirit hidden in each soul and develop the qualities which it will use in the next realm. The child born into the human realm comes equipped with eyes, ears and other senses, which are already formed and ready for use. In the same way we are spiritually in the uterine world of eternal life and the most scientific knowledge which we can obtain is to learn to acquire the DIVINE qualities, because the awakening spirit can take with it to the higher realm only those DIVINE qualities which it acquires here. It is important that we strive to prepare ourselves as well as possible for rapid progress because we feel that it is in our power to continue our life on another plane.'

Unfortunately, Martha had chosen the wrong Esperanto word to translate 'plane' so that her statement came out: 'we feel that it is in our power to continue our life on another planet'. When the talk was published as a booklet, it was duly reviewed in a German Esperanto magazine by Arnold Behrendt, a prominent German Esperantist who was to play an ignominious role in the movement during the years ahead. He took exception in his review, saying, 'I confess: I also . . . believe in the life of the spirit after death. But my belief is not the same as is apparently the belief of the author . . . I don't believe that our spirit will continue to live on another planet . . .' Of course Martha Root did not either.

On Sunday, near the seaside spa town of Zoppot, in a little square surrounded by young fir trees, called the 'Esperanto Ground', a 'Jubilee Oak' was to be planted to commemorate the fortieth anniversary of Esperanto. The Esperantists had brought earth from their homelands to place symbolically around the roots of the young tree.

The sun was hot and it was a long walk from Zoppot to the Esperanto Ground. As flags of Danzig and Zoppot and the Green Banner flew above, the Esperantists and some curious onlookers crowded into the small area prepared for the ceremony. After several speeches, Lidia came forward to pour earth from her father's tomb upon the roots of the Jubilee Oak. Then others approached with soil they had brought for the occasion. Taking the event very seriously, Martha Root had brought earth from the Tomb of Bahá'u'lláh in 'Akká and from the Tombs of the Báb and 'Abdu'l-Bahá on Mount Carmel in Haifa, as well as some sent by an American friend from a place 'Abdu'l-Bahá had once visited in New Jersey.

It was a solemn, symbolic moment as people from many countries offered their native and holy soils, bound together to nurture the tree that stood for unity and understanding. But the outside world intruded with symbolism of its own. A journalist observed that in the sweltering weather, most of the dry earth brought for the ceremony ended up not in the ground but in the air – as dust on the wind.

And, almost three months later, the *Zoppoter Zeitung* reported that the Jubilee Oak had been maliciously destroyed by vandals. Although it was later replanted, in 1937 it was again destroyed and the large commemorative plaque torn down by German Nazis.

The hope of peace that many people had clung to during the years following the Great War was fading. Idealists of Lidia's generation had placed their faith in the League of Nations to keep peace and settle international disputes. But as these children of the war grew to adulthood, it became clear that this hope was doomed: the League, which the United States had refused to join, was impotent. All over the world, fanatic nationalism and sectarian hatreds were stronger than ever. Lidia's generation watched as the dictatorships arose, contemptuously rejecting the League and the Treaty of Versailles. All too soon it became obvious that another global war, more devastating than the first, was inevitable.

While many people were cynical about the chances for peace, some, including Lidia, still clung to the hope that through righteousness and education the hearts could be changed, and peace could become a reality and not just a dream. But these were already beginning to see themselves as a besieged few. In his congress speech in Danzig, Edmond Privat evoked this feeling when he told the gathering: 'Now we stand at the bonfire of our great Esperantist encampment. All of you – bring your cares, your yearnings, your inner weeds and your dry branches and throw them into the fire. Let us sincerely grasp one another's hands, let us form a circle round the beautiful flame. May it grow, may it crackle, may it warm our hearts. Outside, in the world, it is still night.'

In Warsaw Lidia had begun to teach Esperanto classes for the Concord Society. Though she earned very little from her classes, she liked teaching and was good at it. She had also begun to publish stories of her own in *Pola Esperantisto* ('Polish Esperantist'). Through them she had found another way to spread the ideas dearest to her. In her writing she often clothed in allegory the issue or principle she wanted to express. A chance glimpse of a scene – a family in the park, a sticker on a letter, an article she had read, or a person she met, might move her to write about the deeper meaning she perceived. In the space of about a year she published five articles and stories in *Pola Esperantisto*.

One of those stories, which would prove ironic in the light of events to come, reflected the worsening relations between the peoples, but also the hope of those like Lidia that there was an answer and that it could conquer even hatred.

In her story, she described a traveler passing through an alien land called Chauvinia. 'Already the sun was setting and only tiny clouds in the west, colored red as if by blood, showed where it disappeared,' she wrote. 'It was very warm, almost stifling. Nature seemed ready for a storm . . .

'Long I marched on a rocky, mountainous path. At last I met a man. He looked at me unkindly and suspiciously. I greeted him and asked if he could give me refuge for the night. "Who are you, foreigner? What land do you come from? What do you want in Chauvinia?" His voice had a harsh, unpleasant tone; we understood each other with difficulty.

'"I come from a distant land and journey far. I only wish to spend this night in your land."

'"What is the name of your homeland?" he asked.

'I said its name. The features of the Chauvinian became contorted, like the features of an enraged dog ready to bite. "We do not give refuge to your citizens!" he said and turned his back to me.

'Alone, I continued on with heavy heart and tears in my eyes. So, because I was a foreigner I was refused refuge here. I decided not to search further and to cross the inhospitable land as quickly as possible. I walked the whole night. Sometimes clouds covered the moon – then I had to stop and await its reappearance, because without its pale light I would lose my way. Sometimes a tempest arose, as if barring the way, so difficult was it then to go on. Mountain echoes mimicked the clatter of my steps and repeated them many times. Loudly, resoundingly . . . It seemed to me that around me marched some unseen, enemy army . . .'

In the story as Lidia wrote it, the traveler was finally welcomed in green and pleasant 'Esperantoland'. But the ending of the story as Lidia was to live it would prove quite different.

Ten years had passed since Dr Zamenhof's death. Once it had been Ludwik who sat up late, tapping at the keys of the old typewriter. Now it was Lidia who had taken his place. In December *Pola Esperantisto* published a reminiscence of hers, called 'My Father's Typewriter'. 'The old machine stands on its little table,' she wrote. 'Compared with the latest ones it doesn't offer much of value. It lacks some important arrangements and stenotypists regard it with pity, almost with disdain. I, however, respect it. And when I take off the cover it is as if the friendly face is smiling, and before my eyes appears the bright shiny inscription carved on the machine: "Let us work and hope."'

TEN

Believer

There had been a Bahá'í meeting at the yearly Universal Congresses of Esperanto ever since 1925. Martha Root had organized those first meetings, but now more and more Lidia helped with the arrangements and took part in the sessions. At the 1928 congress in Antwerp, Belgium, Lidia served as honorary president at both Bahá'í sessions and spoke eloquently at the opening. This, her debut as a public speaker, attracted considerable attention: until now she had never consented to make a speech of any kind at the Esperanto congresses.

During the Bahá'í sessions, held in the Cercle Royale Artistique, Lidia listened as a Persian Bahá'í reported about the progress of the religion in his homeland. In the past, he said, the Muslim clergy had obstructed education in Persia. Schools were only for boys, and only the Persian and Arabic languages were taught. Now, he said, thanks to the teachings of Bahá'u'lláh, new thought was spreading, which the clergy could not hinder. Bahá'í schools, open to all religions, were teaching both boys and girls. The learning of Esperanto was spreading, chiefly by Bahá'ís, he told them; most of the Universal Esperanto Association delegates were Bahá'ís, and they were sending teachers to various parts of the land.

Once again Shoghi Effendi had sent greetings to the congress. 'I can assure you', he wrote, 'that the members of the world-wide Bahá'í community follow with increasing interest and genuine hope the progress of your labors, and feel that by your high endeavors you are promoting one of the outstanding principles proclaimed by Bahá'u'lláh.

'They share with me the fervent hope that in the days to come closer bonds of co-operation and fellowship may bind the Esperantists of the world with our beloved Faith, and that the establishment and maintenance of intimate relationships between Bahá'ís and Esperantists may prove conducive to the betterment of mankind.'

Shoghi Effendi's words moved Lidia, as did the news of the teaching of her beloved language in the homeland of Bahá'u'lláh. Two goals began to crystallize in her mind – she determined to forge those 'closer bonds of cooperation and fellowship' between Esperantists and

Bahá'ís and to travel to Iran to bring Esperanto to the cradle of the Bahá'í Faith.

As during the lifetime of Ludwik Zamenhof, there was still controversy among the Esperantists over the 'inner idea'. Some still felt that spreading the neutral language should be the only goal of the Esperanto movement. Others felt that the ideas of brotherhood and justice ought to be part of it. Lidia believed those ideas could not be separated from Esperanto, and often said so courageously in articles and allegorical tales in the Esperanto press. In one of her stories in *Pola Esperantisto* she wrote of the old Jewish legend of the 'golem'; in which a medieval rabbi had tried to create a man of earth and clay. The creator of Esperanto, Lidia said, had given 'his own warm heart' to his creation, and it was this fire of idealism that gave the language life. 'But there are people who say, "Yes, it is lovely, graceful, but the fire – that fire within it – is unnecessary." And they put their hands, cold as cadavers, upon the warm heart, blow on it in mockery, try to smother it . . . Oh, *samideanoj*,' she pleaded, 'don't put out the fire.'

While some resented linking Esperanto with any idea, there were others who, though they might share the ideals of brotherhood and justice, just as strongly opposed linking Esperanto or the name of Zamenhof with any religious belief or organization. Just as Ludwik Zamenhof himself had suffered the displeasure of some of his followers when he presented his program of Homaranismo, now when word spread that his daughter was publicly promoting the Bahá'í Faith, some prominent Esperantists disapproved. Years later Lidia revealed that after she became a Bahá'í, people harangued her, accusing her of 'endangering the position of Esperanto, especially in Poland, if I identified myself, bearing the name of the creator of Esperanto, with a new, unfamiliar and still unrecognized religion.' During this time, Lidia felt, she 'made many enemies' but 'didn't care about that'. She explained: 'I value more highly my sincere relationship to God, whom I recognized revealing Himself in Bahá'u'lláh, than I do pleasing "public opinion".'

It has been written that some of Lidia's relatives accused her of betraying the Jewish religion and even persecuted her for her beliefs. Although Lidia admitted in a letter to Shoghi Effendi that her family were opposed to her Bahá'í activity, there is no evidence that their objections were strong enough to be called persecution. Nor were the family's objections of a religious nature. As the Zamenhofs were not religious, they did not react in the strong way that orthodox Jews might have to a conversion. An extremely pious family might even say the funeral prayers for the convert, whom they afterward regarded as dead.

24. *The formal unveiling of the monument on the tomb of Ludwik Zamenhof in April 1926. Professor Odo Bujwid of Krakow stands to the left, his arm resting on the stone*

25. *The secretary of the Universal Esperanto Association reads his speech at the planting of the 'Jubilee Oak' near Zoppot during the Danzig congress, 1927. Martha Root, in white. Ernst Kliemke, a Bahá'í and the president of the German Esperanto Association, is seated beside her. At extreme right: Zofia Zamenhof*

26. *From left: Feliks Zamenhof, Adam's wife Wanda, Zofia, Edmond Privat, Feliks's wife, Julia Isbrücker, Lidia, unknown, Leon Zamenhof, Adam and Joh. R.G. Isbrücker*

27. *The Bahá'í meeting at the Antwerp congress in 1928. Lidia, seated in front row; Martha Root, in the middle of the second row, holds a photograph of 'Abdu'l-Bahá*

For a Jew in Poland, converting to Christianity was indeed seen as a betrayal. Becoming a Bahá'í was something rather different; few knew what to make of it and often mistakenly regarded it as a philosophy rather than a religion, a misconception fostered by the fact that, at the time, it was usually referred to as a 'movement' rather than a religion. There was no Bahá'í community in Poland; in fact, the only other Bahá'ís that the Zamenhofs ever met or knew of were fellow Esperantists – Martha Root, Dr Adelbert Mühlschlegel, Dr Hermann Grossmann, Dr Ernst Kliemke (president of the German Esperanto Association), Professor Paul Christaller and a few others.

It appears that the Zamenhofs' objections arose rather from a concern not to link Esperanto publicly with the Bahá'í Faith, lest the public think the one movement was part of the other. Martha Root's letters, written after visiting Lidia in Warsaw, bear this out. About Adam and Zofia she commented: 'Her people are lovely, but they are not Bahá'ís and I think they would much rather that Lidia did not translate Bahá'í Books or link herself so much and give so much time to Bahá'í work. They would rather her name, the name of Zamenhof, would not be so much associated with Bahá'í. Still they were so kind to me, they were hospitable, they were sincere. I wish to speak them fair . . . They love Lidia devotedly.' But, Martha thought, they did not understand their sister.

Lidia had been saving 'every penny' for her pilgrimage to Haifa. When she told her family that she thought she would not go to the Universal Congress of Esperanto in 1929 but would save the money for her pilgrimage, 'they laughed', Martha told Shoghi Effendi, 'and make a great joke of Lidia's going to Haifa'. Adam and Zofia, Martha added, were '*kind, lovely*, but not so spiritual' . . . Zofia, she said, did not believe in life after death. 'And they do not understand Lidia. She does not say much to them about her praying and study – but last night I talked with them for two hours and I believe that they too might become interested . . . I told Lidia that in time she will bring them all into these Teachings.'

Martha thought some other relatives of Lidia's were sympathetic to the Bahá'í Faith; years later she wrote that she had once met Klara Zamenhof's sister, 'who said she liked the Bahá'í Teachings very much. Their brother, Mr Silbernik [who had lived in New York and died in 1925] . . . wrote for the New York papers a most sympathetic article about the Bahá'í Faith.'

Roan Orloff Stone, who became a close friend and confidante of Lidia in America, recalled in 1980 that Lidia was very close to her family and that she had never mentioned anything to the contrary. At that time, Mrs Stone recalled that some people outside the family accused Lidia of betraying Judaism when she became a Bahá'í.

For her part, Lidia Zamenhof never rejected her Jewish heritage, unlike many Jewish converts to Christianity who often went to great lengths to conceal their background. In fact, Lidia did not feel that by becoming a Bahá'í she had entirely broken with the Jewish community. To her, being Jewish had nothing to do with religion. Though Lidia did not participate in Warsaw's Jewish society, in 1929 she published an article on the Bahá'í Faith in *Nasz Przegląd* ('Our Review'), an important Polish-language Jewish daily newspaper in Warsaw, and she may have been criticized as a result of this. Her family, Martha Root reported, 'was very surprised' by the article.

As the only Bahá'í in Poland, Lidia had to learn about her new Faith on her own. Apart from a rare visit from a traveling Bahá'í, her only contacts with other Bahá'ís were at the yearly Esperanto congresses and by letter. She looked forward especially to Martha Root's journeys to Warsaw, but Martha was not the only one to visit her: Mrs Lorol Schopflocher visited Lidia in Warsaw at least twice. After her visit in 1928 Lidia wrote Shoghi Effendi that Mrs Schopflocher had arrived just when Lidia needed someone to help her understand.

Lidia quickly found that in order to read the scriptures of her new Faith she would have to learn English well. At that time there was no Bahá'í literature in Polish, and, except for the *Hidden Words of Bahá'u'lláh*, no major works had yet been translated into Esperanto. The original literature of the Bahá'í Faith was in Persian and Arabic, and the largest body of translated works was in English. Lidia had begun to study English several years earlier, but now she had a reason to work harder to master it. Eager to study the Bahá'í writings, she felt her efforts were impeded by her lack of English. So she began to take English lessons three hours a week; her teacher was a Russian.

Even as Lidia was learning English, she began to translate Bahá'í literature into Esperanto. And, as she read the Bahá'í scriptures, Bahá'í themes began to show up in her own writing. A statement about life after death in *Some Answered Questions* by 'Abdu'l-Bahá inspired an allegorical tale called *'Birdo en kaĝo!'* ('Bird in a Cage!') which was published in *Pola Esperantisto* in 1929.

When Martha Root visited Lidia in February 1929 for two weeks, she found Lidia working very hard – teaching classes, lecturing about Esperanto, translating and working 'to get the government to introduce Esperanto courses in the schools'. This effort was brave but not finding much success.

Lidia was not having better luck with her efforts to interest people in Warsaw in the Bahá'í Faith. She had written a lecture called 'What Is the Bahá'í Faith?' which she offered to present before a club in Warsaw. They refused. Undaunted, Lidia decided to present it at the next Esperanto congress.

She had begun translating into Esperanto J. E. Esslemont's introductory book *Bahá'u'lláh and the New Era*, which, to Lidia's pleasure, also contained a section about the language invented by her father. Esslemont, who died in 1925, had been, according to Martha Root, 'the very best Esperantist in the Bahá'í world'. Vuk Echtner, a Bahá'í in Prague, had been helping Lidia with the translation, but she did not feel sure of her English yet, so she put the project aside and began to work on 'Abdu'l-Bahá's *Paris Talks*. When Martha Root arrived in Warsaw, Lidia took up her work on Esslemont again, feeling more confident with Martha there to help.

Every day, morning and afternoon, Lidia visited Martha at her hotel to work on the translation. She would read aloud parts of the book and ask her about points she was unsure of. Every night, Lidia worked till one o'clock preparing for the following day's session with Martha. Martha had more confidence in Lidia's abilities than did Lidia herself: 'Oh, how much I admire her capacity!' Martha told Shoghi Effendi. 'She knows a dozen words and instantly selects the one that is just the very best. This will be such a great translation I can hardly wait until I possess it! How much it will help me in my lectures!'

'She is so *thorough*!' Martha wrote Julia Culver. 'It will be a wonderful translation and one of the greatest things that could happen in our Cause. Shoghi Effendi is very pleased.' He had already written Lidia three times.

To Shoghi Effendi, Guardian of the Bahá'í Faith, Martha Root revealed her innermost feelings about Lidia. 'Lidia is so CONFIRMED, so deeply in earnest . . .' she told him. 'She has such a fine mind, so sane, so balanced, so logical . . . She has such excellent judgment about everything. She is her father's child "spiritually" as well as physically. She is so JUST, so modest, so sincere, and she is one of the finest translators I have ever met . . .

'She was very happy over your message to her, but she is so modest she says (I forget the words but the thought is, that she would be very sorry to have you think she is a good Bahá'í when she is only just beginning to TRY to be a Bahá'í, but she says she certainly longs to become a Bahá'í).'

'She so loves the chapter on "Prayer",' Martha told him in the same letter. '. . . Lidia and I are together every minute possible. In her room yesterday we prayed together, she so loved the Dawn Prayer "O my God Thou seest me holding to Thy Name", she prays all the prayers, she is so eager to learn to pray. Today, in my room we stopped to rest from translating and to pray some of the beautiful prayers. I try to tell her how I pray and always wait for the Guidance. I tell her how hard I am praying to Bahá'u'lláh that He will show me how to help HER. I tell her she has one of the greatest opportunities and tasks of this century, for she can arise with the Help of Bahá'u'lláh to link these two great movements, Esperanto with the Bahá'í Movement. She can do a work almost as great as her father did.'

Martha indeed foresaw a great future for her 'spiritual daughter'. To the Guardian she prophesied: 'Lidia may become the apostle for Poland, I see it in my vision Shoghi Effendi.'

That summer of 1929, Martha and Lidia were together again in Vienna for the opening of the International Esperanto Museum just before the Universal Congress of Esperanto in Budapest, and at the congress itself. They had planned the Bahá'í sessions together during Martha's visit in Warsaw.

In Vienna, the delegates attended a reception with the president of Austria. Under the chandeliers Lidia stood out in a bright print dress and cloche hat, clutching her handbag under one arm. At the opening of the Museum, under the dome of the formal hall of the Austrian National Library, Lidia presented to the Museum an original manuscript of her father's from the year 1881.

Some fifty years later, a Viennese Bahá'í, Mrs Luise Lappinger, at the age of 92 recalled entertaining Lidia twice in her flat in the third district of Vienna. Franz Pöllinger, a German Bahá'í, brought Lidia to the Lappinger home, which at that time was a meeting place for the Bahá'ís in Vienna, many of whom were of Jewish background. In the traditional Viennese parlor, dominated by the dining table and chairs, over which a brass chandelier in a tassled shade created an intimate cozy atmosphere, Mrs Lappinger had Lidia sit in the chair reserved for special guests. 'She was agreeable, very gentle, very petite,' Mrs Lappinger recalled.

Bathed in the light of the brass chandelier, they drank tea and ate pastries. Lidia spoke quietly of the difficulties her father had faced. 'She seemed to have a spiritual aura that radiated from her', recalled Mrs Lappinger. 'She was a quiet, fine, noble person.'

After Lidia's visit, Mrs Lappinger recalled, she and Mr Pöllinger found a reference in Bahá'í literature encouraging the learning of Esperanto, so they took a course in the language. 'But people kept falling by the wayside', she recalled, 'until no one was left.'

Lidia and her uncle Dr Feliks Zamenhof were the only Zamenhof family members attending the congress in Budapest. At the opening session, the congress president greeted them and asked them to sit at the table with the officials on the platform. The audience affirmed the invitation with vigorous applause.

At the first working session, Lidia spoke up during a discussion of pronunciation. Arnold Behrendt, a postal official from Berlin, said he felt the matter had been discussed enough. Not so, said Lidia. For there were always new Esperantists, and especially for them such discussion would be useful and instructive. Later, again Lidia spoke up in disagreement with Mr Behrendt on another subject.

During the congress the German representatives proposed that a delegation place a wreath in the name of the congress at the Tomb of the Unknown Soldier. Lidia described the event:

'There, where Andrassy Street ends, near the beautiful city park, a tall monument stretches toward the sky. A heap of flowers lies there, a mounted soldier stands guard . . .

'Tomb of the unknown soldier! How many similar tombs, how many monuments of bronze or marble does one see in postwar Europe!' Long after the war's end, she observed, 'the monuments remain – unknown Abels accuse unknown Cains'. Those who saw such monuments as tributes to military glory were wrong, Lidia wrote. 'They do not see the tears, mingling with the flowers, do not feel the silent prayer of thousands of hearts that never again should unknown soldiers perish in bloody battles; they do not understand that such a monument, though outwardly glorifying the specter of war, is in its profoundest sense a powerful cry for peace.'

No eloquent speeches rang out that day. The Esperantists bowed their heads in silence. Lidia watched the group of people there, among them Frenchmen and Germans 'who have not yet forgotten the turbulent times when, lying in wait in the trenches, they pointed their guns at the enemy' – each other. '. . . And only God knows', she observed, 'whether the bullet that pierced the body of the unknown soldier had not been discharged by the hand of one of those present.'

Two Bahá'í meetings were held during the congress. Lidia spoke at both, and served as honorary president. Her lecture on the Bahá'í Faith was drawn from Esslemont's book, which she had been translating. Her speech was 'excellent', said Professor Paul Christaller, a Stuttgart Bahá'í. During the discussion, people in the audience raised questions which, as Dr Christaller noted, Lidia answered directly and well. Her talk was reprinted in the Bahá'í Esperanto magazine *La Nova Tago* ('The New Day'), published in Germany, as well as in the international Esperanto newspaper *Heroldo de Esperanto*. It was the same lecture that the club in Warsaw had turned down.

Lidia and Martha parted at the train station in Budapest, Lidia going to Poland, Martha to the Orient. At home in Warsaw, Lidia feared she would not see her dear Martha again soon. 'I love her very much', Lidia told Agnes Alexander, a Bahá'í Esperantist with whom she had begun to correspond. The descendant of Christian missionaries to the Hawaiian Islands, Agnes Alexander had been a Bahá'í teacher in Japan since 1914. She had been an Esperantist since the days of Ludwik Zamenhof. 'I heard about you from our dear Martha Root and recognized your name in Bahá'í books,' Lidia wrote to Agnes. 'It was a great honor and pleasure to receive your letter.'

Lidia included a special message for a Japanese Esperanto group called the *Klara Rondo* (Klara Circle): 'With joy I hear of the spread of Esperanto in Japan', she told them. 'The Japanese have great understanding of the practical utility of international language. I would be glad if I knew also that they understood as well the high ideal of humanity of this language.

'Bahá'u'lláh, the great Prophet of the last century, said some decades ago that international language is necessary to attain eternal peace. That was also the motive of the Author of Esperanto, and that is the star, which not only through green but through all colors of the rainbow enlightens and brightens our horizon.'

ELEVEN

Pilgrim

Lidia still longed to make a pilgrimage to Haifa. During Martha Root's visit to Warsaw in 1929, Lidia had written to Shoghi Effendi asking permission to visit him in the autumn. But it was not until almost a year later that she received permission to go. Although Lidia had been disappointed when the Guardian asked her (apparently more than once) to postpone her journey, she later called his instructions 'fortunate'. 'I came to realize', she explained, 'that had I come too early, I could not have withstood the assailing force of tests that must needs try every soul.'

Lidia made plans to sail from Trieste to Haifa in the middle of April 1930. She wrote the Guardian to tell him that she had been continuing her studies of the Bahá'í writings and that she hoped to gain a fuller understanding of her Faith while in the Holy Land.

That understanding came in an unexpected way as a severe spiritual test. But out of the test emerged a profound insight which Lidia Zamenhof would carry with her the rest of her life. It came to her in the form of an allegory, a chance occurrence, which she perceived as a powerful symbol of a spiritual truth. Years later, she described her experiences in Haifa:

'The steamer did not arrive at the pier. It stopped in a certain distance from which passengers were transported to the shore by means of small motorboats. As I was leaving the steamer to step into the motorboat, a strong wave pushed the motorboat. For a moment I lost my equilibrium. Had not someone sustained me, I would have fallen into the water. I often recalled this episode during my stay in Haifa.

'At that time I had no idea that Haifa was to be a testing ground for me as it is for many. I wondered why, almost as soon as I put my feet on the soil of the Holy Land, a strange depression, for which there was no apparent reason, seized my soul. I wondered why my faith, which I considered already firmly rooted, was shaken as a reed by wind and, even as the reed, was almost bent to the ground. Where was the Light of which I already had some glimpses? Why this darkness, this sadness, this depression and these doubts, trying to uproot all I had acquired? I was fighting a desperate battle – a battle for spiritual life or spiritual death. I had already understood the value of this life enough to feel that were I to lose in this battle, it would be ten thousand times more terrible than to lose my physical life. And as there were moments when defeat seemed to be inevitable, I wished I were never born. How often did I recall then the episode of the motorboat, wishing I were drowned in the sea before I drowned in despair!

'In that battle, however, I still had a weapon, a weapon to which I clung to the utmost of my forces. This was prayer. It was in fact only in Haifa that I learned how to pray.'

The object of pilgrimage to the Holy Land for a Bahá'í was to pray at the holy shrines in 'Akká and Haifa. The most important of the Bahá'í holy places was the Shrine of Bahá'u'lláh in Bahjí, near 'Akká. On Mount Carmel, in Haifa, was the Shrine of the Báb. After 'Alí-Muḥammad, known as the Báb ('Gate'), was martyred in 1850 in Tabriz, Iran, His remains had been hidden to prevent their desecration at the hands of fanatical Muslims, and eventually transported to the Holy Land. In 1909 they had finally been interred in the mausoleum 'Abdu'l-Bahá had built for the purpose on the mountainside, at a site chosen by Bahá'u'lláh. When 'Abdu'l-Bahá died, he had been laid to rest in an adjoining room of the building. But when Lidia made her pilgrimage, the superstructure and golden dome that crown the Shrine of the Báb today were not yet built. The Shrine was a simple structure of native stone beside a stand of three large cypress trees on the rugged hillside above the Mediterranean.

'Every morning I would go to the Holy Shrines,' Lidia wrote, 'and, forgetting my Occidental stiffness, I would beat my head against the Holy Thresholds. But for a long time there was no answer. The heavens seemed to be closed to my supplications.

'But one morning, when I arose after a long prayer, my eyes fell on a flower that was lying on the threshold. A red spider, a very tiny one, not larger than a pin-head, was running around the calyx of the flower. I stretched out my hand and gave it a careless push with my finger. Slight as the push was for me, it was a terrible blow to the little spider. It seemed to grow still weaker and smaller and it fell down from the flower, down from the Threshold, down toward the ground. But suddenly there happened something that made me stare with a strange feeling: the little spider did not fall to the ground. It stopped half way as if the law of gravity ceased suddenly to exist for him – and then, as if in spite of this law it drew itself higher and higher, till the calyx of the flower gave him refuge again and hid him from my sight. Quick as lightning and dazzling as lightning there came to me a sudden realization that this little spider was a sign sent me by God. A sign to tell me that a soul who still knew how to keep a ray of faith, be that ray as tiny as a spider's thread, is not to be lost in despair; even from the

28. *Shoghi Effendi, Guardian of the Bahá'í Faith; taken in 1922*

29. *The Shrine of the Báb on Mount Carmel, as it looked when Lidia made her pilgrimage in 1930*

30. *In Arnhem, Netherlands, July 1930, at the Cseh teacher's course*

depths of a chasm it will be led upward, till it reaches its heavenly abode, till it comes to God.'

'It was a promise of protection', Lidia felt, 'as a sign that Heaven was not an impenetrable vault over my head, that it was possible to pierce through that vault and get light from there.

'But what hard work it was for me to pierce through to God! Having received the sign, I should have been assured – but I was not. Still I was as a child crying in darkness. But God was a merciful Father who had much patience with me. I did not feel confirmed yet. I did not know where I was and what was that feeling of utter nothingness which was sometimes completely crushing me. I was being told that these were tests – but it did not make things easier for me. The depression came back. When the last day of my stay in Haifa came and I was making a balance of my experiences, I trembled.

'Here I was in the Holy Land, sanctified again through the appearance of a new Manifestation of God, this Manifestation promised ages ago and waited for through ages. Here I was in the Land where this Manifestation, Bahá'u'lláh, the Glory of God, was kept prisoner in the prison city of 'Akká, that city which was, in His own words, 'as though the metropolis of the owl'; that city from where this Spiritual King addressed His letters of warning to the kings of earth and summoned all mankind to the Most Great Peace. Here I was in the Land trodden by the feet of the tireless servant of God and the Center of His Covenant, 'Abdu'l-Bahá. Here I was in the land where pilgrims from all over the world come as to the Source of Life, and here, at the foot of Mount Carmel, the resting-place of Bahá'u'lláh's Predecessor, the Báb, and of His Son and First Servant, 'Abdu'l-Bahá, I was standing, telling myself that I was unable to draw therefrom the Water of Life.

'Again I was sad, very sad on that last morning, ascending Mount Carmel for the last time. I was downcast entering the Shrines and bowing myself for the last time before the Holy Thresholds. My heart, my head, my soul, the air itself seemed to be made of lead.

'I prostrated myself for the last prayer. And as I was praying, the feeling of despondency began to grow less heavy. Little by little the despondency disappeared. And when it had disappeared a joy came. A joy with no outward cause. A joy born in the heart as if the heart was suddenly touched by a smiling sunray. That joy kept growing as a sea-tide, until it flooded my soul. And still it kept growing until it was so great that if it were one degree greater, it would simply cause my heart to burst! All sadness, all doubts, all the dark hours of battle were gone and the joy was there, a heaven-sent joy, a divine confirmation.

'Whoever receives such a confirmation, forgets his doubts.

'Whoever experiences once such a joy, cannot be truly unhappy even in the darkest hours of his life.'

TWELVE

Cseh Teacher

Lidia remained in Palestine two weeks after her pilgrimage to Haifa. She traveled to Jerusalem and visited the five-year-old Hebrew University on Mount Scopus, presenting to the University a manuscript her father had written – a grammar of the Yiddish language. Lidia herself had never learned to read Yiddish.

By the middle of June 1930 she was home in Warsaw again, but not for long. The Universal Congress of Esperanto was to be held in Oxford, England, at the beginning of August, but Lidia planned to make a trip to the Netherlands before attending the congress.

For some years, Lidia had been interested in the Cseh method of teaching Esperanto. At the congresses in Edinburgh and Danzig she had attended individual Cseh lessons, and, impressed by what she saw, she decided that she wanted to become a certified Cseh teacher. Thus, she set out for Arnhem, Holland, to attend a teacher's course in the technique.

The Cseh method was the creation of Andrei Cseh, a Catholic priest from Romania who had turned his efforts to the promotion of Esperanto. He had developed his direct teaching method out of necessity when, after the war, he found himself teaching Esperanto classes under difficult conditions, without textbooks, to students who spoke different languages. The technique he developed proved surprisingly successful, and he was called upon to train others in his method.

Using only a blackboard and some simple objects for illustration – pieces of paper, rubber animals, etc. – the Cseh-method teacher would begin by speaking to the class very simply in Esperanto about everyday subjects. Gradually, through conversation, the students were introduced to the grammar and vocabulary of the language. So popular was this direct method – a refreshing change from the traditional grammar-oriented styles of language teaching – that an International Cseh Institute was established in the Hague in 1930 to train and certify Cseh-method teachers.*

* In 1937 the Cseh Institute claimed 439 certified Cseh teachers, 34 of whom were traveling internationally to give Cseh-method Esperanto courses.

No textbook was used, though at certain points in the course the teacher distributed supplementary leaflets containing little stories for reading practice. No homework was required, but during the course four humorous questionnaires were given to the students to answer. During the twenty two-hour sessions the teacher spoke only Esperanto. For the first few lessons a helper called the *aparato* translated for the teacher, but as soon as the students started learning the language, the *aparato* became unnecessary. The teacher held the class's interest through lively conversation with the students, who answered questions and repeated phrases in chorus. Rather than the teacher explaining grammatical rules, the students were guided to discover the rules of the language through using them.

After forty hours of instruction, the students were expected to have a solid foundation and a basic ability to communicate in Esperanto. They could then go on to perfect their command of the language through advanced courses, conversation at Esperanto club meetings, correspondence and private study. The Cseh Institute published a monthly magazine, *La Praktiko* ('Practice'), with articles, news, grammar discussions and a column listing the addresses of those desiring to correspond with pen pals in various countries.

Lidia was entranced by the Cseh method. 'The pupils completely lose awareness of the lesson', she wrote of her experience at Arnhem. '"*Forte, kuraĝe, elegante*" [Loudly, courageously, elegantly] they answer, almost unaware that new words, new forms, new rules have crept into the conversation.'

Lidia saw at once that the Cseh teacher had to be 'a wise psychologist'. During the course, which ordinarily took place in the evenings, when the pupils were tired, the teacher had to 'continually nourish the students' interest, make them pay complete attention and make them not yawn, but laugh!'

The Cseh course in Arnhem ended on 29 July and Lidia went on to England for the congress. The city of Oxford had been 'preparing for the invasion' of the Esperantists. According to the *Oxford Mail*, 'More than one hundred' shopkeepers had been learning Esperanto to serve the visitors, and in one cafe fifteen waitresses had learned to speak the language, the newspaper boasted, 'fluently'.

As the Esperantists streamed into Oxford, the local inhabitants streamed out, in cars, coaches and motorcycles, bound for the sea or the moors. Once again the Esperantists had come to Britain on August Bank Holiday. But this time it was a dismal and cheerless holiday with pouring rain.

The congress was held in the Town Hall. The Duke of Connaught, brother of the King, was the high patron, and other patrons included the Minister of Education and a number of university professors. Once again Lidia and her uncle Feliks, as representatives of the Zamenhof family, were persuaded – amid much applause – to join the dignitaries on the platform. They both 'gave short but moving speeches in the very spirit of the inventor of this wonderful language', Evelyn Baxter of London remarked. Later Lidia greeted the congress as the official representative from Poland. She was pleased that Shoghi Effendi's letter of greeting was one of a very few chosen to be read before the congress.

During the meetings, there was concern about recent attacks against Esperanto 'for our supposed inclination to one or another party or sect' and accusations in the British press that Esperanto was subversive. There was wide popular prejudice against Esperanto in rightist extreme nationalist circles all over Europe. The fact that Dr Zamenhof was a Jew was enough to convince some fanatics of the absurd notion that Esperanto was a Jewish-Communist conspiracy to enslave Europe. These scurrilous claims originated especially in Germany, where National Socialism was consolidating its power, and the propaganda organs of the Nazis were spewing out false and repulsive accusations against the Jews, and attempting to link them – and anything, such as Esperanto, that might be connected to them – with communism.

The Bahá'í meeting at the Oxford congress took place on a rainy day in an ancient lecture hall in Christ Church. The sixty people in attendance filled the room. Professor Paul Christaller opened the meeting, and Lidia spoke on the topic of 'Man, God, Prophet'. It was clear from the text of her speech that the spells of doubt, during which belief ebbed and flowed 'as a sea-tide', were over. Lidia Zamenhof had found a deeply rooted faith in God once more.

In dark times of crisis, when mankind was wandering aimlessly like a flock of sheep, Lidia told her audience in Oxford, prophets appeared to lead humanity out of its erring ways. Was the prophet human or divine? She spoke of the nature of man and of God. Something sublime, which the senses could not perceive, lifted man above the rest of the creatures – his spirit. The prophet was greater than man, yet not God. The prophets, she said, could be compared to rays of sunlight that warmed the earth. They were not the great sun itself, although they brought to the earth the sun's essence: light and warmth. And the prophets were like the moon, shining down upon the earth, although their light came not from themselves but from the sun.

Who was God, and what was His essence, His nature? 'Stand before a portrait of Leonardo da Vinci', Lidia said, 'and ask it who was its author, who gave birth to him, where he came from. The portrait, even if it knew how to speak, would not respond. It could speak only of the talent of the artist, of the power of his inspiration, of his artistic fervor and his industrious work, but nothing of his person. It could speak only about the qualities of the creator, not about the creator himself. Because a creation does not understand its creator, who is separate from it; only the creator has full knowledge of the creation.

'. . . We, and the whole world, and the entire realm of creation attest to the Creator, Who, having given existence to all, remains Himself outside and above all. We cannot know His essence, we can only know Him through his creation.'

The essential teachings of all the prophets of the past were the same, she went on. Each of them brought rays of the same sun, each of them taught love – love of God, love of one's fellow man. Although the prophets had disappeared from the material world, their words had not. 'The Divine Inspiration which spoke through the mouth of each of them did not die but, like a phoenix, is always reborn of its own ashes. In this day once again its song can be heard. Whoever has ears, let him hear.'

Afterward, one of those in the audience wrote: 'The words of the world language, truly masterfully spoken by her and raised to artistic perfection, became harmonic tunes of pure spiritual music which her talk presented. The sun broke through the rain clouds and sent warm and bright rays through the ancient windows, and in the room of Christ Church College the spirit of a new, auspicious epoch for mankind reigned.'

When Lidia's talk was published as a booklet, the Esperantist reviewer and journalist Max Butin wrote of it: 'Very wise words, not to be criticized by profane words. Between God and man, as it were, stands the prophet – mediator, advisor, reflection of the divinity and echo of the music of eternity. The linguistically good text extraordinarily warms the heart and liberates the soul.'

When the congress ended Lidia traveled to London and spoke at a meeting on August 13 at the Bahá'í Reading Room on Regent Street. Again the room was crowded, and the people stayed long after the speeches had ended. A number of Esperantists attended, and, Lidia confided to Shoghi Effendi, it was gratifying to hear words of appreciation from those who had not shown much interest before.

At this meeting Lidia spoke of mankind as children who had wandered into a forest against the warnings of their elders and had become lost. Just when, perhaps, the eyes of wolves glowed in the distance, or enticing will-o'-the-wisps were dancing on the marshes, the father's voice rang out, leading the way home. 'Children would immediately run home', she said. 'And mankind? If it obeys the Voice it also will be saved from the forest at night; otherwise it will become the victim of the wolves.

'In these last days mankind has entered a forest where thorns wound the body and the feet sink in a bog. It is not the first time it has turned aside from the path. Many times has the Father saved it from danger. But now the people have entered such a wilderness that they have lost the hope that the Father will find them there, that His voice will reach them; they even doubt whether they have a Father.

'But the Father loves his children and does not leave them to perish helpless.

'The Father's voice calling to mankind is the teachings of the prophets. The voice that is calling through the dense forest in these last days of despair is Bahá'u'lláh. His teachings lead again to tranquility, peace and safety.

'He reminds us that we are children of one Father, members of one family, dwellers in one home; that we must make this home a sanctuary of peace, not a battlefield.'

By August 18 Lidia was back in Warsaw. Though she had many pleasant memories of the Oxford congress, it was the Cseh course that had most deeply impressed her. 'I myself am a teacher of Esperanto,' she wrote to Julia Isbrücker, one of the founders of the Cseh Institute, telling her of her enthusiasm for the course and the Cseh method. 'I know all the difficulties of teaching and thus am competent to accurately evaluate the inestimable course of Mr Cseh. I feel sincere admiration for that truly brilliant teacher.'

A month later Lidia traveled to Lodz, about 130 kilometres southwest of Warsaw, to participate in the Fourth All-Poland Esperanto Congress. It was held in 'a beautiful, great, green-ornamented hall with a large portrait of Zamenhof'. Soon the room was full, with many people standing. Professor Odo Bujwid opened the congress. As the orchestra began to play *La Espero*, suddenly all the lights in the hall came on. As the speakers were delivering the usual greetings, the meeting was suddenly disrupted: a representative of one of the workers' groups abruptly took the floor, greeted the audience in Polish, and, after a few insulting remarks to the 'neutral' Esperantists, sent them 'to the devil'.

But when Lidia stood up to address the audience, 'a hurricane of applause shook the hall'. 'Miss Lidia Zamenhof is already known to the Esperantists of the world as an eloquent public speaker', one person noted. 'This time she chose as her theme the symbolic fact that at the moment when the orchestra began to play our anthem, from the many lamps and chandeliers of the hall, light poured forth. A good sign, a moment of good omen. She told an allegory about the light of the Green Star and captured the green hearts of the crowd. The speech left a profound impression.'

Another remarked: 'The opening speech of Miss Zamenhof was very charming. I like very much to listen and to read the words of Miss

Lidia . . . There is always a kind of golden autumn feeling in her words and, listening to her speak about letting the light come into our Esperanto lives just as during her talk it entered the dim congress hall, I involuntarily compared such a brilliant turn of phrase with that of our chief orator, Mr Privat. But he lacks those notes of romantic melancholy which Miss Zamenhof gives to us.'

The next day, Sunday, in the rain under a forest of umbrellas, a hundred and fifty Esperantists dedicated a plaque on Zamenhof Street in the city center. The event took place in spite of the fact that the police had forbidden mass gatherings because it was just before an election.

By mid-October Lidia's translation of *Bahá'u'lláh and the New Era* had not yet gone to press. Lidia had been working on correcting the proofs and was anxious to see it in print. 'I hope it will serve the Cause', she wrote Agnes Alexander in Japan. 'When this letter reaches you, our dear Martha Root will be with you. I envy you for that!'

THIRTEEN

An Independent Woman

Lidia had not had any formal preparation for teaching apart from the instructor's course in the Cseh method, which she had begun to use in her Esperanto classes in Warsaw. This style of teaching was very demanding, requiring the teacher, in effect, to be on stage during the entire class, holding the students' attention like an actor. But quiet and serious Lidia Zamenhof took to it with a flair that always astonished those who watched her become transformed from a plain little sad-faced woman to a self-assured actress who made learning the international language not a chore but an entertainment. Lidia had at last found her calling. Demanding and tiring as it was, teaching Esperanto was what she wanted to do. Inquisitive journalists would often ask her why she did not marry, and Lidia would tell them that her teaching would suffer if she married. For Lidia, teaching Esperanto had become more than an occupation: it was a mission. Years later she admitted, 'It is even my recreation.'

During this period, the early 1930s, the student Esperantist group in Warsaw often called on Lidia for help in their publicity efforts. Eugen Rytenberg later recalled that audiences always listened with great attention when she spoke – 'slowly, very clearly, with a strong but at the same time gentle voice . . . She was always there when we needed her.'

Eugen Rytenberg, who was teaching Esperanto in the Warsaw State Institute for the Blind, once invited Lidia to test his pupils at the end of the elementary course. As she spoke with the new Esperantists, he could see she was a talented teacher. Afterward, he recalled, she told them an amusing little story. 'When I was a child', she said, 'I had a small lovely white cat. But my cat was not well mannered: it bit [with appropriate pantomime] and tore up my beloved doll. Then I said to it, "Listen, Kitty, I don't love you anymore, do you *hear*?" The cat replied, "*Miaow-das!*"' ('*Mi aŭdas*' means 'I hear' in Esperanto.) And the students burst into laughter.

Lidia then said to them, 'Don't you believe the cat said that?'

One of the pupils boldly replied, 'It didn't say -*das*.'

When she was not teaching or preparing for her classes, Lidia was working on her translations or writing. Her translation of *Bahá'u'lláh and the New Era* had been published at the end of 1930. And her stories and articles were being printed with more frequency. In 1931 the Esperanto literary journal *Literatura Mondo* published two short stories she had written. One was called '*Halinjo*'. Unlike her usual allegories, in which she couched Esperantist or Bahá'í ideas in the form of a fable, '*Halinjo*' was literary fiction. Dark and rather pessimistic, it told of an innocent neglected child named Halinjo who becomes a tragic victim of her decadent parents' selfishness.

The other story was called '*La araneo*' ('The Spider'). In it Lidia cast her experience in Haifa into the form of a story. She wrote of a pilgrim come from far away, hoping to find again the belief he had lost. The pilgrim is alone in the shrine. Outside, people throng; birds sing. But inside, only a colored ray of sun penetrates the arched window. Touching his forehead to the step covered with roses, the pilgrim cries 'for a sign, for some miracle . . .' In his moment of despair he sees a little spider so small it seems only a bit of dust. He flicks it away with his finger, and it tumbles from the flower but stops in midair, its fall broken by the delicate line of web. The spider scurries to hide among the roses. The pilgrim has his sign.

'Thus the heavens did not open,' she wrote, 'nor the earth tremble. Trumpets did not blow, to attest to the presence of the All-Powerful.' But the pilgrim goes back into the world 'tranquilized and confident that whoever can still find in his heart a single ray of faith, as delicate and tiny as a spider's thread, will not perish in the abyss . . .'

Pola Esperantisto had also published one of her short stories. Entitled '*Saluto al steloj*' ('Greeting to the Stars'), it was almost science fiction. But instead of regarding beings from other planets as hostile, alien creatures, Lidia envisioned other worlds populated by brother-beings with whom humans must someday communicate. The hero in her story sacrifices everything he possesses – even his life – to reach out to them in one immense, blazing signal of light, even though he would never know if his message ever reached anyone.

In 1931, however, not everyone around Lidia approved of the message that she had chosen to promote, especially in public. As Lidia had continued to take part conspicuously in the Bahá'í meetings at the Esperanto congresses, she had met increasing disapproval from her family and some of the Esperantists. The Twenty-Third Congress in August 1931 was to be in Krakow, Poland. As the time for the congress approached, Lidia found herself facing opposition from none other than the congress president himself, Odo Bujwid, a professor at the University of Krakow and an eminent Esperantist who had been a friend of Lidia's father. Professor Bujwid's attitude was evidently becoming known and talked about among the Esperantists such that

Martha Root heard of it from acquaintances in Europe. '[He] does not wish a member of the Zamenhof family to take such a great part in the Bahá'í Movement,' Martha wrote. 'He is afraid people will think that Esperanto is something Bahá'í. Especially in the Universal Congresses of Esperanto he wishes Lidia to stop doing so much . . . Lidia is so modest, she never mentioned all this trouble, but the other Esperantists here in Europe have told me.'

Lidia did confide her anguish to Shoghi Effendi, telling him her situation was 'very difficult' as prominent Esperantists and her family were against her 'because of the Bahá'í connection'. Odo Bujwid had warned her, she said, 'not to mix the two', especially before the Krakow congress, as he feared it could be damaging to the Esperanto cause.

While some Esperantists, like Professor Bujwid, were openly disapproving of Lidia's Bahá'í activities, not all the Esperantists were unsympathetic. Martha Root considered Andrei Cseh 'a true friend' of the Bahá'í Faith. Dr Edmond Privat, who shared Zamenhof's ideals, increasingly recognized their similarity to Bahá'í teachings. Many years later, in 1955, he would speak out in the Swiss press against the wave of persecution by the Muslim clergy against the Bahá'ís in Iran. Soon after the Krakow congress, Privat attended the funeral of August Forel, former Professor of Psychiatry at the University of Zurich, where Forel's philosophical will was read. Privat later remarked that 'it was a very impressive moment when the conclusion came telling all his friends about his belief in the Bahá'í Message and his conviction that it is the one needed by the suffering world.'

But Lidia Zamenhof was, after all, the daughter of the Majstro. To some this meant that, while her private beliefs were her own affair, she should not speak out publicly for any other movement. But to those who understood her better and had known Dr Zamenhof's own dedication to his ideals, it meant she could not do otherwise. Around 1931 the great Hungarian Esperanto poet Kálmán Kalocsay published a collection of *Rhyme Portraits* of famous Esperantists, subtitled *A Gallery of Esperanto Stars*. It included a verse portrait, a rondel, of Lidia:

> *Lidia Zamenhof*, kor' fervora
> Vartante patran sent-heredon,
> Jen, serĉas sorĉan sav-rimedon
> Por mond' amara kaj dolora.
>
> Kaj kun entuziasmo kora
> Servadas la Bahaan kredon,
> *Lidia Zamenhof*, kor' fervora,
> Vartante patran sent-heredon.

El sent' profunda, pens' valora,
En sino havas riĉan bedon,
El ili plektas flor-bukedon:
Novelojn kun enhav' trezora,
Lidia Zamenhof, kor' fervora.

(Lidia Zamenhof, fervent heart,
heir to her father's tenderness,
seeks healing spells to save and bless
this suffering world in bitter smart;

and passionately plays her part,
of Bahá'í a votaress,
Lidia Zamenhof, fervent heart,
heir to her father's tenderness.

From thoughts and feelings set apart,
her garden in the mind's recess,
she makes a treasure to possess,
a bunch of stories by her art,

Lidia Zamenhof, fervent heart.

Knowing of the disapproval surely caused Lidia pain. Of course, she would never have done anything she felt might endanger Esperanto. Like the other Esperantists, she knew how quickly Esperanto could become tainted in the minds of others for its supposed connection to some unpopular movement or religious group. In Poland Zamenhof's Jewishness had been enough to cause most Poles to dismiss it; in Germany Hitler had already denounced it; in some other countries, Esperanto was suspected of ties to leftist movements. The very nature of the movement – outside the mainstream of society – and the variety of people who were attracted to it, as well as the almost cultic veneration of Zamenhof and the sometimes excessive use of Esperantist green stars and green flags, led some to judge it a collection of cranks. The Esperantists would continue to suffer from this stereotype up to the present day, and many still wince at the idea of being identified too closely with groups like the vegetarians or the Bahá'ís.

But Lidia sincerely did not believe her actions as a Bahá'í could jeopardize Esperanto. After all, the doom-sayers who had warned Dr Zamenhof not to promote Homaranismo had been proven wrong. Though Homaranismo had failed as a movement, Esperanto had prospered – and the connection had done it no lasting harm. Although it must have been difficult for her, Lidia refused to bend to pressure.

'Lidia has stood FIRM,' wrote Martha Root proudly. But doing so set Lidia apart, even in her beloved Esperantoland.

In August 1931 Lidia went to Krakow for the Esperanto congress. The streets and buildings of the city were decorated with the green star, and overhead the green banners flapped in the warm summer air. But the congress, Lidia wrote Agnes Alexander, 'because of the general economic crisis, which prevented many from coming, was not so well attended as one might hope in other times.' Even so, she told Shoghi Effendi, it proved to be more satisfying than she had expected.

To the Esperantists' delight, some of Krakow's restaurants and cafes had menus printed in Esperanto and a number of the city's tram conductors, postal workers, shopkeepers and waiters had learned enough of the language to serve the nine hundred congress-goers. In one restaurant the Esperantists were so highly esteemed as patrons that, one observer reported, when the waiters saw a green star on a lapel, they rushed to fall into line, military style, and shout 'Bonan tagon!' (Good day).

A few of Krakow's policemen had even learned some Esperanto. They wore green stars to identify themselves, affably gave directions to the foreign visitors, and, an Esperantist noted wryly, 'They didn't arrest any of us.'

But one evening's program – all in Polish – irritated the Esperantists, who had come all the way to Poland to hear the international language. The public had been invited to attend the festivities, and the Krakow audience 'was very gay and laughed a lot all evening', an observer wrote, 'apparently because for the first time in Esperanto history the wearers of the green star understood nothing, in spite of their boasts of mutual understanding'. 'There was a moment', he added, 'when the congress-goers had their revenge and brightened up. That was at the end of the evening, when they were allowed to leave.'

The editors of *Literatura Mondo* organized a 'literary morning' during the congress, with speeches and poetry readings by some of the most famous Esperanto writers. Lidia was asked to participate, and she read with emotion from Mickiewicz's epic poem *Pan Tadeusz* in Esperanto translation. One day, after the speeches, Lidia played a rare cylinder recording of the voice of Ludwik Zamenhof. In spite of the 'technical difficulties' they had getting the ancient machine to work, and the deficiencies of the aged recording, the sound of Dr Zamenhof's voice resounding through the congress hall 'caused much emotion' among the listeners.

A Bahá'í session was held at the congress, and more than fifty attended. In spite of Professor Bujwid's displeasure, Lidia gave a speech at the meeting. Her talk, about the development of mankind since ancient times, was entitled 'Man and Mankind on the Way of Progress'. The report in *La Nova Tago* said Lidia's 'eloquent' speech 'captured the attention of all'.

After the Krakow congress, there were post-congresses in Warsaw and Bialystok. In Warsaw the Zamenhofs – Lidia, Adam and Zofia – invited some of the Esperantists to a reception at their home. They entertained them with tea and cakes and home movies of Adam's young son Ludwik, and a rare film of his namesake, Dr Zamenhof.

Julio Baghy, the novelist and poet of the Budapest School, described a visit he made to the Zamenhof home, possibly on this occasion. Lidia and Zofia led him through the little museum of their father's study with all its relics and memories. Baghy, who had been devoted to Zamenhof, was impressed that they did so in such an easy, unceremonious manner, explaining the various objects simply and without the extravagance with which many Esperantists referred to the Majstro. But Baghy recognized that 'this very spontaneity proves that the father's soul lives on in both'. They 'remind one of the modesty' of their father, he wrote.

Baghy surveyed them with curiosity. 'To which one did fate give more of the father's riches?' he wondered. 'Not possible to know,' he decided. He found them equally kind and equally modest. Only in temperament did he perceive a difference. It seemed to him that Lidia had a 'more dreamy nature' and a readiness to 'do battle for beautiful ideals'.

On August 12, in Bialystok, the birthplace of Ludwik Zamenhof, Lidia and Zofia helped to place the foundation stone for a monument that was to be constructed – a 'Tower of Babel' twelve meters high. Although the event was surrounded in official pomp, with speeches by government functionaries, brisk marches played by a military band, and an honor guard from the fire brigade, the monument was never built.

In 1932 the economic situation in Poland was very bad, and few could afford the luxury of Esperanto classes. Though Lidia worked hard, she earned very little teaching Esperanto in Warsaw. If she earned anything from her writing or her translations, it could not have been much. In any case her Bahá'í translations were done as a labor of love, not for money.

She had been devoting much time to translating Bahá'í scriptures under Shoghi Effendi's direction: her Esperanto edition of the *Paris Talks* of 'Abdu'l-Bahá was to be published in 1932 – specimen pages were included with the January 31 edition of *Heroldo de Esperanto*. She had also finished translating *Some Answered Questions* and was beginning the *Kitáb-i-Íqán* ('The Book of Certitude'), a volume by

Bahá'u'lláh. She was having difficulty with it, but it seemed she was working from an outdated, poor English translation. Shoghi Effendi sent her a new edition.

She also found time to translate Polish literature. The firm of N. Szapiro in Warsaw was publishing her translation of two stories by Polish author Boleslaw Prus, and her translation of the novel *Quo Vadis?* by Henryk Sienkiewicz, would soon appear. Lidia had been named to the editorial committee of *La Nova Tago* in 1929 and contributed articles to the *Encyclopedia of Esperanto*, the first volume of which was published in 1933.

Since she lived in the family flat with her sister and brother and his family, Lidia was able to devote her time to her teaching and her translating without worrying about having to depend on this work for her daily bread. She probably could have continued to let her brother support her, but Lidia was not satisfied to do that. Although at that time it was not expected that a woman would support herself through her own work, Lidia was something of a feminist, and was dismayed by what she called 'that lamentable type of doll-woman, educated only to find a husband'. More and more, she had seen, there was 'a new type of woman, independent and capable, earning her own bread'. Lidia wanted to be one of those women. But prospects for doing so in Warsaw were bleak.

Some Esperanto teachers, like Tiberiu Morariu, a Romanian, had had enormous success giving Cseh courses in other European countries. Lidia had attended her second Cseh teacher's course just before the Krakow congress, after which she was more enthusiastic than ever about the Cseh method. She decided she wanted to go abroad to teach Esperanto. Outside Poland, where there was more interest in such matters, perhaps she could have more success spreading the international language and at the same time make teaching Esperanto a real career.

Martha Root, who was in Europe again, learned Lidia hoped to leave Poland, and she changed her plans and hurried to Warsaw to be with her. Martha wrote: 'I reached Warsaw the morning of May 18, and Lidia Zamenhof my precious spiritual child was at the train to meet me.' Over the years Martha's respect for Lidia had deepened. 'I consider her one of the great souls of Europe,' Martha wrote of Lidia. 'She is a BORN translator, she has a genius for it, and the books she has translated into Esperanto will be a great "leaven" not only in Europe but also in the Far East . . . Her mind is keen and logical and I have met few people in my life more just than Lidia.'

Martha hoped to find people in Poland who would be interested in the Bahá'í Faith, but found few. 'People are very devout Catholics or very devout Jews,' she observed. 'Lidia thought that I should only stay two weeks this time. She said: "You KNOW I want you to stay a year! But it is better to go slowly!"' Martha stayed eighteen days.

Martha and Lidia visited the University Library to place Bahá'í books there and paid a call on the Polish Minister of Religions. They were told that the Ministry would have to give permission to introduce a new religion into Poland.

Martha, as was her custom, gave teas for the people she met, including a secretary of Marshal Piłsudski, dictator of Poland; a Polish writer; the American Consul-General and 'the young girl at the Consulate who had been so nice about my mail'. 'I just gave two teas downstairs in the lobby, a quiet corner,' she wrote, '. . . the others I gave up in my room and prepared it myself which was much cheaper.'

'I met Lidia's friends,' Martha wrote to Shoghi Effendi, 'had them to tea in my room and made the tea myself. She has done her best, but they do not have much interest in spiritual matters. I wish I could tell you all Lidia has done. She went to Lodz to visit one lady whom she thought had a little interest . . .'

Lidia and Martha also spent time together alone, reading the *Kitáb-i-Íqán* aloud and talking about the book, which Lidia was translating. To her close friend, Lidia confided her feelings and her dreams.

Martha already had great plans for Lidia. 'Sometime I hope Lidia can go to the US and to Persia,' she had written even before she arrived in Warsaw. Martha had traveled through Persia in 1930, and she surely told Lidia stories about her experiences there, stories that kindled in Lidia a desire to visit that land. After leaving Warsaw, Martha wrote to Shoghi Effendi: 'Lidia would like to study Persian . . .'

But there was no way Lidia could learn Persian in Warsaw, where there was no Persian consulate, and the Persian language was not taught in the university. Martha was enthusiastic about the idea nevertheless, and she began to concoct plans for Lidia. 'I wish that Lidia had the opportunity to become a fine Persian and Arabic scholar,' she wrote. 'If she could go to Egypt in September and teach Esperanto in Cairo for a year and study Persian and Arabic and the following year go to Persia for a year and teach Esperanto, then a wonderful something would be done! She does not know that I am writing this, she is so modest, so reserved, she works very hard, but the economic situation is such that she can only earn a little, but if she ever could, I know she would love to go to Cairo or work in any city in Egypt.'

Martha Root sensed that life would be very difficult for Lidia in Poland. As a Bahá'í she would be virtually alone. The pressure from others not to link her name with Bahá'í would be a difficult test. Though Lidia was outwardly very determined and 'ready to do battle' for ideas, like her father she was a quiet and sensitive person. 'Lidia is my loved spiritual child,' wrote Martha, 'but strange as it may seem, I feel it would be good for Lidia to leave Poland and work elsewhere (you know how the Bible says about one having no honor [standing] in his own country. She has a very high standing as an individual) . . . She is so YOUNG in the Cause, I do not wish her spirit crushed, and I wish her capacity developed and used to its highest.'

In late July 1932, Lidia and Martha met again in Paris at the Universal Congress of Esperanto. When Lidia rose to give her speech at the Bahá'í meeting, it was clear that the pressure on her had had no effect. Her talk on 'Modern Man and Religion' was bold, earnest and challenging. Could twentieth-century scientific man, she asked the audience, still *believe*? In the heart of the greatest skeptic there was still a corner in which there was room for belief, she told them, and her words had the confidence of a skeptic who had discovered such a corner in her own heart. But, Lidia said, religion need not rely on 'superstitions, naive beliefs in an underground hell where horned devils fry the bodily souls of sinners in pitch' or a paradise made of 'clouds and winged blue-eyed blond angels playing in the heavenly blue'. Could not hell be the condition in which thousands of souls already lived, ignorant of spirituality, condemning themselves to an ephemeral life after which they expected utter nothingness? Could not the very consciousness of a sin committed be, in itself, more burning than boiling pitch, more painful than devilish pitchforks? And heaven – was it not eternal harmony with the cosmic Order and Light?

The literal interpretation of religious concepts, which reason could not accept, was due not to the prophets but to their 'small-minded servants, who did not know how to understand the word of God other than literally', she said. 'According to Bahá'u'lláh, religion goes hand in hand with science. Religion and science are as two rails on which the wheels of human progress run. Those rails are parallel, and only upon them can the wheels of true civilization go forward.'

Her talk was, Professor Christaller pronounced, 'excellent'. But it, and the meeting, went ignored by all the Esperanto journals that usually reported on the various gatherings at the congress.

Lidia went home to Warsaw. By the end of the summer, it seemed that her desire to go abroad to teach Esperanto – and Martha Root's, to get Lidia out of Poland – was about to come true. The Esperanto Society in Gävle, Sweden, had written to the Cseh Institute requesting a teacher for some beginning courses they wished to hold in the fall. Mr Cseh suggested they invite Lidia. Excited at the chance to have 'such a famous guest', the Gävle Esperantists wrote to her at once. She accepted and said she was ready to leave immediately. She finished the translation she was working on – the *Kitáb-i-Íqán* – and sent it off quickly to Dr Grossmann. *

* It was never published.

But then the difficulties began. Lidia had trouble getting her documents to go to Sweden. Twice she had to delay the trip, and the Gävle Esperantists despaired she would ever arrive. But at last she cabled them saying all was arranged. It was just the first of many times when trouble with passports and visas would plague Lidia. In September 1932 she set off from home, at the age of twenty-eight, to become a traveling Esperanto teacher – and an 'independent woman'.

As her ship sailed through the cold waters of the Baltic Sea toward Sweden, she found her thoughts going back to the warm Mediterranean. She 'thought much of Haifa on the ship', and the sea and the seagulls reminded her vividly of her trip to Palestine. Lidia hoped she might return to the Holy Land some day.

At the end of September Lidia arrived in Gävle and was ushered from the train station to a radio station, just in time to say a few words of greeting at the end of an Esperanto broadcast. To attract the public to sign up for the course, she gave demonstration lessons in four towns: Skutskär, Uplandsbodarne, Strömsbro and Gävle. In Gävle 250 people came to the school auditorium where she was to speak. After a musical presentation, Lidia stepped up to the podium and gave a short lecture about Esperanto which her *aparato*, or helper, translated into Swedish. Then she began her introductory lesson according to the Cseh method. It 'pleased the audience very much', reported one participant, and Lidia showed herself 'an excellent teacher'. But only twenty-five people signed up for the course.

Lidia began to teach courses in Gävle, Strömsbro and Skutskär. The classes were small; none had more than thirty students. Apparently interest was not great enough in the fourth town to start a class. The effects of the Depression were evident: not everyone could afford to pay for Esperanto lessons, though workers' Esperanto groups provided scholarships for some unemployed students. Still Lidia must have been disappointed: the Romanian Cseh teacher Tiberiu Morariu had hundreds in his classes! And she was the daughter of Zamenhof . . .

Winter had come, stretching 'its cold fingers over the Swedish land'. Sometimes, on a clear night, Lidia could see the Northern Lights, 'weaving shining curtains over the polar regions'. Perhaps somewhere in a distant desert, she mused, some thirsty wanderer was just as startled to see the shimmering mirage of a watery oasis. It was not going to be easy, this being an independent woman, earning her own bread. And it would be very, very lonely.

Before leaving Poland, Lidia had received from the Polish Ministry of Foreign Affairs a set of slides showing scenes of Poland and people in Polish folk costumes. Along with some gramophone records of Polish music, she put together a program about Poland which she presented at public meetings in a number of Swedish cities. But she was careful never to touch on politics.

On other occasions, when only Esperantists were present, she gave a talk reminiscing about her father, which always touched the audience deeply. On December 15, the anniversary of her father's birth, she spoke on an Esperanto radio broadcast, reminding the listeners how in 1914 at the outbreak of the Great War her parents had made an anguished journey through Sweden, trying to reach home. 'He did not get to know your lovely northern land,' she told them. 'He did not see cheering crowds of Esperantists, did not hear the song of hope from a thousand voices . . . He heard only words of despair . . .'

How large the world was! Against it, one person seemed like a grain of sand. But just as there were in the universe natural forces which joined atoms into rocks, she told them, so there were also forces which could bring together the souls. 'Let us exert our efforts,' she said, 'so that thanks to the international language the human spirits may be united by mutual understanding. Then man will not be a powerless grain of sand. Then something will come into being of which today we can barely feel a presentiment . . . the powerful rock of mankind . . .'

Her classes ended in mid-December and the Esperanto Society held a farewell party in her honor at a Gävle restaurant, where her pupils thanked her in Esperanto and gave her flowers and gifts. On the last day of 1932 Lidia left Gävle.

Toward the end of her stay in Sweden, Lidia had received an invitation from an Esperanto group in Lyon, France, asking her to come to their city to give a Cseh course. Lidia had accepted. Now a long trip across Europe lay ahead of her, and she probably faced it with some anxiety. In Sweden attitudes had always been tolerant toward Esperanto, yet her classes in Sweden had been disappointingly small. France was another story. Though Esperanto had spread in France during Zamenhof's time, it had suffered there because of de Beaufront's activities and the war. It was the French delegate to the League of Nations who had led the opposition to Esperanto; for a time, in response to a rumor that Esperanto was to be taught officially in the Soviet Union, the language had been forbidden in French schools. What awaited the daughter of Zamenhof there?

FOURTEEN

Light and Shadow

The train journey through wintry northern Europe was, as Lidia described it, 'torture'. Outside it was freezing. Inside her railway compartment the heaters under the benches blazed 'like infernal fire', but whenever the windows were opened, a 'glacial blast' blew in. Lidia arrived in Lyon with 'a lovely grippe'.

Lyon was an ancient city, once the Roman town of Lugdunum. Since the fifteenth century, it had been famous for its silk industry. Families of silk weavers called *canuts* wove, at the rate of a few centimeters a day, ornate brocades and silk fabrics for the French court at Versailles. Although mechanization was putting an end to the traditional silk industry, in the 1930s the characteristic clattering of the busy looms: *bis-tan-clac, bis-tan-clac*, could still be heard throughout the district of La Croix-Rousse.

Lidia had arrived in Lyon sooner than expected. The course was not to begin for some time, but this proved to be fortunate since she was ill. An Esperantist couple, Emile and Marie Borel, took Lidia into their home. Mrs Borel immediately set about curing her, applying various remedies and looking after her with such care that Lidia found that even being sick 'under the wing of Mrs Borel . . . was not disagreeable'.

When Lidia recovered, she was impressed by how hard the Lyon Esperantists were working to publicize her course. They had put up posters, handed out leaflets, sent invitations, and broadcast announcements over the radio station of Lyon-la-Doua (of which Emile Borel was the manager). 'Imagine the important radio station manager of imposing stature, how he personally visited offices, shops, etc., asking for a place to put up posters for the course,' Lidia wrote. 'About the work of Mrs Borel I will say nothing, because she liked to carry out her task anonymously and she would complain terribly if I betrayed her . . . And here, the out-of-work *samideano* who during a frosty night pasted up posters, putting all his heart into that work which always goes unrecognized.'

It was the Borels themselves who had been largely responsible for bringing Lidia to Lyon. In 1932 they had proposed to the *Amicale*, an

Esperanto group in Lyon, that Lidia be invited to come from Sweden to teach a course. But the cautious committee members had 'reservations'. The public of Lyon seemed indifferent to Esperanto. If ten people could be gotten together for a course, it was considered a great success. Four thousand francs – a large sum – would be necessary to bring Lidia from Sweden and pay for publicity. Where could they find so much money? Marie Borel said: 'We will find it,' and somehow they did.

Lidia was to present her introductory lesson in the Edgar-Quinet Hall of the University of Lyon. The time had been announced for 8:30 p.m. with the secret intention of beginning, at the earliest, at 8:45. But in spite of inclement weather, by 8:33 the hall was packed with more than four hundred people and some had to remain outside.

Law professor André Philip introduced Lidia to the audience, remarking that she was carrying on her father's work like an apostle. After the Polish consul in Lyon spoke a few words, expressing sympathy with the idea of international language, Lidia gave a short talk, with Emile Borel serving as her translator.

'Then the lesson began', the reporter for the newspaper *Le Progrès de Lyon* wrote, 'and it was a real delight to listen to the new teacher teach . . . initiate and ardently convert to the international language all those who listened.

'The method is extremely picturesque, amazing', he went on. 'Instantaneously, and as if under an irresistible suggestion, the entire rows of listeners apply themselves to repeating, with the singsong pronunciation of the initiates, the words and phrases which the teacher illustrates with familiar objects and expressive gestures. A veritable ovation was given Mademoiselle Zamenhof.'

'Never has a course of Esperanto, or even, perhaps, a course in any other language, won such great success at the Faculty of Letters,' was the evaluation of *Le Progrès*.

The next evening the course began. Lidia had been afraid that the students would not want to come every evening, and even she herself was surprised to see how 'young and old, laborers, merchants, scouts, teachers and various important people hurried every day not to be late and to get a good seat'. During the class 'the pupils worked, the rubber animals worked – cat, dog, donkey, pig – the usual tools of the Cseh course. The photographers also worked.' The Lyon papers reported favorably on the course, with articles and photographs that aroused greát interest. In spite of unusually cold weather and a wave of grippe, for three weeks every night the students came. And every night, the appearance of the diminutive teacher was greeted with a thunderous applause. Dr André Védrine, who attended the course, later recalled: 'the atmosphere was extraordinary. Lidia Zamenhof was a remarkable teacher. Plain in appearance, she demonstrated a sprightliness and a joyful spirit which could leave none indifferent. A few objects skill-fully handled, a few pieces of colored chalk, an expressive pantomime, and all the students understood.' The translator was hardly needed.

Raymond Gonin recalled: 'Often one heard the students say, "What a good teacher!" because she made them enthusiastic.' Mrs Borel told him that before the course began she had feared it would not be successful because Lidia was somewhat timid, but during the course Lidia spoke so forcefully, she conquered her shyness.

'With these three weeks of amazing lessons by Lidia Zamenhof', raved *Le Progrès*, '. . . the universal language which already counted so many eloquent followers in Lyon has been given an impetus which should be decisive.

'Upon seeing the hundreds of pupils of all ages, of all social classes, looking and listening so attentively in order not to miss the slightest gesture, the slightest intonation of the charming teacher – because it is a veritable charm which Lidia quite naturally, without knowing French, radiates among her audience – to see all these radiant faces, eager to understand and to make themselves understood, one gets the feeling of a new faith, an irresistible blazing-up of minds which should not come to a standstill now.

'By this vigorous demonstration, this unprecedented educational triumph, the universal auxiliary language proves its irresistible impetus, its effective power in human progress.'

When the course ended, the number of students had risen from 144 to 170. On the last evening Mr Borel installed a radio microphone in the classroom. Before beginning the lesson, Lidia gave a farewell speech which was broadcast over the air. Then, to her polite questions: 'Are you well? Are you happy?' her class responded as usual in chorus.

Lidia left the university that night sad to be departing. At the emotional farewell party in the Maison-Dorée, a large crowd of her students gathered to say good-bye to their teacher and offer her gifts. The table was so crowded with the flowers they had brought that, she noted, 'there was hardly room for a cup of chocolate'. But most satisfying of all to Lidia was hearing her pupils speak to her in Esperanto – people who three weeks earlier had known nothing of the language. When she left Lyon she wrote, 'although the day was cold, my eyes were sweating'.

News of Lidia's tremendously successful course in Lyon stirred up enthusiasm and excitement among the Esperantists in other cities in France, and invitations poured in asking her to come and teach courses. She left Lyon for Montbéliard, Belfort and Valentigny, in a region where up to now there were very few Esperantists. After she left, there were 140 new ones.

Her next course, in Saint-Étienne, began with 80 and grew to 103. In

Bordeaux, again there were 80. Her successes were so encouraging that the committee in Lyon asked her to continue teaching in France for another year, and Lidia consented.

After her classes ended that summer, Lidia and the Borels traveled to the Netherlands to spend several weeks at the new Esperanto House in Arnhem, attending a seminar for Cseh-method teachers. On July 26, which the Esperantists celebrated as the birthday of Esperanto, people in one of the classes presented Lidia with a basket of flowers. Touched and surprised by the gesture, she thanked them but, one observer noted, 'gently directed the honor' to her father.

Although Lidia had seen her father idolized by the Esperantists, she did not expect this attitude of awe to carry over to herself simply because she was Dr Zamenhof's daughter and was continuing his work. She was well aware of the visible position she held, but besides the position she had also inherited from her father the attitude that the Esperanto work was all-important, and that any status that people attributed to her was only useful as far as it helped to get the work done. Like Dr Zamenhof, she did not seek or expect special attention to be paid to her but – through her – to Esperanto.

At Arnhem, after class, there was time to relax on chaises in the garden or take a rowboat out on the River Rhine. Mies Bakker-Smith remembered Lidia from that summer as 'a very serious person, who was never seen to laugh'. Lidia impressed her as very determined and inflexible, even 'somewhat dictatorial'.

At the end of July Lidia traveled to Bergen-op-Zoom in North Brabant for the dedication of a monument to her father. The tall granite pedestal, on which was a five-sided column surmounted by a world globe made of Venetian glass, had been built by local neutral and Catholic Esperanto groups. As Lidia formally unveiled the monument, the orchestra played the Polish anthem. When the music stopped Lidia spoke about the great ideal of her father: that Esperanto was not merely a language; most important was its spirit of unity and brotherhood among the peoples.

August came and with it, as always, the Universal Congress of Esperanto. Since 1924 Lidia had attended all the congresses, but although in Arnhem she was less than 150 kilometres from the congress city, this year – 1933 – she did not go. The congress was to be in Cologne, Germany.

Even while Lidia had been enjoying her phenomenal success in Lyon, frightening events were taking place in Germany. Adolf Hitler had become Chancellor and was moving to consolidate the power of his National Socialist German Workers' (Nazi) Party in order to take complete control of Germany. Under the guise of preventing a communist revolution, Hitler had enacted emergency measures, imprisoning thousands of people and suspending civil liberties. By July 1933 all other political parties had been suppressed, and the Nazi party was the only one allowed in Germany.

The instrument of Hitler's authority was the *Schutzstaffel* (Defense Corps), or SS. From an elite bodyguard for Nazi party leaders, the SS grew into a huge organization with immense power, whose members swore to Adolf Hitler an oath of 'obedience unto death'. Their black uniforms and lightning-flash insignia had already become sinister symbols of terror in Germany. As early as March of that year, 1933, the SS had set up, at Dachau, the first of its concentration camps where it imprisoned suspected anti-Nazis and other people considered undesirable, many of them Jews. The designation of the camps' elite guard units foreshadowed what was to come: they were called the *Totenkopfverbände* – Death's Head Units.

Nazism was not just the aberration of one madman. Its historical and intellectual roots were deep in German history and philosophy. Its exaltation of war, its conviction of the 'destiny' of the Germans to rule as a 'master race', derived from the ideas of earlier philosophers. Its hatred of the Jews was a cancer that had existed in Germany, as in Poland, for centuries.

At the time, many refused to believe the enormity of Hitler's program. But early in the 1920s Hitler had clearly laid out his ultimate plans for the state he intended to build based on the 'superiority' of the German 'master race'. He had written that his philosophy was 'obligated to promote the victory of the better and stronger and demand the subordination of the inferior and weaker'. 'All who are not of good race in this world are chaff', he had said.

In spite of the intellectual trappings with which the Nazis sometimes clothed their racist theories, these views had not even a shred of scientific truth. Yet many highly educated Germans, including a great many youth, embraced them. During the 1920s and 30s the youth of Germany, especially university students, were, as Lucy Dawidowicz writes in *The War Against the Jews*, 'overwhelmingly anti-Semitic'. It helps one realize just how pervasive anti-Semitism was when one considers that during the period between the wars there were some seven hundred anti-Jewish periodicals in circulation in Germany and over four hundred anti-Semitic organizations.

But Hitler did not come to power only because of his program of anti-Semitism. Many Germans welcomed Hitler because they believed that the 'New Order' he promised them offered the nation its only chance to rise again to its rightful state of greatness and prosperity. The economic chaos and demoralization Germany had suffered after the Great War provided a hothouse in which hatred flourished. Just as in Russia traditional anti-Semitism had been manipulated to channel the discontent of the masses into pogroms, in the twenties and thirties, when the Nazis blamed the Jews for Germany's defeat and for the social, economic and political troubles that had plagued the country since the armistice, many Germans were only too willing to listen.

In the spring of 1933 in Germany, anti-Jewish violence had been organized and carried out by Storm Troops – the Nazi party's private army. When reports of the violence reached abroad, triggering criticism of Germany and calls for a boycott of German products, Hitler blamed the Jews and accused them of spreading lies to undermine the state. Threatened by Nazi Minister Hermann Göring with a pogrom, Jewish leaders were forced to deny the atrocities.

An anti-Jewish boycott was carried out, enforced by Storm Troops under the supervision of the SS, and there was violence throughout Germany. By force and by legislation, Jews were ejected from their jobs in the civil service, on newspapers, in universities and even in orchestras. Most Jewish lawyers were forbidden to practice; Jewish judges were forcibly 'retired'. Eventually laws were enacted virtually removing Jews from public life in Germany.

In April the Cologne congress committee had tried to assure worried Esperantists that foreign guests in Cologne 'need not fear any difficulties because in Germany absolute order reigns'. There was no danger to the Esperantists, assured *Heroldo*, which was published in Cologne and thus subject to censorship. Security in Germany was greater than it had been in recent years, and, the article added somewhat ominously, 'from day to day it is becoming even greater'.

But in fact the Cologne congress was not as well attended as some previous congresses. The Depression made it difficult for some to afford the journey, but others stayed away in fear or in protest. One of those who stayed away was Lidia.

In Cologne the meetings went on as usual, only, *Heroldo* remarked, 'more accurately on time'. There were the usual speeches, songs, dancing and entertainment. But besides the green stars and flags that always decorated the congress hall, this time there were also swastikas. The president of the congress was Arnold Behrendt from Berlin, who had become president of the German Esperanto Association in 1929 following the death of Dr Ernst Kliemke. In his address Behrendt asked the audience to believe that Adolf Hitler was truly building a new state which would show the world that it ought to restore trade and political relations with Germany.

The Esperanto movement in Germany had been taking an alarming direction in an attempt to accommodate itself to the Nazi regime. Some leaders of the movement there naively hoped that by renouncing the ideals of Zamenhof they could prevent the language from being

31. *Young French Esperantists paste up a poster advertising Lidia's Cseh course in Lyon. Second from right: Dr André Védrine*

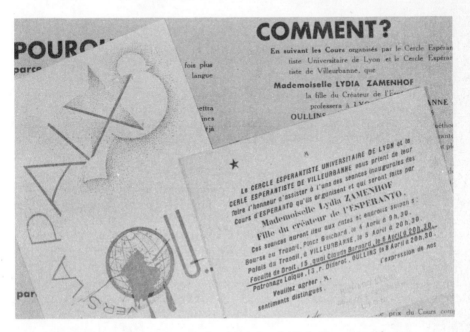

32. *Flyers and invitation card publicizing Lidia's Esperanto classes*

33. *Marie Borel, 'La Pastrino'*

34. *The first course in Lyon, January 1933*

35. *Arnhem, 1933: In the garden of the Esperanto House, on 26 July, the birthday of Esperanto*

36. *Relaxing between classes. From right: Hans Bakker, Lidia, Mies Bakker-Smith*

37. *Lidia awaits the unveiling of the monument to Ludwik Zamenhof in Bergen-op-Zoom*

38. *An outing in the countryside near Lyon. First row, third from right: Emile and Marie Borel, Lidia*

suppressed and might even be able to persuade Nazi leaders of Esperanto's usefulness. But in *Mein Kampf*, published in 1925, Hitler had stated his opinion of Esperanto: 'So long as the Jew has not become master of the other peoples,' Hitler had written, 'he must speak their languages whether or no; but let them once be his slaves, and they would have to learn a universal language (Esperanto, for instance!) so that Jewry could rule them more easily by this means as well.'

By April 1933, *Heroldo* reported, more and more Esperanto groups were 'becoming absorbed into the prevailing situation'. The Esperanto club of Oppeln had done so: it now consisted only of members or sympathizers of the Nazi party. At the annual convention of the German Esperanto Association under President Behrendt, it was decided to change the organization in accord with new Reich regulations. From now on Behrendt would no longer be president of the GEA but its 'Führer'. Behrendt did not live to see the results of the new Nazi order to which he tried to adapt Esperanto: he died less than two years later.

The Summer University at the Cologne congress was a fiasco. Two of the four speakers did not show up, including a Dr Mutarelli who was to lecture on 'Public Works of Fascism in Architecture'.

A group of German Bahá'í Esperantists held a small meeting at the congress in spite of all, and without either Lidia or Martha Root. Lidia, however, had sent a short speech to be read at the meeting by Elsa Maria Grossmann, a German Bahá'í Lidia had known for several years.

Now, when men were raising ever-higher barriers between themselves, Lidia's statement said, the Bahá'í teachings offered a doctrine of harmony and unity. But to understand that unity, a certain degree of evolution was necessary. From an ancient time when people had believed the world to be ruled by different gods, mankind had evolved to a stage where it could understand that the Creative Power of the universe was one. And from the time when the family or the clan, and later the nation, claimed man's loyalty, much social evolution had to take place before he could grasp the concept of one humanity.

The law of the prophets had always been: love. 'It is the same eternal light, carried by different light-bearers. This light shone once from an ancient torch. Later from a newer lamp it sent forth its rays, although the light was always the same, as was its purpose: to make mankind see . . .

'All are children of the same beloved Father. All are drops of one sea, leaves of one branch, flowers of one garden. That applies equally to human groups as it does to individuals. "Do ye know why We have created ye from the same clay? So that none shall exalt himself above the other"', she quoted the words of Bahá'u'lláh.

But in Cologne, Germany, in 1933 few heard her words.

FIFTEEN

From Place to Place

Instead of going to Cologne, Lidia returned to Lyon and spent two weeks with the Borels, preparing for her autumn courses. The first was to be in Romans, a small city south of Lyon in the department of Drôme, with, as Lidia described it, 'an old clocktower, narrow little streets, from which the wind of the past seems to blow'. There were eighty in her course.

One evening, a public meeting had been planned. Lidia showed her slides of Poland and spoke of her country and its customs, 'its thorns and roses'. Then she played her gramophone records of Polish folk music. During the evening, she noticed a woman in the third row who seemed spellbound, tears shining in her eyes, and, elsewhere in the room, a simple worker, listening with a strange melancholy.

At the end, as the audience was leaving and Lidia was packing up her records and slides, the two people approached her timidly. The woman spoke to her. She was a Pole who had lived in France seven years and would never return to Poland. The man was also a Pole, long away from his country. He revealed to Lidia that he had been walking around outside the hall for hours before her talk, waiting 'to capture the echoes of his distant native land'. Lidia was profoundly touched by these two fellow-countrymen nostalgic for their homeland. She herself had been traveling for a year now, and as she would later admit to a correspondent, during this time she 'suffered greatly from home-sickness'. She had found that she didn't especially enjoy traveling, with its discomforts, annoyances and frequent changes of lodging. But to accomplish her goal – to teach Esperanto – she had to travel almost constantly. The work was far more important to her than her own comfort, and the joy of hearing the words of her father's language thunder back at her from an audience who before that evening had known nothing of Esperanto was worth all the sacrifice.

Lidia wrote to Shoghi Effendi that because she was constantly traveling and teaching Esperanto, she could not do much directly for the Bahá'í Faith. But, she added, she considered her work for Esperanto to be 'part of the divine program for improving the conditions of the world'. When Shoghi Effendi read her letter, he made a note on it: 'urge her study Persian as preliminary to a visit to Persia where she would be most welcome and where her services are already deeply appreciated.'

Lidia's next course was in Châteauroux, where Félicien Baronnet made the arrangements. Wherever Lidia went, she had to rely on the local Esperantists to publicize the course – contacting the newspapers and local officials, printing and distributing posters and handbills. The publicity was crucial in attracting people to the introductory lesson. 'The demonstration lesson is extremely important', she wrote Mr Baronnet. 'It is, one may say, the general battle of the course campaign and on it to a great extent depends the success of the course.' From experience, Lidia had learned that it was important to get as large a crowd as possible to attend the demonstration lesson. A local dignitary always attracted attention. 'It would be good if you could get as chairman a local authority, for example, the mayor, a city councilman or school official. That always impresses the public!' Baronnet managed to get the vice-mayor of Châteauroux, and about two hundred attended, though only forty-five signed up for the course.

Mr Baronnet found Lidia a modest *pension* in the town, where she stayed during the weeks of the course. One day the Baronnets took Lidia for an automobile excursion through the picturesque valley of the river Creuse, which, Mr Baronnet recalled, Lidia seemed to enjoy. He also recalled that when Lidia left Châteauroux, her students gathered in an enthusiastic demonstration at the train station to say good-bye and present her a gift.

In November Lidia returned to Lyon to begin her second course in the city where she had had such great success. But would that success be repeated? *Esperanto* reported that the opening of the course was 'a triumph. More than five hundred people attended. In Lyon five hundred really is five hundred. A favorable wind is blowing.' After Lidia's introductory lesson, 161 signed up for the course. It seemed to her that in France interest in Esperanto was indeed growing.

When the course in Lyon ended, she went on to Marseille where she had seventy students. Georges Cau, who was sixteen when he attended that course, long remembered how she used many objects of diverse forms and colors, showing them in succession and loudly saying the name of each, after which the students repeated the words in chorus. 'I never forgot the "golden key" which miraculously opened the door to the main question words in Esperanto grammar', he recalled fifty years later.

In early December, while Lidia was teaching in Marseille, she received news from her family that her uncle Feliks Zamenhof, whom she 'loved very much', had died in Warsaw. Lidia could not leave her course in France and go home to Warsaw for the funeral. That blow was followed a short time later by the death of another of her father's brothers, her uncle Leon Zamenhof.

In January 1934 Lidia finished the course in Marseille and began teaching in Vallauris, Saint-Raphaël and Cannes, on the Côte d'Azur. In Cannes the Cseh course again attracted over a hundred students.

Now Lidia had much less free time to devote to writing and translating. Although she hoped to find time 'when I am not wandering all over the world but sitting quietly at home' to translate some modern Polish novels, she never did. She had still not found a publisher for the play *Iridion* which she had translated long ago.

But her translation of *Quo Vadis?*, Henryk Sienkiewicz's novel about the early days of Christianity in imperial Rome, had recently been published in Amsterdam, and the reviews began to appear. *Esperanto* praised the 'smooth, pleasing, very easily readable language' of the translator, but noted that the printer had made too many typographical errors. 'The style deserves all praise for its correctness and immediate clarity', wrote the reviewer, who nevertheless managed to find some minor grammatical points to quibble over. The reviewer in the *British Esperantist* even remarked that Lidia's translation of the novel was 'much more complete than the French and English translations', better conveying the nuances of the original Polish.

Lidia remained in the south of France during the spring of 1934, beginning new courses in Grasse and Vence, then returning in May to Bordeaux, where she had been invited to give a second course and was honorary president at the French National Esperanto Congress.

From Bordeaux she wrote 'Auntie' Victoria Bedikian, a well-known Bahá'í in the United States: 'I feel very guilty that I have been silent so long, that for such a long time I have not answered your sweet letters and haven't thanked you for your beautiful drawings . . . because of [my] constant traveling my correspondence suffers a great deal. Will you please forgive me? . . .

'With constant interest I read of the continuing construction of the Temple [the Bahá'í House of Worship being built on the shore of Lake Michigan in Wilmette, Illinois]. I hope some time to see it, but I don't know if and when I will be able to come to America. Probably I shall have to stay longer in Europe, especially in France, where I have much work before me. Later, it is my heart's desire to go to Persia to teach Esperanto in the land of Bahá'u'lláh. But that cannot be for several years. Who knows, whether before that I won't see you in America?

'With extreme regret I read of the death of Keith Ransom-Kehler.* I always hoped that I would meet her, but never had the opportunity.

---

* Mrs Keith Ransom-Kehler was an American Bahá'í who had gone to Iran to appeal to the Persian government to annul the ban on the importation and circulation of Bahá'í literature in that country; she died of smallpox in Isfahan on October 23, 1933.

But although that is no longer possible in this life, I haven't lost hope that God will permit that meeting in the next life.'

Lidia was enjoying considerable success wherever she went in France, her classes usually attracting from 50 to 150 pupils. Frequently the number of students increased by the end of the course. People were not dropping out; they were hurrying to join – even after the lessons had begun.

In the summer Lidia returned to Warsaw for a short visit. It was her first trip home in two years. At the house on Królewska Street, the swallows were still in their nests under the eaves. Lidia had only a few weeks at home before she would be sailing to Stockholm for the Twenty-Sixth Universal Congress of Esperanto. Before she left Warsaw, she made a farewell visit to the Jewish cemetery.

'Always, unforgettably engraved on my heart is that gray granite, brought from misty Scotland,' she wrote, 'and here, in Poland, now caressed by sunny rays, now showered by autumn rains, now decorated with flowers placed upon it by faithful hands.' Coming closer to the monument that stood upon her father's grave, Lidia became filled with dismay. A large mark of dirty violet color, like spilled ink, covered part of one side of the stone. 'Rain had smeared the color over the granite, and the monument stood defiled, stained.'

A few thick letters could be made out. Someone had written 'Long live the Esperantist Movement' and a name.

The name scrawled on the monument seemed to her symbolic of what she saw occurring in the Esperanto movement. That movement itself was the real monument to her father, she believed, 'more lasting than the granite and the only truly immortal one'. It had been built, brick by brick, as the life work of Ludwik Zamenhof. This monument, Esperanto, ought to be considered, as the stone was inscribed, 'erected by the Esperantists of the whole world'. No person should try to write his own name on it – this would be nothing less than to stain that monument as well. But, she warned, some among the builders came 'bringing in one hand a brick for the monument, in the other hiding a red pencil to inscribe their names in thick letters on the brick.

'The winds of ambition,' she cautioned, 'bring the rains of jealousy, and few wish to remain unknown among the known. Instead of placing brick upon brick in harmony and order, doesn't it sometimes happen that someone even tries to tear out a brick if it seems too beautiful alongside the others?

'History itself will do justice,' she wrote, 'and will inscribe upon its pages the names of the truly meritorious. Let us only work, each according to his ability, for the beloved Cause, not for our own glory, and sacrificing our efforts and labor, let us not ring the bells of hypocrisy and not conceal with our hands the red pencil [used to write upon the monument].

'We are building a great, beautiful monument. May it remain clean!'

The day came to leave for Sweden. Lidia noticed that even as she was leaving to go north, the swallows under the eaves were also taking their leave, flying south to Africa, escaping Europe's winter.

Martha Root arrived in Stockholm first. Just as the congress was to open, Martha was, she herself wrote, 'so ill with grippe, only Bahá'u'lláh knows!' Although she had a raging fever, on the day the congress began she went to the station to meet Lidia, who had been looking forward to this visit with her 'dear Martha' for months.

The Stockholm papers were full of momentous news from Germany. The *Svenska Dagbladet* carried pictures of German soldiers giving the Nazi salute. The day before, it had carried the screaming black headlines: 'HINDENBURG DEAD. *The entire world shares Germany's grief.* ADOLF HITLER *Chief of State submits the decision to a referendum – wants to be called Head of State but not President . . . Hitler, who only two years ago did not even have German citizenship, is now dictator over 65 million people.'* Hitler's takeover of Germany was complete. The article about the Zamenhof family at the congress was dwarfed by the news.

All week the papers were full of Hitler and of Hindenburg's funeral, but this news seemed unable to cast much of a pall over the Esperanto congress taking place in neutral Sweden. Over two thousand Esperantists were in attendance. Martha Root commented, 'All delegates remarked that the Swedish atmosphere had a tranquilizing and friendly-making influence upon all guests. Even the little foibles which always occur in big congresses were met with such good humor and forbearing mind that everything in and outside the congress was sunshine here in Sweden.'

The congress sessions were held in the Swedish Parliament House, though the opening was in the splendid Concert Hall. Martha Root dragged herself out of bed again with a temperature 'much over one hundred' to be there and deliver Shoghi Effendi's greetings to the congress.

After the official representatives had made their remarks, Lidia arose to give a short address. 'Once again the Esperanto congress has brought us together,' she told them, 'once again the Green Banner waves above our heads, and once again the beautiful language sounds from mouth to mouth. That language indeed seems to us like a telescope through which we can better see the future, which seems to be rosier than the present. Sweden is a miraculous land; even in the region of Midnight, the sun shines. And if it seems that night is now covering the world, the Esperanto star gives us hope for better days.

Let us have faith in the future!' The audience burst into loud and prolonged applause.

The Esperantists had grown to regard Lidia with affection. Her successful courses in France had become known through reports in the Esperanto press. The magazine *Esperanto*, in an allusion to the anthem *La Espero*, referred to her as the 'esteemed daughter of our Majstro who on the wings of the easy Cseh method flies from place to place, gathering new adherents for the ideal of her high-minded father'. At a time when those ideals were under attack, even by some of the Esperantists, Lidia was admired by many for 'faithfully guarding the spirit of our dear Majstro'.

Edmond Privat had not attended the congress. But by telephone-radio hookup, he spoke to the gathering from Switzerland. 'Breathlessly this seated international audience listened to every word,' Martha Root reported, 'even every nuance as his loved voice carried his light-bringing message over the air to them.' Both Privat and Lidia, remarked Martha, 'that day, had their lips touched with Fire of God!'

As usual, there was a Bahá'í meeting at the congress. 'The power of the Holy Spirit was in our midst,' Martha reported. 'It was held in a marvelous Council Chamber of the great Parliament, all chairs were wide, comfortable, very high backs like throne chairs. Every seat was taken, twenty nations were represented; on the long center table we had a fine exhibition of English and Esperanto Bahá'í books and the Esslemont book in many languages. We had a rich, soft-tone silk cover on the table and the books were placed on this. We had flowers, it was all very artistic . . .'

Martha herself had arranged the exhibition quickly just before the meeting began, reported Almida Zetterlund, a Bahá'í Esperantist from Stockholm, who chaired the meeting. 'From the first moment', Miss Zetterlund wrote, 'one felt a special spiritual atmosphere which itself inspired the speakers.' When Lidia rose to give her speech, her words 'went right to the hearts of all. The expressions on the faces of the listeners showed rapt attention.'

Lidia spoke, remarked Martha, 'as one inspired'. Her speech was 'much applauded and was praised in the newspapers. (Between you and me, I made a careful résumé of it the day before and took it myself to the press, for if they quoted her I wished it to be exact . . .)'

Lidia's speech showed how far she had traveled in the course of her own spiritual journey. It revealed a belief in God that had become strongly rooted, and a view of life and death which saw death not as the end of life, but merely a passage to another level of existence. 'Perhaps [death is] not disappearance,' Ludwik Zamenhof had written as he himself lay dying. 'Perhaps death is a miracle . . . that something is guiding us for a high purpose.' Now, at last, Lidia felt confident she knew what that purpose was.

'Our whole life is ceaseless learning,' Lidia told the audience. 'The child first learns to speak and to walk . . . and later he goes to school, where, having begun with the alphabet and the elements of mathematics, he enlarges his knowledge until his mind rises above the earth to explore the mysteries of the solar systems and milky ways.

'And if his mind also inclines toward analytical work he will begin to investigate the material universe until finally in the structure of the atom, that tiny universe, he will uncover the same laws that rule the solar systems . . .

'And he will bow his head before that eternal law, before that unwritten code of universal harmony. He will begin to feel himself only one small note in that eternal symphony, and he will realize that he must not be a squeak but a note in harmony with the symphony of existence.

'What is that eternal harmony, that potency, penetrating through and holding in its power the universe? It is exactly that which we understand by the word "God". We may call it by a thousand names, in a thousand different tongues – no matter – the essence remains the same. It is only important that we understand that those thousand names refer to one sole and identical, eternal and infinite Being.

'There are people who deny the existence of that Power. Some, truly the most naive, deny because they cannot see, hear and feel that power. They cannot "capture" God in the net of their perception . . . They deny, saying that the idea of God is a childish fantasy which no serious proofs confirm. They fail to comprehend that everything that exists eloquently attests to the potency of that which created – that one green leaf attests to that Power better than thick volumes could possibly do, that the hum of summer insects . . . is a voice stronger than the loud talk of those who do not understand that there exists no effect without a cause; that where there is a creature, there must be a Creator. Seeing a table, they realize that there must have been a woodcutter who cut the wood, a furniture-maker who gave it form, but seeing before them worlds and suns, they do not comprehend that there must have been an Intellect that planned them, a Will that brought them into being, a Hand that directs them.

'There are people who believed and lost their faith. Oh, that is the fate of many of those who prayed but found their prayers unfulfilled; those who in sickness begged for health; those who in misery asked for help; those whom death robbed of their best beloved; finally millions of those who lived through the inferno of the war who, having avoided the bombs and gases, vainly eke out the most miserable existence. All those hopeless, rebellious ones ask: 'Does God really exist? Where is

He? How could He create so much misery and cause so many tears to flow?"

'Or it appears to these people that besides God another and equal power reigns in the world, which is the scene of an eternal battle between the good God and the prince of darkness.

'The Bahá'í teachings proclaim the nonexistence of evil. Is it possible to imagine a power which would be able to stand against the Creator of everything? To believe in Satan means in fact not to believe in God, for it means not to believe in His most essential attributes: His power over everything and His goodness . . .

'That which we call evil is only lack of good. Darkness is only lack of light. Blindness is only lack of vision. These are but passing circumstances, often created by ourselves. They will pass, for eternity is an attribute of God, and to Him only good belongs.

'One may say, on the contrary, that it is small consolation to the blind to assert that his blindness will pass – together with his life. But that is the viewpoint of the short-sighted. For life does not pass . . .

'With full assurance the Bahá'í teachings assert the immortality of the human spirit. The body is only an instrument, which the spirit uses for a time to express itself. Even if the instrument becomes defective, the hand that uses it does not perish. The body is like a garment that becomes outworn and is cast away. But its wearer is not cast away along with the garment. The body is like a cage in which dwells the bird of the spirit, before it breaks the cage and flies to heavenly heights.

'And when bodily life shall cease, when the blind eyes are closed, other eyes will open and the joys of the spiritual world will recompense the sufferings of those whose physical eyes saw not the brilliance of the material sun . . .

'What is true of man', she concluded, 'is also true of mankind. It also must learn the lesson of harmony, and that harmony it must find, before all else, in itself. It must be like a chord in which one note does not grate against another, but together with the others forms a beautiful harmony. It must be fragrant as a garden where many diverse flowers bloom one beside another. It must feel as one tree rich with many brother-leaves, one sea abounding with many brother-drops . . .'

While in Stockholm Lidia gave another powerful speech, this time before a gathering of the Union of Esperantist Women. She appealed to them to rise to the challenge that was theirs, as women and as mothers, to work for peace, in a world that was moving ever more swiftly toward war.

'In the work for peace', she told them 'the first and chief place should belong to the women. War is an affair of men . . . the male love of power and authority . . . the result of that primitive social order which always had as its leader and ruler – the man.

'But today women are rapidly rising from the low status they have held. In many respects they are now equal to men; in others, they surpass. That superiority exists in those spheres which deal with sensitivity and feeling, and this sensitivity dictates to us dislike of force and coercion.

'For too many centuries, we women have been told that our main role in life is motherhood, and that is what we were supposed to remember. The feeling of a woman's heart, especially a mother, must hate war, which destroys her nest and leads her dearly loved ones to the fields of horrible death. For a long time, men have said that the task of the woman is to give, and to look after the man. Let them then understand that no compromise is possible between us and war . . .

'Let us unite to bring peace to the war-tortured world. And we women can do that better than men. What have they done in that respect? Disarmament conferences, which are only futile chatter as long as souls lack the feeling for peace.

'To inspire that peaceful sentiment is the role of the woman. It is she who educates, she who first forms the mentality of future state leaders. You who are mothers: never put toy soldiers into the hands of your child. Teach him that blood must not be shed, that violence is ignoble. Teach him to love not only the nearest neighbor, but also the neighbor across the border.

'See how we, fellow-idealists from diverse lands, are linked together through Esperanto . . . Our hearts beat with the same rhythm and in harmony sing the melody of love and peace. Let us join hands. Let us increase our ranks. Let us form the legion of peace across boundaries. Our road is very long. But let us be patient and courageous, for our goal is great . . .

'Even if you think that you humble teachers and secretaries can do very little, still do not hesitate to offer your "widow's mite" to the cause of peace. Because it may happen that war will break out again and pitilessly engulf those who are dearest to you in the world. And then your heartache will be greater when you think, "I could have worked for Peace, but I did not."'

After the congress Lidia and Martha remained a while in Stockholm. That week, wrote Martha, 'my room was like a "Birunih" (a place where I served tea and told people about the Cause).' One evening Lidia and Martha went to an Esperanto conference; Martha stayed till midnight, but Lidia left early. This time it was she who was ill.

On August 18 Lidia left Stockholm for Warsaw. Martha wrote: 'At five p.m. Lidia sailed. I introduced her to the captain, for this was the same ship in which I had crossed over to Sweden, and he said he would do everything for her comfort and happiness. He gave her about twenty long paper ribbons, those garlands in rainbow colors one throws from the deck. I caught them from her as she tossed them down, and holding the "rainbow" of colors – one of us at each end of this "arc" – we looked into each other's eyes, until my spiritual child moved out to sea, our Lidia!'

Lidia Zamenhof and Martha Root would never see each other again.

SIXTEEN

Forte, Kuraĝe, Elegante!

After the congress in Stockholm, Lidia returned to France to begin new classes in the fall, this time in Châteaurenard, Orléans and Thiers. It was the end of November 1934 when she arrived in Thiers. In spite of bad weather which kept many away, a large audience filled the parterre and galleries of the Theatre Bazola for her introductory lesson. The curtain rose. On the stage stood the diminutive Lidia, her *aparato* or translator and two other Esperantists from Thiers who welcomed her.

A participant, M. Deculty, described the evening: 'She does not wish to give a class but to make conversation. Because the first rule of conversational etiquette is the introduction, she elegantly offers her visiting card, saying, "I am Miss Lidia Zamenhof".'

'The second rule is the introduction of the public. Having asked the occupation of several young people, she succeeds in making them understand and speak.

'Now she talks of linguistic diversity. Why do people not understand each other? Look: in the trees chimpanzee understands chimpanzee . . . Man has conquered space and time through radio and aviation, but before a man who speaks another tongue, he is as mute as a fish . . .

'Mankind is drowning in a deluge of languages, it flounders and searches for an ark. Do they not know that ark exists? It proudly stands out, unafraid of the waves. It is our Esperanto . . .

'And now the lesson begins. Very skillful and effective is the method of our *samideanino*, and wondrously masterfully she teaches. Soon the rules are understood. Miraculously, one listens to all the participants loudly, elegantly respond to her frequent questions.' Lidia's students long remembered how she urged them to respond '*forte, kuraĝe, elegante!*' (loudly, courageously, elegantly!), using the phrase that was the hallmark of the Cseh instructor, designed to encourage bashful – or lazy – students to participate.

'The hour grew late. Wishing them good-night, Miss Zamenhof said she hoped that having awakened interest in our cause, the people of Thiers would kindly attend the three-week course. The long applause was proof of great success . . .'

While she was staying in Thiers, the Esperantists of Moulins invited her to speak in their city. She responded, to their delight, 'immediately', and one December day, Esperantists from Thiers, Vichy and Clermont-Ferrand formed a caravan of four cars decorated with green flags and Esperanto slogans to take her to Moulins. Local Esperantists were on hand to greet Lidia on her arrival and whisked her into one of the city's main restaurants, where, soon after, one person observed, 'one could see . . . a large group of people eating together, each wearing a little green star, whether on a jacket lapel or pinned to a dress, speaking a language unknown to the astonished diners around them'.

At three, in the *université populaire*, the mayor of Moulins introduced Lidia, who spoke on 'Esperanto – Universal Language'. The hall was full, and the audience included local dignitaries, professors and teachers.

'From the first sentences', one person observed, 'she knew how to carefully capture her audience and after several minutes each was astounded seeing that he understood, and often that the translator seemed almost unnecessary.'

She had been asked to give a Cseh lesson there. 'That lesson was masterful. In less than ten minutes she succeeded in getting the entire audience to speak Esperanto! Immediately after the questions, at first very simple, which she asked, each realized with surprise that he could answer, and even answer quite correctly. Soon the translator was abandoned and the questions become longer and longer, more and more difficult. However, all responded, and one may say with real enthusiasm.'

Lidia's fame was spreading through the Esperanto world, both for her teaching successes and for her outspoken advocacy of idealism and peace. Although now she was busier than ever, hurrying from one town to another to teach courses, she was increasingly called on to serve in various, mostly honorary, positions. She had been a 'correspondent' of the Academy of Esperanto and now was elected to the prestigious Language Committee. Her name appeared on the editorial boards of several Esperanto periodicals including *Pola Esperantisto* and *La Ligilo* ('The Bond'), a magazine for blind Esperantists, to which she contributed several articles. The Association of Blind Esperantists named her its honorary president, as did the University Esperantist Circle of Lyon.

Her first courses of 1935 were in Romans, Perpignan and Châteaurenard. The Chamber of Commerce of the province of Pyrénées-Orientales donated two hundred francs toward the course in Perpignan. The tuition was twenty francs for the forty hours of lessons but, as she had done before, Lidia allowed those without jobs to attend without paying, even though the tuition from the classes was her only income.

In April 1935 Lidia returned to Lyon to teach there for the third time. As she always did, she stayed at the home of the Borels on the Quai Claude Bernard, beside the River Rhône. She gave four courses, two in the city of Lyon and one each in Villeurbanne and Oullins. Leaflets with her picture on them were distributed to publicize the courses, and the University Esperantist Circle printed large posters that were pasted on walls all over town. For the next three weeks she worked six days a week teaching a total of almost four hundred students.

Lidia's first courses in Lyon had begun a period of great prosperity for Esperanto in that city; she had awakened considerable public interest, and new Esperantists were coming in by the hundreds. 'We owe our success chiefly to the teaching talent of Miss Zamenhof', Mrs Borel told a radio audience one day. 'Her skill and charm, and also the name she carries and worthily represents, speak to the public more than anything else.' When Lidia had come to Lyon two years ago, the University Esperantist Circle had only fifteen members. Now it counted more than three hundred.

From the first moment Lidia had arrived in Lyon and was taken under the wing of Marie Borel, her friendship with the couple had grown. She came to be considered the 'adopted daughter' of the Borels, Dr André Védrine recalled many years later. Lidia and the couple had affectionate nicknames for each other. Lidia called Mr Borel '*aparato*', for he served in that role for her classes. Mrs Borel she teasingly called '*pastrino*' or 'lady reverend' because Mrs Borel, the moving spirit of Esperanto in Lyon, was 'almost like a minister of the Esperanto Faith'. The Borels fondly called Lidia '*la diino*', 'the goddess'.

It is not hard to understand how Lidia and Marie Borel became so close. They shared a devotion to Esperanto, and both would be remembered by their friends as being rather romantic and idealistic. It seems that Marie Borel was also a Bahá'í, or at least sympathetic enough that she held Bahá'í meetings in her home.

Because Lidia spent more time in Lyon than anywhere else in France, the Esperantists of that city had more opportunity to get to know her, most often at the home of the Borels. Even so, Gabriel Eyssautier recalled, outside the classroom Lidia kept to herself much of the time and was not a talkative person. She was 'a bit timid', recalled Raymond Gonin, 'certainly very modest. She wasn't a person who tried to impose herself.'

When she could, she tried to interest the Esperantists in her religion. Nearly fifty years later, one lady still lovingly kept the faded little Bahá'í pamphlet Lidia had once given her.

Lidia impressed the Esperantists of Lyon as a dreamy, intellectual type, with little experience in practical matters. Once, Cécile Pral recalled, the fire in the room stove had gone out. It used anthracite coal, which was very hard to light. Lidia wanted to start it again. But, not being experienced, she hesitantly dropped the flaming matches onto the anthracite, hoping it would catch fire, much to the amusement of Miss Pral.

Others who knew Lidia in Poland agreed she was a dreamy, mystical type, not given to practical matters, but added that anthracite was not commonly used in Poland, where wood and soft coal were more typical fuels. And like other families in their social class, the Zamenhofs had always had a servant who took care of such things.

Although Lidia seemed frail and delicate in ordinary life, all who knew her agreed that she became 'another person altogether', when she walked onstage to teach. René Lemaire recalled her as 'a person who was almost invisible in the street, who walked along slowly, looking at the ground. But when she was in the classroom teaching a lesson, she was a lion.' 'She gave the course like an actress playing a role,' recalled Cécile Pral. 'She threw herself into it, and during the day she rested to have the strength for it. She wasn't interested in sightseeing. She used to say, "I've visited so many monuments. I'm tired; I have to keep my strength for my classes."' It seemed odd to them because Lidia was young; Cécile Pral guessed she might not be in good health.

Lidia did not talk much about her family, Pierre Dehan recalled, although once he remembered her talking about the situation in Poland. He could tell from the deep affection with which she spoke of her country that 'for her Poland was something very dear, it was her fatherland'.

Although Lidia had studied French in school, her knowledge of the language was limited and she did not know French slang. The Esperantists of Lyon long remembered with fond amusement how once on the tram Lidia overhead someone say a certain word she had not heard before. It caught her attention because of its peculiar sound. She asked the Borels what the word meant and they responded with embarrassment, 'Oh, you mustn't say that. It's vulgar!'

'Oh,' replied Lidia sadly. 'What a pity! It has such a nice sound.'

The French Esperantists had made up a slang phrase from a rather rude French remark which meant 'buzz off' or 'go away'. In Esperanto the phrase didn't mean anything unless you knew the French. It amused Lidia when she heard it, and Mrs Borel once told Raymond Gonin, 'Imagine! We taught a new Esperanto expression to Lidia Zamenhof – we taught her "buzz off!"'

Pierre Dehan, who lived near the Borels, was a student in Lidia's course. Once, Lidia put an announcement for him in *La Praktiko*'s 'I Wish to Correspond' column. He received twenty or thirty postcards in reply and had to answer them all at least once for courtesy's sake. After he wrote the letters, he took them to the Borels, with the intention of asking Mr Borel to correct them for him. Lidia happened to be there. Mr Dehan recalled that she said, 'Oh, good! Give them to me. I'll correct them myself.'

'And she laughed a lot,' Mr Dehan remembered, 'apparently because of some peculiar incorrect phrase I had used. Then she turned to me and said, "When I have such a student I tell him, 'Buzz off!'"' Evidently she said that because we were with Mr Borel who was quite a wit.' Later, Lidia autographed an anthology of L. L. Zamenhof's writings for Pierre Dehan with the words: 'Learn Esperanto well. That is what I want.'

Once, Dr André Védrine recalled, during a lesson in Lyon she told the students that they were her children. Sometime later she was asking the students, as she always did, '*Kiu estas vi?*' (Who are you?) and they, of course, answered with their names. Védrine, at the back of the room, was the last to be called upon. When Lidia asked him, 'Who are you?' he called out: 'I am your son!' That made her laugh and she said, 'Yes, you are my Esperanto son.' After the course she autographed a book for him: 'To my Esperanto son.'

Raymond Gonin recalled another time when she was asking the students the same question. She came to a lady and said, 'Who are you?' and the woman answered, '*Mi estas malnova esperantistino*' (I am an old Esperantist). Taken by surprise but pleased, Lidia cried: 'Oh! I like your name very much!'

Mr Gonin recalled how once, during a lesson, a very shy boy found himself being interrogated by Lidia. '*Ĉu vi amas min?*' (Do you love me?) she demanded.

'I blushed and my ears were ringing,' the boy later told Raymond Gonin, 'and I didn't know what to say. She laughed and once more she asked me, "Do you love me?" I blurted out, "Yes! I love you!"' And after that, when he became a teacher himself, he always told his own students, 'You must never be shy. I was once shy.' And he would tell them that story.

Although Lidia's students and friends in Lyon regarded her with affection and admiration, not everyone in France loved Lidia. The workers' Esperanto groups, with few exceptions, did not support her courses. Lidia was considered to belong to the 'neutral' Esperanto movement and she did not participate in anything having to do with the politically leftist workers' movement. 'I have no contact with SAT' [*Sennacieca Asocio Tutmonda* (World Association of Non-Nationalists), the major organization of the workers' Esperanto movement], she

39. *Lidia demonstrates* kato *to a class while Emile Borel, 'Aparato', looks on*

F-ino Lydia Zamenhof.

40. *Caricature from* La France du Sud-Ouest, *Bordeaux, May 1934*

41. *Lidia with her nephew Ludwik in Italy during the Twenty-Seventh Universal Congress of Esperanto in 1935*

42. *An alfresco meal in Rome during the congress. From left: Adam, Ludwik, Lidia, Wanda*

43. *The introductory lesson in Moulins drew more than 180 to the course*

44. *Lidia in Geneva on her way to the Vienna congress in 1936*

45. *Speaking at the dedication of Zamenhof Street in Thiers, May 1936*

46. *Formal opening of the Jubilee Congress in Philharmonic Hall, Warsaw, in August 1937*

once wrote a correspondent. 'I wish to belong to no struggle, thus also not to class struggle.' Lidia appears to have had at least one real enemy in France, although whoever it was remained anonymous. From Paris, once the stronghold of the traitorous Louis de Beaufront, came rumors which some of the Lyon Esperantists heard, claiming that Lidia Zamenhof was a spy. Nothing could have been more preposterous. The Lyon Esperantists suggested this was probably the work of one person, and was a result of the fanatical nationalism and suspicion of the time. If Lidia ever knew of the rumor, she seems not to have mentioned it, as was her way, and continued with her work.

Once, while Lidia was in Lyon, Mrs Borel and several other Esperantists took her to visit a blind and deaf Esperantist named Antoinette Niquet who lived in a hospital near Lyon. Lidia had a special sympathy for the blind, remembering from her childhood the patients in her father's waiting room and Dr Zamenhof's long years of work to save their sight. The visit to Antoinette touched Lidia so deeply that she later spoke about it over the radio station of Lyon-la-Doua. Many years afterward, Raymond Gonin, also blind, recalled that on the journey Lidia wondered how she could possibly make herself understood since the woman did not hear or see and Lidia did not know the Braille alphabet. But when Lidia arrived, she found the matter quickly solved. 'I wrote with my finger on the palm of her hand', said Lidia, 'words in ordinary letters which she "read" very well. She didn't even wait for me to finish the word, guessing from a part of it, or even the first letter, what I wanted to say.'

Antoinette Niquet had been struck blind and deaf by illness at the age of fifteen and for many years had lived in the hospital in a ward with ten beds. 'But', Lidia observed, 'the other patients are there as temporary guests. The real mistress of the hospital room seems to be Antoinette.'

'Watching her lively movements, one can hardly believe she does not see. With complete sureness, she passes through the room, taking from the corners chairs for her guests, and placing them near the open window, through which comes the fresh smell of the countryside.'

Antoinette showed Lidia her library of Braille volumes and spoke of her many correspondents in various lands. 'One sensed no deprivation in her words', Lidia observed. 'She speaks of the joy Esperanto gives her, linking her with those who share her fate.'

She had made a gift for her visitor – a notebook with thick pages, which she had pierced so that the letters could be felt as well as read. On them Antoinette had painstakingly copied some poetry by Lidia's father. Raymond Gonin recalled the gift 'touched and impressed Lidia'.

At last it was time for them to leave. Lidia took Antoinette's arm to help her, but soon found the blind woman did not need help.

'And when we walked together', said Lidia, 'it seemed to me that I myself was being guided by Antoinette.' As they walked through the street, Antoinette explained to Lidia about the buildings they passed. The shop keepers all knew Antoinette, who ran errands for the other hospital patients. Suddenly, Antoinette dropped Lidia's arm and disappeared into a doorway. 'After a few minutes she reappeared, with a radiant face, bringing me a beautiful bouquet of flowers – a fragrant gift from the blind–deaf *samideanino*.' The tram came, Lidia said good-bye and climbed aboard, throwing a last look at Antoinette, who, tapping the pavement with her white cane, was walking back to the hospital, her home. 'In my hand lies the flower bouquet,' Lidia mused, 'in my heart – in memory of the doubly unfortunate, yet brave and courageous lady.'

The Twenty-Seventh Universal Congress of Esperanto was to be held in Italy during the first two weeks of August, 1935. Although that country was in the grip of fascism under Mussolini, Lidia went to the congress. Martha Root, who was traveling in Scandinavia, did not attend. But Adam Zamenhof, his wife and son traveled from Warsaw to the congress and Lidia was happy to be with them again.

This year, no Bahá'í meeting was planned. Instead, for the first time, a Bahá'í talk, which Lidia was to present, was on the program of the congress itself, as part of the Summer University lectures held at the University of Naples. In her speech Lidia spoke of the nature of man and the existence of God and His relationship to His creatures, about the immortality of the spirit, about free will and destiny, about the meaning of suffering.

How free *was* man? Did he not, as a creation, depend entirely on the Power that had created him? If God was indeed all-knowing, He must know in advance all human actions. Was fate predestined then? If so, could man ever escape the destiny that had been laid out for him?

'Foreknowledge is not the cause of the destiny,' Lidia asserted. 'For example, we all know that in a few hours the sun will disappear beneath the horizon, but our foreknowledge is not the cause of the fact; on the contrary it itself comes from that fact. Similarly, although in the foreknowledge of the Highest Creative Power our fate is written, that foreknowledge does not mean destiny, it is only one of the attributes of the Creative Power.

'Fate is of two kinds: absolute and accidental . . . According to its destiny, when the oil in a lamp is consumed, the lamp must go out. But it can happen that, even before the oil is gone, by chance a strong wind may extinguish the flame. The absolute fate of man is to come into the world, to mature, and having attained the state of maturity, to begin to age, and finally, when the time is come, to return his body to the earth

– but it can happen that a brick falls on his head and cuts the thread of his earthly life sooner. We cannot avoid absolute fate, but we can avoid those other causes, and it is wise to guard oneself against them. Man is responsible for all the actions he performs by his own choice. If no free will existed, there would be no responsibility – neither merit nor guilt . . .

'Along his way he often encounters difficulties. Disappointment and sorrow are with him often throughout life. But they do not come by chance. They are sent to us from above, so that we may learn and perfect ourselves through them. It is easy to sail on tranquil seas – but that sailor is truly brave who in the midst of great waves and hurricanes does not lose his head but knows how to guide the ship to a safe port. We learn and become strong through difficulties . . . The greater the suffering, the greater the harvest of spiritual virtues appearing in man.

'Sometimes happiness makes man self-assured and forgetful. But when sorrow comes, man remembers his smallness and powerlessness and turns upward to the Power above, which alone can save him from his difficulties. And thus his self-assurance dissolves and his spirituality grows . . .' But as she spoke Lidia looked out over the audience with disappointment, seeing that there were not many in attendance. A tour planned at the same time as her lecture had lured the congress-goers to less serious pursuits.

As in previous years, at the congress Lidia also addressed the Union of Esperantist Women. She told them, as she had the year before, that they could become a force for peace. She urged them not to let their children play with war toys 'because the toy of childhood will become a terrible reality in adulthood', and to teach them that children of other races and other lands were just like themselves. Children, she said, should be encouraged to cultivate friendships 'not only with children of their own race or people, but with children of other lands, above all, with children of those lands from which they are separated by the barriers of political hatred and prejudice'.

This they could easily do through Esperanto, she said, and she encouraged her audience to teach the international language to the children in their care. By this means, Lidia concluded, 'Above and beyond the borders a wondrous bridge will be built of the children's hearts. Upon that bridge the mature generation will meet sometime and build a new, better future.'

After the business meetings of the congress ended, Lidia, with her family, went on the congress cruise across the Mediterranean to Malta and Tripoli, Libya, on a chartered ship flying the Green Banner.

When Lidia returned to France to begin her autumn courses, she was exhausted. The first course was to be in Haguenau, Alsace, in the farthest northeast corner of France, and immediately after it she would have to travel south to teach in Saint-Étienne, Hyères and Toulon. From Haguenau she wrote her friends Mies and Hans Bakker that she had done so much during the summer in connection with the congress and cruise that she was very tired. She had hardly rested at all, she admitted. Now she had a heavy schedule ahead of her, but Lidia was confident she could, as she always did, summon up the strength and vitality that always amazed her students so. The fatigue, she was sure, would soon pass.

SEVENTEEN

Let Our Star Be the Beacon

Lidia's presence in France had indeed begun a renaissance of Esperanto in that country. But even as adoring crowds of new Esperantists and sympathizers listened to her exhortations to carry out the ideals of Zamenhof, in the international Esperanto movement another crisis was brewing. Once again the principles of Zamenhof were at stake, and the question of neutrality became the cause of division among the Esperantists.

'Neutral' did not mean the same thing to everyone. To Zamenhof it had meant that no one nation or group of people should be favored over any other; it meant equality of treatment and justice equally for all. But now some Esperantists, abandoning the spirit of Zamenhof's intent, asserted that the international language should be so absolutely neutral that it would have no moral content whatsoever. Esperanto, they felt, should be regarded merely as a tool, which even Nazis and fascists should be encouraged to use for their own purposes if it pleased them. In some countries, including France, there were calls for the creation of special nationalist Esperanto societies. Some even disparaged the ideals of Zamenhof as old-fashioned nineteenth-century notions which should be abandoned.

In Geneva a significant change had taken place in the leadership of the Universal Esperanto Association (UEA), the international organization of the 'neutral' movement, founded in 1908. For some time the organization had been beset by financial problems, caused, among other things, by the high cost of living in Geneva, where the organization's office was located. In addition, among the leaders there was division about the role of the national societies in the UEA as well as the stand Esperantist organizations ought to take on the matter of nationalism. The UEA was reorganized, but Andrei Cseh and Edmond Privat – prominent supporters of Zamenhof's ideals – were not reelected to its governing committee, and in protest several other leaders resigned.

The new UEA officials felt the movement ought to shed the idealism of men like Cseh and Privat and 'adapt to the needs of the times'. The new president was Louis Bastien, a French general; the vice-president was Anton Vogt, a German member of the Nazi party. Until now the political situation in Germany had been avoided in the Esperanto press in an attempt to remain 'neutral'. But following the change of leadership in the UEA, its official journal *Esperanto* printed an article entitled 'The German View on the Racial Problem'. It attempted to present the Nazi racist theories of 'racial purity' and the absurd idea that the 'blurring of lines between races' was 'the most dangerous and gravest sin against life'. The article claimed not to judge the relative value of any group of people, merely that races were 'internally and externally different'. Had Ludwik Zamenhof been alive, he would have been outraged and saddened that an Esperanto journal could even consider printing such lies, which struck at the heart of everything he had struggled for. But Ludwik Zamenhof was not there to protest.

Instead, it was Lidia who spoke out, in an article called '*Nia misio*' ('Our Mission'), which, to the credit of *Esperanto*, appeared in the same issue. Lidia was alarmed at what was happening in the Esperanto movement, especially in Germany. The Nazi party members within the movement were moving against the Jewish Esperantists. In 1934 about twenty Jewish delegates of UEA were forced out of their positions.

From the pages of *Esperanto*, Lidia challenged the Esperantists to fight against the current attitude of anti-internationalism. As Dr Zamenhof had done so often during his lifetime, in strong words she asserted that Esperanto could not be separated from its inner idea.

The Great War, Lidia wrote, 'not only killed millions of people, it also poisoned the spirits of millions . . . revived the primitive blind cult of force and the belief that might makes right. Brotherhood between peoples, the solidarity of the human race, good will in international relations – all this became a mist, vapor. All this now seems to millions only unrealistic babble, a naive fairy tale for overgrown children. The bloody battles changed people into beasts, but although the bloodletting stopped, the brutality did not cease. Because that terrible hate . . . did not end. The thick walls still stand, more strongly than ever, between the divided peoples.'

Now, all that sought to break down those walls, or to preach the brotherhood of mankind or love toward one's enemy, had become suspect. 'This mentality', she asserted, 'is Esperanto's greatest enemy . . . We must battle it. As long as chauvinism rules in the world, as long as everything international is odious to it, Esperanto has no chance of victory.'

The battle for Esperanto, she asserted, could not be separated from the struggle for the vaster world concept of mankind. 'The international language and its inner idea are not two separate things, one of which we can put away in the desk drawer if we wish and show only the other. They form one living whole, whose body is the language, and [whose] soul – the spirit [behind that language]. If we choose to separate the body from the soul, nothing would remain but a rotting cadaver.

'We must propagate everywhere not only the language Esperanto, but also that for which it was created – the coming together of and friendship between peoples. And we must in no way become tired or discouraged in the struggle, because for us it is a battle of life and death. Woe to our Cause, if humanity's bloody nightmare should return. For too long a time, it will delay the victory of Esperanto! . . .

'We must not permit national ambitions to raise their heads among us . . . Esperanto was created so that the peoples should feel equal with each other, not so that through it they should try to raise one above the others . . .'

She concluded: 'If Esperanto had come into the world in some blessed era of universal peace, it would be only a language. But Esperanto stepped into the world-arena at a time when that arena resembles the bloody arenas of ancient Rome. It follows therefore that according to the will of destiny, Esperanto . . . has a mission to fulfill. That mission is – to hasten Universal Peace. Let us not turn away from that mission. Let us work for more than the international vocabulary and international grammar. Let us work courageously and openly so that because of the international language, better relations may prevail among the children of humanity.'

In another article called '*En la mondon venis nova sento*' ('Into the World Came a New Feeling') – the title was taken from the first line of *La Espero* – Lidia spoke out again about nationalism and hypocrisy and alluded to the anti-Semitism that was breaking out among the German Esperantists. She called to mind the first congress at Boulogne-sur-Mer when, 'free of national prejudices, free of blind dogmas, they met and in brotherhood clasped hands – not Frenchmen with Germans, not Russians with Poles, but men with men.' At that time, she continued, 'into the hearts came a new feeling! . . . From mouths to ears went the new language, but more important, more beautiful and holy than the language, from heart to heart went the new Feeling.'

But, 'the old feeling came back into the world' – the monster of hatred. 'The monster is chained for the moment,' she wrote, 'but not dead yet. At any moment it can break its chains and throw itself anew into the world, more terrible than ever, more bloodthirsty than ever.

'Oh, the lovely days of Boulogne, how distant you are!' she lamented. 'Today even the hearts of the Esperantists are not always free from that accursed old feeling. Today, if the Majstro were to come back among us, perhaps in many he would not recognize his disciples, and perhaps he would even find doors that would remain closed to him.'

'And yet,' she observed, 'above our heads the Green Banner still waves. Our voices still sing of the new Feeling . . . Let us be worthy of our banner, of our anthem . . . If night envelops the earth and furious waves foam, let our star be the beacon to mankind that has lost its way. If the waves toss a castaway onto the shores of our spiritual land, let him know that here he will find a fatherland, that all extend a hand to him in friendship, and, without asking about his origin and religion, will say to him sincerely, "Welcome, *samideano!*"

'Then, and only then, will we have the right to sing about the new Feeling that came into the world.'

As for those who wanted to jettison the ideals of Zamenhof in favor of current trends, Lidia vigorously expressed her opposition in an article she wrote about the current state of 'Idealism in the Esperanto Movement'. Now, she asserted, idealists were considered by many fellow Esperantists to be only 'irresponsible children whom they indulged for a while'.

'We cannot tolerate that . . .' she exclaimed. 'We must call for fuller recognition . . . The times are too serious to sit hesitatingly on the fence. The world has never been in a situation like that of today; and that terrible situation is the result not only of economic misery, but also the most lamentable of all, spiritual misery. Mankind is suffocating in the pure atmosphere of materialism. A breath of idealism, the human feeling of the solidarity of mankind is necessary.

'But many in our ranks still do not understand that. Many believe that the concept of materialism is a sign of the times, that it is the fashion of the present era; and fearing to be out of date they turn away from the ideal as if from something long out of style. Fearing to be mocked, they often recant that which they once proclaimed to be their guiding light. When among them someone talks about the inner idea of Esperanto . . . they are annoyed: they'd prefer not to speak of such things.

'It is time to put an end to that cowardly attitude,' she asserted. 'Time to stand up and proclaim to the whole world that the international language opens not only human mouths and ears but also hearts.'

The Esperanto movement seemed endangered from within by those who wanted to rip the language from its idealistic roots. Lidia knew that the Bahá'ís, at least, were committed to the ideals at the core of the Esperanto's inner idea. If Bahá'ís were to learn Esperanto in large numbers, it would help ensure that the Esperanto movement would stay on a firm ideological foundation. Even while Lidia was calling on the Esperantists to support the ideal behind the international language, she was urging the Bahá'ís to learn Esperanto.

In an article in *The Bahá'í Magazine* she wrote: 'Bahá'ís watch the growth of the Esperanto movement with sympathy and good wishes. Many of them are already Esperantists, but many are only lookers-on. This is not enough. For as Christ says, "Not everyone who says 'Lord, Lord' shall enter the Kingdom of Heaven, only he who does the will of my Father which is in heaven." It is not enough to watch with sympathy. We must accept and follow.

'Once I met a Bahá'í who told me he did not intend to learn Esperanto as he knew four languages and that was enough for him. Unfortunately, Polish was not one of the four, and the language in which he was speaking I could hardly understand. So that as far as I was concerned, his knowing four languages did not suffice. One day I asked him if he never meant to visit Poland. He answered that Poland was beyond him, as one cannot easily get about in a country whose language one does not understand. So for him, too, four languages were not enough . . .

'The international language is part of the Divine Plan which is given effect in the era of Bahá'u'lláh. And the creation and spread of Esperanto are proofs of the creative power of Bahá'u'lláh's words.'

The crisis in the movement invaded even Lidia's dreams. She wrote about it in *Pola Esperantisto*. 'I dreamed a strange dream,' she mused. 'I dreamed that I had to take an examination. An examination on gardening. A practical examination. I was in a garden. It was a beautiful garden, but long uncared for. And the task which was given to me was: to clear the garden, to make of this disorderly wilderness a place of beauty, to make the flowers grow and bloom, and tear out and throw away the weeds.

'I had to fulfill the task as best I could. Dismayed, I asked myself: which plants should stay, and which should I tear out? I looked around. I saw flowers that I myself had planted, and flowers whose seeds an unknown wind had brought and which the black earth had accepted and nurtured. And it seemed to me that the most logical solution would be to leave in the earth and tend that which I myself had sowed, and to tear out all the rest.

'But was I right? Doubt nagged me. I asked advice of the old gardener, who plowed the earth in the garden. He raised his face to me, full of furrows, like the plowed earth. He looked at me with his deep-set eyes, and slowly moved his head in a negative gesture. "No," he said. "Do not arrange the garden that way. Do not ask whose hand sowed the seeds. That is not important. But look around and try to understand what the master of the garden intended when he founded this beautiful garden. Whatever fits into his plan, leave it and care for it.

Other plants, even if they stand proudly, tear them up: there is no place for them here."

'At that moment I woke up. A strange dream, I thought, and a strange examination. What did that garden mean, full of flowers of diverse origin; what did the task mean, which had been given to me, and the advice of the gardener? And the exam? Why? . . .'

Lidia tried to analyze it. 'Our whole life is an unceasing test of our strengths', she wrote. 'And the garden? Each of us has in our soul a garden . . . and the great examination of our life is: to keep it in order. Let us not allow the weeds to take the place of the noble plants. And let us not ask whether this or that little flower pleases our taste, because few of us are competent in gardening. Let us only strive that the way in which we arrange our garden conforms to the plan according to which it was founded, to the goal for which it exists.

'And there can be another explanation of that dream. We are all like plants. Sometimes we have brilliant colors, but often we are only weeds of vanity and ambition. For the moment, perhaps, we can be proud; but woe to us when the gardener comes, for he will tear us from the earth and throw us where there is not the aroma of roses but the odor of putrefaction . . .

'And if some of you wish to consider that green garden the arena of the Esperanto world, consider also how orderly we keep it, so that he who founded it will be content, and so that it may flower for the eternal blessing of mankind.'

EIGHTEEN

A Chord Played

The winter of 1935–36 found Lidia once more in northern France. She gave three courses in Le Havre and Sanvic, Normandy, to more than 250 people – the neutral and workers' groups cooperating to bring her there. So favorably did the city government of Le Havre regard the courses that it gave a grant of 1,000 francs so that they could take place, and the Chamber of Commerce donated 450 francs. In Sanvic, following the course, her pupils formed an Esperanto club called the 'Lidia Zamenhof Group'.

In February a reporter from *Le Petit Havre* interviewed Lidia. 'A small woman, petite, with blond plastered-down hair, nordic, receives us in the modest guesthouse on the Boulevard François I,' wrote the reporter. 'In a clear and joyous voice she welcomes us at the threshold, uttering a phrase which I don't understand but to which I all the same respond as best I can.' The reporter asked Lidia if she thought Esperanto had made much progress in France.

'I am profoundly convinced of it,' Lidia answered. 'In the cities I have visited, and notably in Lyon and Toulon, Esperanto has gained a multitude of adherents. But it is certain that France is not in the first rank of Esperantist nations and that the efforts of countries like Holland, Sweden, or even all the way over in Japan are much more sustained than in France. That is, moreover, why I have come to your country.'

The reporter asked her how she thought an international language might bring about peace.

'We are not naive!' exclaimed Lidia. 'We know very well that Esperanto will change neither the face of the world nor the feelings of men, but we believe that an international language will contribute powerfully to a better understanding among people, and we also know that without understanding there cannot be love.'

The reporter concluded the article: '"Forcefully, courageously, elegantly!" Thus Mademoiselle Lidia Zamenhof begins all her classes. And this is how she goes gradually to victory, with so much energy, so much courage, and so much elegance that she is certain to reach one fine day the goal she so passionately seeks to achieve.'

Over a hundred people attended Lidia's good-bye party in Le Havre in March and she set off for Moulins, where the introductory lesson drew more than 180 to the course. Her course in Moulins proved that Esperanto 'brought together the hearts': three couples who met there eventually married.

In the spring, she was invited to return to the cities of Thiers and Romans to give courses. Paule Raynaud Delafouilhouze, who attended the class in Thiers, recalled how Lidia taught with gestures, mime and acting. Mrs Raynaud, a new teacher herself, said she often thought of Lidia in later years when, in her own classes, she was inspired by Lidia's method of teaching, so 'lively and liked by the pupils'. She long remembered Lidia in a certain green coat. 'Green, the Esperanto color,' she recalled, 'suited her well.'

The prediction Leo Belmont had made at Ludwik Zamenhof's funeral, that in every city monuments would be raised in his honor, seemed to be beginning to come true. Over the years, through the efforts of Esperantists, in various countries monuments and plaques had been dedicated, and streets and squares in many cities had been named for Ludwik Zamenhof. By 1935 there were some forty Zamenhof Streets including the street in the Jewish quarter of Warsaw where the Zamenhofs had once lived – Dzika. Lidia's visible presence in France had led to several new Zamenhof Streets in that country. When she could, she would attend the dedication as the guest of honor, speak a few words about her father to the crowd and cut the ribbon or unveil the stone, as the occasion required.

The city of Thiers had decided to name one of its streets in honor of Zamenhof, and Lidia was to attend the inauguration. Despite the rainy day, the town dignitaries were out in force, and Esperanto flags decorated the streets. Once again the Esperantists had outdone themselves. It was reported that three thousand attended, including two bands and a ballet troupe. Lidia spoke a few words to the crowd, a sea of umbrellas, under a great sign that proclaimed 'Honor to Zamenhof, Creator of Esperanto'. Within a period of eight days, three towns in France had dedicated Zamenhof Streets.

Naming Zamenhof Streets was all very well, but it did not have much effect on the deteriorating world situation. Twenty-two years had passed since the shots fired in Sarajevo had ignited the Great War, and Europe seemed headed for catastrophe once again. On July 11, the eve of the anniversary of the Battle of Verdun, as thousands gathered on the site of the battlefield, Lidia gave a moving speech over the radio about that event. She urged the audience to swear to guard the peace. 'Let us learn the lesson of the days past,' she said, 'and let us swear that those days shall never return.'

In 1936 once again the Universal Congress of Esperanto took place in a country where Nazi influence was strong – in Vienna, Austria. In spite of that, Lidia attended, as did Zofia and Adam along with his family. Austria itself was still free, though not for long. On her way to the congress, Lidia passed through Geneva, visiting for two days at the International Bahá'í Bureau.

The Esperanto congress was held in the Hofburg, the former imperial palace. There were the usual get-acquainted evening, opening ceremony, religious services, working sessions, section meetings, theatre, ball and excursions. At the ball in the Hofburg, two uniformed Austrian police orchestras played Viennese waltzes and modern dance tunes while couples in their native costumes danced till two.

But the feeling at the congress was different this year. The opening ceremony, one reporter noted, 'left no profound impression, in spite of all the pomp. It lacked soul, it lacked spirit, it lacked enthusiasm.' At other congresses the opening had been an occasion for inspiring oratory on Esperantism, stimulating the audience to go forward to carry out its high ideals. This time it was about excursions to the Schönbrunn and the Danube.

A shadow cast its chill over the congress. Many were thinking about what had happened just the month before, across the border in Germany.

The attempts of the German Esperanto Association to accommodate itself to the National Socialist regime had failed. Nazi party members had taken over the organization, expelling all its Jewish members. A new society had been formed called the *Neue Deutsche Esperanto-Bewegung* (New German Esperanto Movement) which was completely pro-Nazi. But even this organization found it could not hold the allegiance of the Esperantists and at the same time convince the German government of Esperanto's usefulness.

The first blow had been struck in May 1935 when the German Minister of Education, Bernhard Rust, ordered educational authorities in Germany to cease all support for the Esperanto movement, issuing a statement that 'In the National Socialist state, there is no place for the growth of an artificial world auxiliary language, such as Esperanto. Its use weakens the essential values of the national character . . .' This decree nullified one of 1924 which had recommended the instruction of Esperanto in Germany. The Nazi leaders were unconvinced by arguments that, since Esperanto was neutral, it could serve the new Germany. Officials hotly asserted that the only suitable world language was German. Still the Esperantists persisted, confident that Esperanto would never be forbidden in Germany. Unknown to them, the leaders of the SS were already taking measures to stamp out the movement.

The surveillance arm of the SS was the *Sicherheitsdienst* (Security Service) or SD, under Reinhard Heydrich, a fierce anti-Semite whom Hitler himself would call 'the man with the iron heart'. By 1935 Heydrich had also become head of the *Geheime Staatspolizeiamt* – the Gestapo – an organization whose name would be known soon enough to all Europe as the embodiment of Nazi terror. Head of the SS Heinrich Himmler and SD chief Heydrich were well aware of Esperanto, its principles and the fact that its founder Dr Zamenhof was a Jew.

A month after the Minister of Education's pronouncement against Esperanto, Heydrich warned Minister of the Interior Wilhelm Frick about the increasing activity of the Esperanto movement and recommended that Esperanto groups in Germany be dissolved and their possessions confiscated. When the matter came to the attention of Josef Goebbels, Minister of Propaganda, Goebbels pointed out that if this were done, it would only show the world that such organizations were persecuted in the Third Reich. The foreign Esperantists and the international press, he feared, would use the opportunity to propagandize against Germany. Goebbels recommended that, rather than officially forbid them, the government should request the Esperanto societies 'with some pressure' to dissolve themselves.

But three months went by and the Esperantist organizations stubbornly refused to comply. Heydrich complained to the Führer's deputy, Rudolf Hess, that the Esperantists were still working against the state and asked for a party order against membership in Esperanto organizations and for Goebbels to step up propaganda against the Esperantists. Martin Bormann issued the decree, and Nazi party members were henceforth forbidden to belong even to the New German Esperanto Movement, which had boasted of its good relations with the Gestapo.

Heydrich was not satisfied.

The Esperantists tried to continue their activities, though without many members, but in June 1936 Heydrich decreed in Himmler's name that all organizations of artificial language were to be liquidated by 15 July. All the Esperanto societies ceased activity. Esperanto publishers were closed down. At Hirt & Sohn in Leipzig, which had printed Lidia's first translations, the stock was burned and plates smashed. The Cologne-based newspaper *Heroldo de Esperanto* moved to the Netherlands. Reports reached abroad that individual Esperantists were being arrested. Although there would be some underground activity in the years ahead, especially among workers' groups, the Esperanto movement was officially dead in Germany.

Heydrich gloated that Goebbels had been wrong: his action had not caused the storm of international protest that the Propaganda Minister had predicted, but only one 'interference from the foreign press'.

Without the German Esperantists, the number of congress-goers in Vienna was small. Only 854 attended – it was the smallest congress since 1922. Neither were there any Esperantists from Spain, where bloody civil war had just broken out, or from the Soviet Union, where only socialist Esperanto groups were permitted – and soon even these would be suppressed in Stalin's purges.

At the opening of the congress, a representative of the Czechoslovakian Germans stood up and energetically declared that, in spite of all, the German people remained democratic, and the German Esperantists – faithful to Zamenhof's ideal. His outburst brought a storm of applause and cries of 'Vivu!' but not much else.

Lidia delivered Shoghi Effendi's greetings to the congress at the opening session. She had arranged the Bahá'í meeting herself, but, she wrote Martha Root, it 'was not very large. None of the meetings was large at this congress. I presented (with great approval of Shoghi Effendi) the letter of 'Abdu'l-Bahá to the Central Organization for a Durable Peace in 1919. Do you know that *La Nova Tago* can no longer come out in Germany because Esperanto is officially forbidden there?'

The congress was also marred by the long-standing dispute among the leaders of the neutral movement, which reached a crisis point in Vienna. Some of the leaders were determined to move the headquarters of the Universal Esperanto Association from Geneva to London. During a working session, Lidia found herself in a heated discussion with General Bastien, president of the Association, about the subsequent fate of the UEA's library. 'We live in a dubious era', she reminded the audience, 'when fires are fed by books.'

Some Swiss who did not want the change insisted that the by-laws of the organization did not allow the move. To change the rules would require the delegates to decide the matter by a vote. A vote was then carried out, but some insisted it had not been strictly according to the rules. The two sides could not agree and the Swiss took the matter to court, which ruled in their favor. The faction – a large majority – that was determined to make the move now broke away from the UEA and formed a new organization called the International Esperanto League (IEL). Most members and national societies went over to the new organization, and the UEA was left with only a few hundred individual members. The Esperanto movement would not be reunited until after the war.

Lidia was among those who felt that the letter of the law had not been followed. But to her, the question of moving the central office from one place to another was not the most important issue. Above all, Lidia feared schism, and she urgently reminded the Esperantists of the

damage that had been done to the movement by the Ido episode in
1907. 'Only in unity is our strength', she asserted.

While Zofia Zamenhof eventually joined the IEL, Lidia never
formally transferred her allegiance to the breakaway organization and
remained to the end of her life a member of the UEA.

One bright light at the Vienna congress was Lidia's address to the
International Women's Conference on Wednesday afternoon. The
conference theme was 'The influence of the political and economic
situation in Europe on the situation of women'. The speech Lidia
delivered was one of her best – and most provocative. To read it today,
in the light of history as well as current events, it is even more
poignant. Her words are just as pertinent, if not more so, now than
they were in 1936.

'Mankind consists of two elements,' Lidia began, 'the male element
and the female element, or, speaking in the current style, the strong sex
and the weak sex.' Until now, she told them, the strong sex had ruled
in the world. For thousands of years, women, the weak sex, had been
the slaves or the playthings of men. 'Let us look at the pages of history.
What do we read there? An unending series of battles and wars. Men
made those wars.'

But, she told them, those millennia during which 'women bore the
yoke of male rule' must come to an end. The fruits of the reign of men
had become 'too bitter'. And that bitterness, she asserted, women felt
more than did men. When there was no bread, who suffered for the
children's hunger? When the call to war was sounded, who trembled
for the sons sent into battle? When the news no longer came from the
trenches, when all returned home except her son, whose heart bled
more? It was clear: 'the monster of war . . . sank its claws above all into
the hearts of women'. Those sufferings, she said, must finally jolt
women into throwing off their long oppression. 'Women must arise –
they want to arise – they are arising!' she cried. 'Not to bring down the
men, not to rip from their hands the scepter of rule and capture for
themselves the reins of the world . . . no one wants that, even the most
fanatic feminist. All women want is equality!

'"Mankind is like a bird with two wings,"' said 'Abdu'l-Bahá. One
wing is man, the other – woman. Before both wings are equally strong
and developed, the bird cannot fly. 'And that second, till now weak
wing, little by little is becoming strong. Women are entering all the
professions and succeeding in them as well as men.'

But the way of progress was often thorny. Independent women
who earned their own bread were treated with suspicion, she noted.
'Faith in woman's work is still not general, and such distrust, with the
resulting exploitation, results in the fact that often for work of the same
quantity and quality a woman receives half or a third of the pay given a

man.' But these, she said, were difficulties 'of the transitional period. When that period is over', she was confident, 'woman will be economically equal to man.'

Of all the new fields women were entering, one profession, Lidia believed, seemed 'almost predestined by nature itself for women – that is education. And not only teaching itself, but all that touches the moral, intellectual or even physical culture of the youngest generation.' The child's first education occurred under the eye of the mother – and those early experiences gave direction to the development of the child's character. 'In the hands of women lies a boundless responsibility – the formation of the souls of the young generation, which means in effect, the *future of the world*!

'If the generation which in the year 1914 decided the fate of humanity had had mothers and teachers conscious of their high task – if that generation, instead of playing with lead soldiers and wooden swords in childhood, had been educated in the spirit of respect for life, of love for one's neighbor beyond the threshold of one's native land, would we be where we are today?

'We know not what the next moments have in store for us. Never more right was the warning, "Beware, for ye know neither the day nor the hour!" Tomorrow the bloody phantom may return, a thousand times more terrible than before. Perhaps tomorrow the apocalyptic rider will gallop through the world, to fulfill the power given to it, power over a fourth of mankind!

'But in the end, massacred to the bone, mankind will indeed understand how terrible are those dark forces which it led onto the arena so that there they could tear apart and rend its own body. And it will wish to chain them firmly, once and for all. It will wish for peace – not a parody of peace, not a peace that serves only to prepare better for war. It will wish for eternal Peace, universal and sacred.

'For that Peace to come, men must want it. And for them to want it, they must understand that it alone is beautiful, good and worthy. And for them to understand that, someone must teach it to them, someone must enlighten them about it. And thus, oh women, do not cease your efforts, because a vast field lies before you. Do not lose heart when you hear that today around the ship of mankind a furious ocean howls with a thousand waves. Save that which is to be saved: THE FUTURE OF THE WORLD!

'Show your children, your charges, that glories exist more noble than the bloody crowns of Caesars and Napoleons. Tell them that concord builds up, discord destroys. Teach them that "love" is not merely a banal harangue, that "brotherhood" is not just a utopian dream.

'Explain to them that if they do not make these truths an essential part of their thought, action and life, they will themselves, in their turn, bow low and sigh under the threat of those black clouds which today hang over us.

'Teach them to understand and to love not only the members of their own family, of their city, province and land. Teach them to extend a hand to brothers from beyond the borders. Teach them to understand those human brothers, although borders and languages divide them. And to that end, teach them the language of love and peace, that language which opens the hearts and binds them together like an enchanting bond, teach them Esperanto!

'Say to them that that language must not serve them solely for the exchange of postage stamps and picture post cards, but that above all it must serve for the exchange of thoughts and feelings, so that they may recognize the true face of their neighbor and see that that face is the face of a brother.

'Women, individual effort is always noble and good. But the way of individual effort is long, and we do not have time to lose, because destruction and death move quickly. Unite your efforts! Unite your voices and cry throughout the world: love and peace among the peoples of the world! Let there be understanding among the children of men! Through Esperanto, the language of unity, let understanding reign upon earth! May that language be spread throughout the world! Esperanto in the schools!

'Nothing comes into being without a cause, and nothing passes without causing an effect. A chord played, even when it disappears from our hearing, lives on in space, goes round the world, rises beyond, and flies to worlds we cannot reach, and brings them that chord as our greeting. Will the chords of our planet be grating or harmonious? Will they bring into the music of the spheres a sweet sound or a harsh noise?

'And the rapid-flying lightning-quick waves of light, which pass through the ether, even when their source is long extinguished, what picture will they immortalize in the universe – a picture of burning cities, or the lights of promethean fires, which lead mankind forward on the eternal way of progress?

'At the threshold of the new era stands humanity as a weak, trembling child. Women, extend to it a helping hand, so that that child may not fall on the threshold, so that it may grow in glory and go forward to a better future!'

NINETEEN

Without Eggs and Without Chickens

After the Vienna congress Lidia went home to Warsaw for several weeks, 'very happy to see my hometown, my friends and relatives again'. Then she returned to France and plunged into a busy schedule of classes. In Nantes 300 attended the introductory lesson, and 182 signed up for the course. It was the largest number of students she had ever had in a single class. In the past year, Lidia had developed her own course for those who had already completed the Cseh beginner's lessons. In Nantes, seventy enrolled in her advanced class. Afterward, she gave another course in Lyon, and, once again, over a hundred enrolled.

Meanwhile, Martha Root had been at work on her plan to send Lidia to the United States. From the steamer en route to New York she wrote to the Bahá'ís in the United States to tell them she hoped they would invite Lidia to America. To Della Quinlan, secretary of the Bahá'í International Auxiliary Language Committee, she wrote: 'I wish Lidia Zamenhof could come to New York and teach Esperanto and continue her study in Persian . . . Lidia is trying to learn Persian and it is her great aim to take Esperanto to Iran the land of Bahá'u'lláh, but of course she could not go yet for conditions are so upset there and also the Guardian wishes her to know Persian *well* before she goes. Lidia is the best teacher from Europe to come to our country and she is a most *confirmed* Bahá'í.' Martha underlined 'confirmed' three times.

Martha Root had been in contact with Shoghi Effendi about sending Lidia to America and the Guardian was enthusiastic about the idea. In July 1936 he wrote Lidia: 'It would be splendid if you could visit the United States where the friends are so eager to meet you and accord you a hearty welcome. You will let me know, I trust, whenever you decide to visit them, for I wish to introduce you to them in a befitting manner . . .' Lidia was grateful for his encouragement to go to America. She wrote him that if she went to the US it would be to teach Esperanto there, but she hoped it would lead to opportunities to serve the Bahá'í Faith more directly.

Mrs Della Quinlan, from New York City, would play a major role in Lidia's visit to America. A middle-aged woman, Mrs Quinlan worked in the public relations department of the New York Stock Exchange. She had become an Esperantist and a Bahá'í as a teenager. Both movements were very dear to her, and she hoped that the Bahá'ís and the Esperantists could work together to bring Lidia to the United States. Lidia also placed great importance on such cooperation. She wrote Martha Root that she would not come to America unless both groups were behind her.

But the situation in the United States was unlike that in Europe. In the US there were few Esperantists, and Esperanto classes had traditionally been free. In Europe the inviting Esperantist group had always paid Lidia's travel expenses. The money she received from her lessons depended on the number of students who enrolled. But even in France, where the number of students had ranged from 20 to 182, Lidia never knew if there would be a hundred or a handful of students, so she could never be sure of her income.

Some Americans doubted that Lidia could earn enough from her classes in the US to support herself. The name of Zamenhof was much more familiar in Europe, and Esperanto was much better known there. Previous visits of eminent European Esperantists to America had been, in the words of one Esperantist, 'failures'.

Thus not all the American Esperantists were enthusiastic about sponsoring Lidia's trip. Because the Esperanto Association of North America was in financial difficulty, its general secretary discouraged bringing Lidia to America, but Ernest Dodge, chairman of the Executive Committee, was wholeheartedly in favor, saying he thought the idea 'inspiring and gripping'. Another well-known Esperantist felt that a visit by Lidia Zamenhof would 'not be a success' and that his 'local group would not care to take the responsibility of inviting Miss Zamenhof here, as it would be very unlikely that a class could be gotten together . . .' Some seemed uneasy about Lidia's Bahá'í affiliation. 'It appears', wrote Samuel Eby from New York, 'that Miss Lidia Zamenhof, daughter of Dr Zamenhof, is a confirmed Bahaist.'

Both the Bahá'ís and the Esperantists decided to postpone considering the matter, and it seemed Lidia's visit might not take place after all. Martha Root was not there to speed matters along: at Shoghi Effendi's instructions she was taking a 'rest cure'.

Without a formal invitation, Lidia could not make plans and did not know what to do. Shoghi Effendi had written to her again in November 1936, and it was clear that he, at least, was in favor of the trip. 'Dear and valued co-worker:' he wrote, 'I have communicated with the American National Assembly and I feel confident that the American believers will be only too glad, and indeed eager, to extend to you a cordial welcome. Your services, past and present, are, I believe, but a prelude to a distinguished record of the services that will enrich the annals of God's Holy Faith. Persevere, nay redouble your valued and highly meritorious efforts.' That was enough for Lidia. Over the years she had formed a spiritual attachment to Shoghi Effendi which was one of loyalty and devotion. Ever since she had met him in Haifa, she had regarded his wishes as a binding command which she must obey, no matter where it might take her.

In January 1937 Martha confided to Della Quinlan: 'Private just to you. P.S. I had a letter from Lidia about two or three weeks ago and she is very eager to come if the Guardian wishes it. I wrote urging her to come if she feels she ought to and I believe Bahá would help her. She had saved a little money to go to Persia for the Guardian told her to go to Persia but she couldn't go yet because of the nationalism there. Poor child, she doesn't know the conditions in our country, doesn't know what to do and she is praying hard for Guidance. Write her a line c/o Mrs Borel . . .'

Besides the question of the formal invitation, something else troubled Lidia about going to America. All her life Lidia had been a public figure in the Esperanto world, even though, apart from her brief work as secretary of the student association, her involvement in the organized movement was mostly in an honorary capacity. As a Cseh teacher, for several years now she had earned her living by speaking to groups of strangers in foreign countries and had given many public speeches in front of hundreds of people. She had often presented Bahá'í talks at the Esperanto congresses and had spoken about the Bahá'í Faith before the Theosophical Society in several cities in France. But she had never spoken before large groups of Bahá'ís, and the prospect of doing so filled Lidia with anxiety. To stand up in front of fellow-believers and teach them something about their own Faith? What could she possibly tell them?

Lidia wrote Martha that she worried the Bahá'ís might be expecting too much of her. 'My dear little mother: . . . Truly it seems that trip will come about . . . I only fear at times that the matter will be misunderstood and that people will think I could be a Bahá'í teacher, that is, that I could give talks, etc., to the believers – which I certainly could not do, and I beg you to make this point clear. I know you well indeed, and your too-high opinion of me, and know that if in conversation I should say that to you, you would at once exclaim, "Oh, yes, you could do it!" Therefore I beg you to present this point with absolute clarity because otherwise perhaps the NSA would be misinformed and even deceived. But certainly, and naturally, when I am among Esperantists I will try, as far as I am able, to acquaint them with the teachings of Bahá'u'lláh.'

Also, she told Martha, she did not feel able to give speeches in

English, even if she could read the text. She often had difficulty understanding Americans when they spoke and feared that in America people would not understand her if she spoke English with her Polish accent. In France she always used an interpreter for her talks.

Although Lidia had traveled throughout Europe, the prospect of going to America frightened her a little. She knew nothing about the country, and it was so far away.

In preparation for Lidia's visit, Della Quinlan sent her a 'Publicity Questionnaire' to fill out with background information in order to prepare press releases and to plan speaking engagements. Lidia's response to two of the questions illustrated the difference between her state of mind, as a Central European, and that of the Americans. The questionnaire asked, 'Are you free to travel anywhere in the country?' and, 'Are you free to travel to neighboring communities?' The Americans, who took their freedom for granted, simply wanted to know if Lidia would be available to travel anywhere. They must have been a bit perplexed by the graver interpretation she gave the questions, thinking they were inquiries as to whether she would be permitted freedom of movement in the United States. She wrote: 'I am not informed about any objections.'

The barriers between the peoples seemed to stand higher now than ever before. But even as the explosive situation in Europe seemed increasingly hopeless and people were becoming ever more cynical, Lidia refused to give up or to surrender to despair. On the contrary, now her work seemed even more crucial, for she knew that the time was short. With more urgency than ever, she raised her voice for unity and peace. In articles, radio broadcasts and lectures – directing her words often to women – she admonished people to work for true understanding among the nations and races, and to demand peace. And she warned those who would listen that the war toward which Europe was rushing would be far more terrible than the 'Great War' of 1914–18. In a chilling allegorical story about a mysterious musician, she wrote of the fascination some people seemed to have for the coming catastrophe.

'Before the strange artist came to the land', she wrote, 'his fame had spread through cities, towns and even villages.' His music was said to shake the very souls of men, and there was great excitement about his coming concert. But the price of tickets was high, very high. Nevertheless, the public besieged the concert hall, eager to see the famed pianist. But it seemed that the secretive musician required the hall to be in complete darkness before he would play. Some, especially the women, protested; but at last, in the name of art, all the lights were put out.

When the artist entered, all could feel his presence. And when the music began, it was like nothing they had ever heard. 'One might think that it was not the voice of the piano, that the artist was hitting the chords of nature itself, making them weep, wail and howl, making them moan, roar, fill with terror . . .'

The music became more frightening. 'Finally it passed all limits. The notes no longer resounded in the space around them, but reverberated within each person, thundered beneath the skull, beat within the heart, seethed in the veins, deafened, squeezed, suffocated, terrified.

'Truly the artist was inspired . . .

'At last they could stand it no longer. Despairing voices began to cry for light.'

When the lights went on, the mysterious musician was revealed, cloaked in black. From beneath his hood the skeletal face of Death itself leered at the audience. '"Ladies and Gentlemen," said Death. "I only played the *Prelude* for you. And now do you want to hear . . . the *Concert?*"

'That Prelude was played in the years 1914–1918,' Lidia wrote. 'Will we still hear the Concert?'

In another, courageous article entitled '*La vojo al superhomo*' ('The Way to Super-Man'), she attacked the prevalent attitude that held physical development above spiritual development. This notion had reached its extreme of depravity in Germany where, at this time, the Nazis were obsessed with German 'racial purity' and with creating a super-race through 'eugenics'. The Nuremberg Laws had been adopted in 1935, making Nazi racist doctrines the law of the Reich.

'In a magazine I read an interesting article,' Lidia wrote. 'A certain Dr Voronov wants to create a super-man. He wants to inject ten-year-old children with extracts of monkey glands. He says that the mother who will permit her child to be given that injection will be a new Eve of mankind: she will provide the beginning of a new, better human race . . .

'Serious scientists consider the idea of Voronov pertinent. And it may have important results. But will it create a super-man?

'Experiments done with sheep may show that one can perhaps improve and strengthen the human body. With the help of his younger brothers-in-Darwin, the monkeys, perhaps the human race will become stronger against disease and more resistant to aging. Perhaps the way shown by Voronov is the right way of physical culture.

'It may be; I don't know. But will Voronov truly create a super-man?

'If the Voronov man, stronger than the ordinary one, will use his powers to attain a depravity beyond that of ordinary man, could he be called a super-man? If he will use his intellect, as our generation has done, to create ever more perfect tools of destruction and death – shall we call him a super-man?

'No extracts, glands, injections, however effective, will make of man a super-man. That cannot be attained solely through physical culture. For that we need spiritual culture and spiritual evolution. And spiritual culture is not attained through the glands of monkeys.

'Spiritual culture is the culture of the heart. Mothers who desire to be new Eves of mankind! Cultivate the hearts of your children. Children's hearts are soft. Beware lest they become hard. The hearts of children are pure. Guard them from impurity. Strive that they receive those injections which are necessary for their evolution: the injections of good will and love. Nurse the hearts of your children. The hearts of mature people are often in a state of degeneracy. May the hearts of your children always remain young. The youth of the heart is true youth. It is worth much more than that youth which is artificially prolonged with the help of chimpanzees.

'Scientists of the world! If you wish to create a super-man, cultivate the hearts. Cultivate the hearts so that they will be free of prejudices, so that they will be filled with love, so that they will become great and encompass the whole of mankind.'

'And', Lidia concluded, 'when calumny, jealousy, hatred, conflict and war will disappear from the world, then understanding, love and peace will reign, then will the world become another world, and mankind – another mankind. And then, only then, the race of super-men will have been created.'

But as time passed, it was clear that conflict and war were not going to disappear from the world. In one of its issues La Praktiko reported an amusing anecdote about a farmer in Texas who was convinced that in two years a new world war would break out. He based his prediction on the fact that in the year 1912 one of his chickens had laid a strange, long egg shaped like a torpedo. At that time, because of the extraordinary shape of the egg, the farmer foretold that war was coming, a prediction fulfilled two years afterward, in 1914. Now another of his chickens was again laying torpedo-shaped eggs, which led him to prophesy that another great war was approaching. 'Well', commented La Praktiko, 'the state of the world is such that even without eggs and without chickens, one can easily foresee catastrophe.'

TWENTY

Now I Am Flying

Lidia was anxious to go to the United States. But would her trip ever take place? She waited for word to come from America. In November 1936, Shoghi Effendi had informed the National Spiritual Assembly of the Bahá'ís of the United States and Canada that he had 'encouraged her to undertake this visit' and advised them 'to extend to her a hearty welcome and to make every effort to facilitate her visit to your country'. But by February 1937 Lidia had still not received an official invitation. Nevertheless, she was determined to go. She wrote Roan Orloff: 'because Shoghi Effendi's wish is for me an order and guidance, I shall do everything possible to come to America in the autumn.'

At last the letter arrived: The National Spiritual Assembly sent Lidia 'an urgent and cordial invitation to visit America'. Lidia accepted, saying, 'I pray that Bahá'u'lláh may enable me to serve in America, to give His Message to some of the Esperantists and to help the Bahá'í friends to know this language that has been created through the creative power of God's word.'

The National Spiritual Assembly offered to pay for her passage to America and her return voyage to Europe, but the Esperantists were asked to take responsibility for arranging her classes. The five hundred dollars that the National Assembly gave Lidia for her ship passage would not cover all her living and travel expenses while she was in the United States; all those involved expected that Lidia would charge a fee for her classes, as she had always done in Europe. She wrote that if she could be sure of having hospitality provided for her so that she did not have to stay in hotels, she would not have to charge for the lessons. But this alternative was never seriously considered. The Bahá'ís asked the Esperantists to arrange for her classes because at first they felt they could not charge the public for education in one of the Bahá'í religious principles. Although they later decided that it would be acceptable to charge a fee for the Esperanto lessons, the matter of arranging Lidia's classes remained with the Esperantists.

In the spring of 1937 Lidia went to Paris to give several Cseh courses. Her classes were held in an Esperantist-owned restaurant called 'The Green Star', as well as in the city hall of the ninth district. A course for teachers was held in a room at the Sorbonne. But her classes in Paris attracted only a handful of pupils. A course in Versailles met with better success. Lidia did not know it, but they were the last Esperanto courses she would ever teach in France.

André Gilles, then a timid eighteen-year-old, recalled sharing a table with Lidia and some other Esperantists one day at a vegetarian restaurant in Paris. But because of his shyness, he was not brave enough to speak to the famous daughter of Dr Zamenhof. He never saw her again, but in the years that followed, as a young soldier he often thought with concern about his chance table companion. After the war, he long remembered the 'peace-loving, high idealistic words of hers' which he had read on various occasions.

Marcel Delcourt recalled meeting Lidia in Paris. He was in the French Air Force stationed at Villacoublay and visited the Esperantist center on the rue Chabrol, where Esperantists gathered to socialize. He remembered that he even danced with Lidia, and she made a teasing comment on his military uniform, greeting him as 'Mr Warrior'. He hastened to correct her: he was just an ordinary 'Mr Soldier'.

Although she teased the young Frenchman, the sight of the military uniform probably wrenched her heart with pity. She might have been remembering another French Esperantist she had met, who had once worn a smart uniform too. He was a blinded war veteran, his eyes covered by a black band. 'He gave his eyes to the fatherland . . .' Lidia had written in an article, 'and the fatherland in gratitude placed upon his breast a red ribbon . . . Whom did that sacrifice serve?' she asked. 'Did the fatherland gain by the crippling of its son? Who was made happier because of it?

'If it were a case of sacrifices freely offered, made with full conviction for a rational end!' she exclaimed. 'If it were a case of pioneers who perish of yellow fever while draining the swamps! If it were a case of the friends of mankind, who die from experimental serum to spare the lives of others! Then we would respectfully bow our heads before those sacrifices, which deserve monuments more than do generals and marshals.

'But those sacrifices that have been exacted from human beings dressed in uniforms have served no purpose. They have brought happiness to no one, and they have brought unhappiness to millions.

'And perhaps soon once more . . .

'None of us knows whether tomorrow his own eyes will not be torn out by a bullet . . . whether tomorrow his own eyes will not be covered with the black band, whether he will even be allowed to tread upon the earth. As long as there is still time, let us exert our efforts to open the blind eyes of those who believe that the red ribbon can ever make up for the shadows of the black band . . . to warn those who, a thousand times blind, are rushing toward the abyss. To cry throughout the world: "Away with war! Peace is sacred!"'

In May at an international conference on 'Esperanto in Modern Life', held by the International Esperanto League and the French Society for the Propagation of Esperanto, Lidia presented her Cseh demonstration lesson and gave several speeches. In one lecture, she spoke of the evolution of human society up to the present – the time of the nations. Was there anything greater that could claim one's loyalty? The answer she gave was: mankind.

Not all in the audience were receptive to her words. Once again, nationalism was strong in France. More than thirty years earlier, Ludwik Zamenhof had stood before an audience in France at a time when nationalistic fervor was strong and had spoken fearlessly of his convictions. Now, as Lidia found herself in a similar situation, this time she spoke of him.

The author of Esperanto, she told them, 'always had a vision: the vision of one great family circle, based on the foundation of neutral language, the vision of humanity reunited through understanding, the vision of a happy era when "we shall pull down the walls between peoples". And that vision was everything in his life. It was his highest goal. All else was secondary: the language itself was only a tool for attaining that goal. And although he never sought influence, although in 1912 he officially rejected the title of Majstro, in order to be free to serve his beloved ideal, Esperanto is so linked with him, his concepts have stamped upon the movement a mark so indelible, that one simply cannot completely understand the Esperanto idea without knowing the ideas of Zamenhof.'

Those ideas were contained in his philosophy of Homaranismo, which was now all but forgotten. Each person, Lidia said, must recognize that whatever nation, race, religion or class he belonged to, he was before all else a human being. The principles of Homaranismo, she added, 'prepared man for a new role': to feel himself a member of humanity.

In another speech at the conference she talked of the Bahá'í Faith, which she believed embodied those principles of her father. 'The Bahá'ís also use Esperanto in practice to propagate their ideas,' Lidia told the gathering. The International Bahá'í Bureau corresponded in Esperanto; Bahá'í literature was available in the language; and there was the Esperanto Bahá'í magazine, *La Nova Tago*, published under the direction of the National Spiritual Assembly of the Bahá'ís of Germany and Austria. (The magazine, as Lidia knew, was now forbidden in the Third Reich. Barely a week after Lidia's speech, the Bahá'í Faith itself would be forbidden in Germany by order of SS chief

Heinrich Himmler, all Bahá'í activities prohibited and the National Spiritual Assembly dissolved soon after.) 'The Bahá'ís', Lidia told her audience, 'see in Esperanto not only a means to spread their Faith . . . They see in it the law of God Himself, one of the God-given principles of the New World Order.'

But the picture she painted of the Bahá'ís' acceptance of Esperanto was more an expression of her fondest wish and desire than it was of reality.

While indeed some Bahá'ís, among them some of the most distinguished and prominent leaders of the Faith, were enthusiastic Esperantists, other Bahá'ís seemed uninterested in the whole question of international language. They applauded the idea, but felt no pressing need to learn Esperanto. The Esperantists could not understand this; if an international language was one of the Bahá'í principles, Esperanto would seem to be its fulfillment. Why, then, they wondered, did not more Bahá'ís learn the language and use it, and why were the Bahá'ís reluctant to claim Esperanto as their own international language? Many Esperantists saw this as hypocrisy.

In fact, the Bahá'ís and the Esperantists differed in the way in which each group believed an international language should be established. The Bahá'í writings stated that in the future the governments of the world and the Universal House of Justice (the supreme administrative institution of the Bahá'í Faith which had not yet come into being at that time), would choose a universal auxiliary language. Most Bahá'ís, therefore, felt they need not be concerned about the matter until that time came.

The Esperantists, on the contrary, believed that the international language must come into being in the same way that native languages did – through practical use, without waiting for an official decision. In 1891 Zamenhof had warned the Esperantists not to wait for governments or important persons to support Esperanto; they would take notice, he had said, only after Esperanto became successful on its own. The Esperantists had learned the truth of his words as for decades they tried in vain to place the matter before governments and international bodies, such as the League of Nations. But the debates about international language always degenerated into a tug-of-war between speakers of various national tongues. Waiting for governments to act would delay the adoption of an official international language perhaps for centuries, they believed, while the problem – lack of communication and understanding among peoples – persisted and even grew worse.

The Bahá'ís and the Esperantists shared the belief that an international language would help to break down the barriers between peoples. But the Esperantists felt its immediate need more acutely and recognized that were the governments of the world ever to reach such a level of co-operation that they could agree on a world language, the *problem* which international language could have helped solve would no longer exist. In such a world of co-operation and mutual agreement between the nations, an international language would be merely a convenience.

Those Bahá'ís who were also Esperantists saw no reason why the two approaches should exclude each other: if Esperanto were to spread as a 'grass-roots' movement throughout the world, when the time came for an official decision to be made, the choice would be obvious. And they knew that, as Dr Zamenhof had warned when he first presented Esperanto, before 'everyone' learned the language, some individual 'ones' must take that step first. If people refused to learn Esperanto, thinking they must wait until an official international language was chosen, they would in effect assure Esperanto's failure.

'Abdu'l-Bahá had made many statements about his hope that Esperanto would spread and become universal. But, many Bahá'ís wondered, was Esperanto destined to become *the* international language ordained in the Bahá'í writings to be chosen by the Universal House of Justice? A statement was circulated that seemed to show 'Abdu'l-Bahá had said definitely that Esperanto would become that language – Lidia quoted it in her Paris speech. But the statement, a translation the original of which was unavailable for authentication, could not be confirmed.

For decades the question kept coming up, and Shoghi Effendi had to explain: no one could say for certain that Esperanto would become *the* international language of the future. He always encouraged Bahá'ís to support and study the language but made it clear that, as he told the National Spiritual Assembly of the Bahá'ís of the United States and Canada in June 1937, '. . . while the teaching of that language has been repeatedly encouraged by 'Abdu'l-Bahá, there is no reference either from Him or from Bahá'u'lláh that can make us believe that it will necessarily develop into the international auxiliary language of the future. Bahá'u'lláh has specified in His writings that such a language will either have to be chosen from one of the existing languages, or an entirely new one should be created to serve as a medium of exchange between the nations and peoples of the world.' But the Guardian continued: 'Pending this final choice, the Bahá'ís are advised to study Esperanto only on consideration of the fact that the learning of this language can considerably facilitate intercommunication between individuals, groups and Assemblies through the Bahá'í world in the present stage of the evolution of the Faith.'

In fact, this was a very significant statement, which supported the Bahá'í Esperantists' position. Earlier statements had generally encouraged the Bahá'ís to associate with the Esperantists because of their common ideal, but now Shoghi Effendi was recommending that the Bahá'ís learn and use Esperanto for its present practical value as a working international auxiliary language. Many who read his words, however, saw only the qualification, and ignored the Guardian's advice to learn Esperanto.

Indifference to Esperanto was especially prevalent among the Bahá'ís in the United States, who shared the general attitude of their countrymen toward foreign languages. Unlike Europeans, most Americans had little contact with speakers of other languages, and they felt no need to learn languages themselves. Their geographical isolation gave them little chance to experience the clash of language differences, and in spite of the fact that their own language was a legacy of English colonialism they were unaware of the contempt in which speakers of other national languages held English.

Officially, relations between the American Bahá'ís and the Esperantists had always been cordial. For many years, classes in Esperanto had been conducted under Bahá'í auspices. Several Bahá'ís held positions of importance in the Esperanto Association of North America (EANA) as well as in local Esperanto societies. James Morton, a New Jersey Bahá'í, was vice-president of the EANA.

The National Spiritual Assembly of the Bahá'ís of the United States and Canada regularly sent greetings to the EANA's annual congresses, quoting Bahá'í scriptures on the topic of universal auxiliary language, and stating that the National Spiritual Assembly was 'in complete unity with the lofty aims of your association'. In 1934 the National Assembly even created a national committee which was to 'find ways and means to make more effective Bahá'í contact with Esperanto groups'. At first it was known as the Esperanto Committee, but was later referred to as the Universal Auxiliary Language Committee. It reported on the formation of new groups of Bahá'í Esperantists, classes in Esperanto and contact with the Esperantists.

Among the American Bahá'ís, however, some were convinced that the universal language of the future was sure to be English. While the question of inviting Lidia to America was under discussion, Bahá'í Esperantist Josephine Kruka wrote Dr Charles Witt, chairman of the Bahá'í International Auxiliary Language Committee: 'Many of [the Esperantists] feel somewhat unkind towards the Bahá'ís because they feel the insincerity of "preaching what you do not practice" for they know the Bahá'ís do nothing to promote an International Language. Many of the Bahá'ís think nothing need be done since they are positive English will be the International Language.'

As Lidia contemplated her coming journey to America, it was with some anxiety but also with hope. Aware of the lukewarm attitude of many American Bahá'ís toward Esperanto and of the wary attitude of the Esperantists toward the Bahá'ís, she secretly determined – she confided to Roan Orloff in Boston – to try to build a bridge of co-operation between her two beloved Causes there. She did not know how she would accomplish this or whether she would succeed, 'but I remember the promise of Bahá'u'lláh', she wrote, 'and I trust that the Supreme Concourse will always help those who arise sincerely to proclaim the Cause of Bahá'u'lláh.'

'To us all is destined a certain task,' she wrote, 'and if we fulfill it with our whole heart, Bahá'u'lláh will sustain us and will lead us to Him.'

The Esperanto Association of North America had appointed a committee of three to undertake Lidia's arrangements in the United States. Two of the committee members were Bahá'ís: Della Quinlan and Josephine Kruka, who was also treasurer of the EANA. The third member of the committee, its chairman, was an elderly man named Samuel Eby. Lidia was told that he was 'friendly but perhaps somewhat conservative' in his ways, an avid proponent of Esperanto although he himself could not speak it well. He was a Swedenborgian minister. These three were to take care of arranging Lidia's itinerary for her stay, communicating with groups who wished her to visit them, and arranging her travel and speaking plans.

Lidia went to the American Consulate in Paris to apply for a visa but was perplexed by the requirements. She applied for a visitor's permit for one year, and found that a deposit of five hundred dollars had to be given the American government as a guarantee that the visitor would leave in the time prescribed. Lidia wrote the National Spiritual Assembly about her confusion over a requirement that one receive a 'waiver from the Contract Labor Clause from the Department of Labor'. She thought this meant assurance she would not have a salary in the United States, yet somehow she connected it with the third provision – proof she would not 'be liable to become a public charge'. She asked the National Assembly secretary Horace Holley to send the necessary legal documents and begged him 'not to postpone these formalities'.

One of the Esperantists who was to play an important role in Lidia's journey to the US was Ernest Dodge, the chairman of the Executive Committee of the EANA. Mr Dodge was a civil service examiner in Washington and a devoted Esperantist. In April he wrote Josephine Kruka about two points that were to become critical: how long could Lidia stay in America? And would there be any governmental restrictions regarding her working there for money? Mr Dodge wrote Samuel Eby, the chairman of Lidia's committee, that he was sure the new committee would take up this phase of the problem at once. But the committee of three was soon preoccupied with other problems and the matter was forgotten for the moment.

Mr Dodge also wrote Lidia of his concern about the attitude of some well-known Bahá'ís toward Esperanto. The Bahá'ís, he felt, should 'all be theoretically very favorable to Esperanto', but he had been dismayed to find among them 'much indifference to the matter of international language and even an attitude of doubt or skepticism about Esperanto itself'. Although Mr Dodge, who was a Unitarian, knew of Shoghi Effendi's supportive attitude and that of the Bahá'í National Spiritual Assembly, he had received reports which disturbed him including the news that 'one of the grandsons of 'Abdu'l-Bahá' (undoubtedly Ruhi Afnan, who was later declared a Covenant-breaker because of his disobedience to the Guardian) had expressed 'skeptical if not unfavorable statements about Esperanto' at the Green Acre Bahá'í Summer School. This sort of thing, Mr Dodge feared, would dampen the enthusiasm of the other Bahá'ís. He told Lidia she had her work cut out for her in America.

By the tenth of June Lidia had not yet heard from the chairman of her organizing committee. Although time was growing short, she still had not been able to make any real plans for her journey.

As she had discovered often during her years of traveling, her own plans could not always be realized. Lidia was aware of the racial problems in the United States, and she was eager to introduce black Americans to Esperanto. Twice she wrote Della Quinlan that she wished to give a Cseh course in Harlem, the black district of New York. But apparently this idea was never seriously considered by those in the US who were responsible for organizing her classes.

In July Lidia, still in Paris, received tragic news. Her close friend and 'adopted mother' Marie Borel had died in Lyon after a long illness. Lidia hurried south to attend Mrs Borel's funeral in Arles. Then she went sadly home to Warsaw.

Poland was still rebuilding from the devastation of the First World War. In Warsaw, on one of the main thoroughfares stood an ominous giant bomb, with an admonition to all to work to keep the peace. But as the decade of the 1930s moved toward its close, the attention of many Poles was focused not on the great looming threat of war from its neighbor Germany, but rather on Poland's own Jews.

Anti-Semitism in Lidia's homeland was growing more intense. During the years Marshal Piłsudski had ruled Poland as dictator, from 1926 to his death in 1935, overt anti-Semitism had been kept somewhat under control. But although Piłsudski was not anti-Semitic himself, the attitudes of the rest of the country had not changed. Poles continued to blame the Jews for the nation's troubles, and two years after Piłsudski's death, in 1937, the new leaders of Poland adopted an official government policy of anti–Semitism. They had concluded that the way to solve Poland's economic problems was to force the Jews out of their jobs. In what has been called a 'cold pogrom', laws were passed directed at squeezing Jews out of their livelihoods, and there were anti-Jewish boycotts, made easier by a law requiring that all shop signs carry the owner's name.

But the Polish government aimed at a more drastic 'solution' than removing the Jews from Polish economic and cultural life. They intended to force the Jews out of Poland altogether and had demanded the League of Nations give them a colony where it could deport them. Throughout the late 1930s, while the attention of the rest of Europe was riveted on the menace of Hitler, Poland – lulled by the nonaggression pact it had signed with Germany – felt its most serious concern was how to get rid of its Jews.

The Universal Congress of Esperanto in August 1937 was to be a Jubilee celebration in honor of the fiftieth anniversary of the publication of the language. For once Lidia did not have to travel to attend the congress, for it was to be held in Warsaw. While other cities, even Krakow, had welcomed the Esperanto congresses, if only for the tourist income that the Esperantist visitors provided, in Warsaw in 1937 the reception was distinctly cold. The congress, Lidia wrote to Shoghi Effendi, had 'many difficulties', for Esperanto had never been popular in Poland, where many considered it 'a Jewish affair'. Some of the newspapers, Lidia told him, printed distortions and falsehoods against the Esperantists, and one of the articles contained an attack on the Bahá'í Faith. As a result of this, however, she added, one of the Warsaw Esperantists had become very interested in the religion.

During the congress, a special visit to the birthplace of Dr Zamenhof in Bialystok had been arranged. Afterward, at lunch, one Esperantist from England found himself seated near Zofia and Lidia. The restaurant was tiny, the Esperantists many and the tables were crowded so closely together that there was hardly space to move between them. A band played as they dined, and every other tune seemed to be *La Espero*. Upon hearing it, the Esperantists traditionally would stand in respect, as for a national anthem. It was difficult to balance the soup and stand up in the cramped space, but every time the anthem was played the Esperantists respectfully rose to their feet, or tried to. When a waitress passing with a bowl of soup spilled it all over the English Esperantist, he recalled that it was Zofia and Lidia who came to his rescue and helped him present himself as a 'decent citizen' afterward.

At the congress, Lidia met Samuel Eby, the chairman of her

organizing committee. They discussed her plans for coming to the US, and he attended her Bahá'í talk. It apparently had considerable effect on him but in a way no one would have expected.

While the Esperantists were gathered in Warsaw, Adam Zamenhof presided at a conference held in the Zamenhof home to try to bring together the two international organizations, the Universal Esperanto Association and the International Esperanto League, which had split the year before. The meeting was unsuccessful, and the schism continued.

Twenty years had passed since the death of Ludwik Zamenhof. Commemorating the anniversary, *La Praktiko* praised his daughter, Lidia, for carrying on the Majstro's lifework. It was a great and unusual favor of fate, commented the article, when a child continued the work of the father 'with fervor and success'. Calling Lidia 'a tireless pioneer', a 'true apostle of the world language', the article noted she had recruited and taught thousands of new Esperantists. 'Lidia propagates not only the language of her father,' added the article, 'she also fervently works for his ideals.' Now, twenty years after the Majstro's death, 'his worthy daughter intrepidly holds his place'. From 1932, when she had first left home to begin her travels, until now Lidia had given some fifty Cseh courses to approximately three thousand students.

The time was approaching for Lidia to leave for America. Although she had been traveling constantly for five years, the journey ahead of her was so long and important to her that, she confessed in a letter to Della Quinlan, she felt worried about it. 'I know that up to now they [the Bahá'ís in the US] are perhaps a bit too skeptical of Esperanto,' Lidia wrote Mrs Quinlan, 'but because my trip is by invitation of the National Assembly and through the encouragement of Shoghi Effendi, I am encouraged to hope for their good will.'

Lidia was disappointed that she would not see Martha Root in America. Martha was traveling in the Orient, and had written to Lidia from Shanghai. In the last speech Martha would ever give in America she had mentioned Lidia. 'I learned Esperanto because I found that most nations preferred a neutral tongue,' she told a gathering at the Bahá'í Nineteen Day Feast in San Francisco. 'Lidia Zamenhof is one of the greatest Esperantists in the world. She is a profound Bahá'í . . . I will not be here to welcome her, but you will take care of her.'

On September 20 or 21, the Polish ship MS *Batory* sailed from the harbor of Gdynia with Lidia Zamenhof on board. She was on her way to America at last.

In New York, Della Quinlan awaited Lidia's arrival with some anxiety. Samuel Eby had returned from Warsaw with a disturbing report for Della. He told her that Lidia could not and would not speak English. Furthermore, he said that her Bahá'í talk at the Jubilee Congress had been a poor one. The impression Mrs Quinlan gained from him was that they would not be able to count on Lidia as a public speaker after all. Even as the *Batory* plowed through the Atlantic toward New York, no doubt Della wondered if inviting Lidia to America would prove to have been a terrible mistake.

TWENTY-ONE

An Entirely New World

The *Batory* was due to arrive in New York harbor on Wednesday, September 29, and when the day came, reporters from every newspaper in New York were waiting in Lidia's hotel room to interview her. But the ship was a day late and they left disappointed.

The next day, early in the morning, a small group of Bahá'ís and Esperantists were waiting at the dock to welcome Lidia. Horace Holley and Della Quinlan – clutching a bunch of dahlias – were among them.

On board the *Batory*, Lidia saw the Statue of Liberty rising out of the morning fog. She watched the other passengers, many of them immigrants, and observed: 'emotion was visible on each face, in spite of a mask of indifference, when the American officials on the ship began checking passports . . . declarations, certificates, to decide on life or death: to admit or not to admit the alien to American territory? What happened', she wondered, 'at the last minute, to that old woman whom I helped to prepare her customs declaration for a samovar and festival candlesticks, the last souvenirs of the old world, of the old life? Only later did the thought of her come to me, because in the meantime I myself experienced some emotion when my passport disappeared into the official's portfolio to "verify" the truth of my assertions about the purpose of my voyage and about the organization that had invited me.'

Horace Holley was waiting to sign the guarantee for her with the immigration officials. Although he had arrived at the port ready to pay the five hundred dollar bond, the officials did not ask for it. But the customs officers gave Lidia a thorough search, suspicious of what appeared to be a bizarre collection of objects in her baggage. They seemed 'somewhat surprised by the battery of pencils, rubber animals and other necessities of the Cseh teacher' in her suitcases.

As Mr Holley drove Lidia to her hotel, New York 'absorbed' her: 'incomparable for its skyscrapers, the feverish traffic, the great crowds of people, of automobiles, of everything that the world possesses. My legs still wobbled and I still felt the roll of the ship, but there wasn't time to think about that. My room in the sixteen-story New Yorker

Hotel quickly filled with journalists and Esperantists. In America one doesn't waste time.'

In fact, this time only four reporters turned up, but they stayed long, asking questions. In the end, only the *New York Sun* and the *New York News* ran the story. One article trumpeted:

'BONAN TAGON!' SAYS THE LADY

Uninformed Reporters are
Unable to Answer

THEY KNEW NO ESPERANTO

'Bonan tagon,' a slender young woman wearing spectacles greeted a group of somewhat startled reporters . . . 'Kiel vi fartas?'

'Let's have it again,' one of them replied. And the young woman answered: 'Bonan tagon, kiel vi fartas.'

. . . And thus the fourth estate was again introduced to Esperanto, the international language, by its principal advocate, Miss Lidia Zamenhof, the youngest daughter of its late founder.

After demonstrating that she could speak English if she were a mind to, Miss Zamenhof lapsed back into Esperanto and there she stayed in the face of much coaxing during the remainder of the interview.

The reporters soon learned that her words of greeting simply meant, 'Good day! How are you?'

The journalists seemed less interested in Esperanto than in asking Lidia personal questions she was not used to being asked by strangers. How old was she and how tall? When the reporter from the *Sun* asked her how much she weighed, she looked puzzled. He cried, 'Let me guess, let me guess,' and made her stand up. He looked her all over, pinched her arm, and announced that she weighed about a hundred pounds. 'She took it', Della Quinlan later recounted, 'without turning a hair. But when he went out, her face was a study! She said slowly and emphatically, "This is an entirely new world."'

One reporter asked Lidia, 'Have you any boyfriends?' and he reported her reply thus: '"No haven time fora such phoolishnessck," her reply or the translation, or both, sounded like.'

Reporter Howard Whitman, whose article, headlined 'ESPERANTO'S DAUGHTER HERE TO FIGHT BABEL', ran in the *Sunday News*, also was not entirely serious in his coverage of Lidia's voyage to carry 'the torch of her sire's life work to America'. Of Esperanto he wrote: 'An essential starting vocabulary may include: Mi salutas vin (Hi, pal), Mi amas vin (I love you), and Donu al mi kvin dolarojn (Lend me five dollars).' Explaining that the Esperantists wore a green star in their lapels to recognize each other, he suggested: 'Next time you see one, try "Donu al mi kvin dolarojn", which is as good a way as any to see how much brotherly love the language has engendered.' The article was accompanied by a photograph of Lidia, 'crusader for Esperanto', surrounded by her rubber animals and other Cseh course demonstration objects, and the caption cried '*Vi Havas Ion Tie!*' (You've got something there!).

Two days after Lidia's arrival, the Spiritual Assembly of the Bahá'ís of New York City held a tea for her at the Bahá'í Center at 119 West Fifty-Seventh Street, and the New York Esperantists gave a dinner to introduce her to the Esperantists.

At the Bahá'í Center that afternoon, a large crowd had gathered to meet Lidia. But those in the audience who knew of Samuel Eby's unfavorable reports about Lidia's speaking ability undoubtedly awaited her speech uneasily. The distinguished lawyer Mountfort Mills opened the meeting, welcoming Lidia on behalf of the National Spiritual Assembly. Della Quinlan greeted her in the name of the Bahá'í Esperantists. 'Then', Della later told Josephine Kruka, 'She came up on the rostrum . . . and she spoke in English with a delightful French accent. And Josephine! She took them by storm. It was a beautifully thoughtful speech, showing a fundamental grasp of the spirit of the Cause. She ended in Esperanto, which Jimmie Morton translated. She had no more than left the platform, than Mr Mills came up to me and said it was one of the best things that had ever been done in New York, would she speak the next Sunday.' Della was overwhelmed by confusion and delight. 'O, Josephine, we "have something here" as they say!'

Della was instantly charmed by Lidia. 'Lidia is so cute', she wrote. 'When she is looking for something about the room, she puts her finger at the side of her nose and says "Nu kie ĝi estas" (Now, where is it?). 'She is such a little thing!' Della told Ernest Dodge. 'Her photographs make her look big for some unknown reason.' 'No picture does her justice. She is too alive!'

That evening, the meeting of the New York Esperanto Society was to be devoted to Lidia's Cseh demonstration lesson. Diana Klotts, a reporter for a Jewish periodical, *The Sentinel*, was there. Earlier that day she had met Lidia in her hotel room. 'Small, blond Lidia Zamenhof is not beautiful. Not, at least, in the accepted sense of the term,' was her first impression. But after viewing the demonstration lesson she wrote: 'It is evening, and the East Room of the New Yorker is packed with people listening to a young woman of about 33 years old whose eyes sparkle behind shellrimmed glasses. With all the courage and wisdom of a modern Minerva she stands before her audience and in a full rich voice says whimsically, by way of introduction, 'Mi estas

Lidia Zamenhof.' And all at once, slight blond Lidia Zamenhof is beautiful, radiating that grace and charm which emanate from the truly great . . .

'As the evening progresses, and her introduction has been completed, she steps down from the platform and lesson one in Esperanto begins. And there is humor – laughter – lots of fun in the little East Room. There is nothing dull about a language as alive as Esperanto . . . She will say 'Mi amas vin' (I love you). And there is the reflection of a strange inner light. Yes, Lidia Zamenhof is beautiful – as is the message she brings.' The article, headlined 'The High Priestess of Esperanto', was syndicated and sent to a hundred Jewish periodicals.

Two weeks later, Lidia spoke again at the Bahá'í Center. Her talk was entitled 'The Return of Spiritual Heroism'. Again it was a success. With delight Della told Josephine: 'Philip Marangella said that he did not see how she could sustain her talk at such a high spiritual level for such a length of time. I think that is the greatest compliment that a speaker has ever received in my hearing.' To Jessie Revell, in Philadelphia, Della wrote: 'Horace said to me tonight that he wished she would settle down here in America. You know he does not praise lightly.' And to Lucy Marshall in San Francisco: 'She has a peculiar quality that I have never run across before. Great simplicity in expression combined with a profound grasp of spiritual reality.'

In spite of the fears Lidia had once confided to Martha Root, that she could not give talks before fellow-believers, Lidia had quickly captured the hearts of the American Bahá'ís.

But troubles were just beginning. Relations between the Esperantists and the Bahá'ís had become strained at the outset by confusion over what role the Bahá'ís expected the Esperantists to play in Lidia's visit. Some of the Esperantists had been hurt because they had never been approached officially by the National Spiritual Assembly itself but only by Dr Charles Witt, chairman of the International Auxiliary Language Committee. They could not understand why Dr Witt never wrote to them again and were puzzled why Della Quinlan was the only one they ever heard from. Somehow she had neglected to tell them that she was the new chairman of the committee. Eventually this problem was resolved, but a certain wariness on both sides remained. It soon became aggravated by a conflict between two members of Lidia's organizing committee, Della Quinlan and Samuel Eby.

In the light of Lidia's first well-received talks in New York, the disparaging statements Mr Eby had made about Lidia's public-speaking ability seemed most peculiar. As events progressed, Della came to feel that, as she put it, the man had 'developed an antagonism to Lidia and to the whole idea of having her here'. She confided to Lucy

Marshall that 'I am afraid this was an indication of antagonism to the Bahá'í Faith'.

Lidia's Esperanto classes in New York began with fifty-three students, who paid five dollars for the series of lessons. The Americans had hoped to attract more students and were disappointed. Yet, a report optimistically stated, 'If one considers the difficulties that the Esperanto Movement has experienced in this large city, those results are indeed satisfactory . . . Many Bahá'ís, who till now were not interested in the world language, have begun the study of Esperanto.'

According to Della, the poor turnout was largely due to lack of advertising. Although Mr Eby had paid for Lidia to stay several days at the New Yorker so that she could be available to reporters, Della claimed that he had refused to advertise the courses. They had been counting on his newspaper contacts; he had worked at the *New York Times* as a proofreader.

Although at first Lidia was unaware of the problems Della was having with Mr Eby, Della thought that Lidia sensed the atmosphere of tension, 'the condition around herself', and that it was giving her 'nervous indigestion'. By the middle of October Lidia was so ill she had to cancel a class.

In fact, Lidia had been ill since her first week in America. At a picnic in the country on a cold rainy day, she had caught a bad cold that lingered on. The strain of the ocean voyage and the adjustment to a foreign country no doubt had also taken their toll on her health. To make matters worse, the conditions in the home where she was living were far from ideal. Mr Eby had arranged for her to stay with an Esperantist family in the Bronx during the rest of her time in New York. It was a long distance from her classes and too far for people to come and visit her easily. Although all Lidia had asked for was a clean, warm room, winter was coming and the heater in the house was broken. The man in whose home she was a guest was 'devoted to her', but he displayed alarming and unpredictable behavior. After experiencing one of his outbursts, Mrs Holley was quite upset that Lidia had been placed there.

In spite of Lidia's illness, she had the same dynamic effect on her students in America as she had had in Europe. 'She appears a very quiet person,' wrote Della, 'but when she gets up before a class, she changes. Then one sees a vivacious, interesting personality. One of my friends said to me after watching her, "She is the most fascinating thing I have ever seen."'

Lidia struggled on with her classes, concealing her illness until it became obvious that she was very sick indeed. Even then she insisted she was only 'a little bit ill' and it was 'nothing serious, probably fatigue'. But after much coaxing, she was persuaded to consult a doctor – an Esperantist who had known her father in Warsaw. He diagnosed her illness as jaundice, and she had to call off her classes for a week.

The tension between Della Quinlan and Samuel Eby was growing steadily. Della felt he had been acting peculiarly ever since his return from Warsaw. She could not understand why he had suddenly developed such an antagonistic attitude, for they had been on very friendly terms for two years. But now he gave Della to understand that he wished to take over the work of the organizing committee himself and would not consult with anyone about plans for Lidia. Della felt that the eighty-one-year-old man might be suffering from some kind of rapidly progressing senile dementia. As chairman of the organizing committee he still held considerable power, and Della worried what he might do next to sabotage Lidia's visit.

To Della, Mr Eby seemed angered that Lidia was so successful, and irritated that the Bahá'ís liked her so much. Della complained to Ernest Dodge: 'He said that he did not intend to send her where there were any "rabid" Bahá'ís.'

At the height of the furor, Mr Dodge reminded Mrs Quinlan about the matter of Lidia's documents and the waiver from the Contract Labor Law. Della told him Lidia's visa was good for a year. 'Everyone assures you that it can be easily renewed,' she asserted confidently. She would try, she said, to get precise information. But Della was busy with many things – her own job at the Stock Exchange, coordinating Lidia's schedule, writing to all the various groups that wished Lidia to visit them, and dealing with the difficult Mr Eby. Mrs Quinlan herself was not well, and had been suffering from cancer. Thus, once again, the matter of the visa seems to have been dropped.

By the end of October Lidia's health was much improved. But the Holleys and Della Quinlan agreed that she must be moved from the house where she was staying, though they were unsure how to get her out without hurting her host's feelings. Mrs Quinlan and Mr Holley went to visit Lidia, and Mr Holley proposed that the Spiritual Assembly be her host for December, so she might have more contact with the Bahá'ís. Lidia agreed.

The doctor who had treated Lidia warned them not to wait that long. According to Della, the conditions he found in the house had shocked him and he did not want her to remain another month there. Lidia was not very strong, he said. She needed to regain her strength and have peace and quiet. He thought there were too many stairs to climb there, the bathroom conditions were not right and she was not being properly nourished.

During these difficult days, Lidia received a letter from Shoghi Effendi in which he sent his 'ardent prayers for your unprecedented success in your historic trip to the States' and told her to 'persevere and be confident'.

In early November, Della and Josephine were stunned to learn that Samuel Eby had lodged a complaint against them with the Executive Committee of the Esperanto Association of North America. Moreover, Mr Eby apparently had expressed his opinion that the Esperantists should not cooperate with the Bahá'ís at all about Lidia's plans. Such cooperation, he felt, meant entangling the neutral Esperanto movement in a dangerous alliance with a religious creed.

Mr Dodge tried to persuade him this was not true and said he hoped that Lidia would awaken interest in Esperanto among the American Bahá'ís.

Mr Eby was continuing to denigrate Lidia as a speaker. Having such an unfavorable opinion about her, his insistence on taking over all her plans made little sense to Della, who felt he simply wanted to keep the Bahá'ís away from her. It seemed apparent to her that he intended to prevent Lidia from giving public talks while she was in America.

Josephine Kruka, to whom Della confided her difficulties in long, anguished letters, pointed out that they ought to 'make of him a friend rather than an enemy'. Della sheepishly accepted the rebuke but continued to be exasperated when Lidia insisted that Della be polite to the man.

If Lidia did not know exactly what was amiss, she knew that something was indeed terribly wrong among the people around her. When Mr Eby completely ignored her at a meeting where she was to be the guest of honor, and refused to discuss her plans with her, Della at last had to explain to Lidia what was going on.

Now Lidia finally understood the reason for the atmosphere of tension and distraction among those who were supposed to be organizing and promoting her classes. But Lidia's response was not to take sides, or to engage in plotting, but to remain above the dissension and to concentrate on her work. Although privately she must have been anguished at the rift between her coworkers, which was plainly hampering the Esperanto efforts and casting a gloomy cloud over her visit to America, Lidia refrained from complaining about it and tried to keep on friendly terms with all.

Samuel Eby hinted to Ernest Dodge that he wanted to have Della and Josephine dropped from Lidia's committee. But when Mr Dodge refused to comply and instead suggested that Della be given the leading role in working out Lidia's itinerary (which she had been doing all along), Mr Eby resigned. It was unfortunate that what may have been a physical illness for which he, of course, was not responsible led him to play the role of the antagonist in Lidia's visit to America. It was to be one of the last things he did: he died a year later.

Whatever the cause of his antipathy toward Lidia – Della later felt it had begun at the congress in Warsaw when Lidia apparently had not paid the visiting American the attention he believed he was due – his behavior so distracted Mrs Quinlan that she neglected to look into the matter of Lidia's documents. At the time it seemed like a minor detail, but in the end it proved to have tragic consequences.

One evening at a Bahá'í Nineteen Day Feast in New York City, Lidia at last met Roan Orloff (later Stone), the young Cseh teacher with whom she had been corresponding. Roan worked at the State House in Boston and lived alone in a hotel. Her mother, a 'fanatically orthodox' Jew, would not have her in the house ever since Roan had become a Bahá'í.

Roan had been eager to meet Lidia. At the Bahá'í Center, the room was full of people milling around, talking in English. Lidia was sitting alone on the edge of a big sofa, with, Mrs Stone later recalled, 'the look of sadness that is so characteristic of so many Jewish expressions'. Roan approached and introduced herself according to the Cseh method: 'Bonan vesperon. Mi estas Roan Orloff. Kiu estas vi?' (Good evening. I am Roan Orloff. Who are you?)

Lidia smiled and said, 'Mi estas Lidia Zamenhof.' But when she realized that Roan was speaking to her in Esperanto, 'all of a sudden she became a changed person', Roan recalled. 'She became vivacious, there was a look of eagerness and joy on her face to realize that there was somebody in the room who could talk to her in her own language.'

Lidia already felt close to Roan and had written her from France: 'I feel we are truly sisters, as Bahá'ís, as Esperantists and finally for our common love of dear Martha Root, whom I always call my spiritual mother . . .'

At the Bahá'í Center in New York Lidia also met Dr Ugo Giachery and his wife Angeline. The Giacherys had been prepared to meet the daughter of the famous Dr Zamenhof, but they were surprised and delighted to find she was a modest, retiring young woman who spoke English very well, with a slight accent, and was devoted to her Faith. 'There are some women who are not beautiful who are attractive,' Dr Giachery recalled many years later, 'but there is something that comes from within. And you are attracted even if they do not have what you would call a well-formed physiognomy; you were attracted to her; she had a charm of her own.'

The Giacherys were especially touched by Lidia's devotion to the Bahá'í Faith. This was, Dr Giachery remarked, 'a rare quality in an Esperantist; of all those we had met before, only a handful had shown any interest in the Bahá'í Faith'. 'As a Bahá'í', he said, 'she was a firm, steadfast, convinced follower of the Faith. And it was not because of a mirage of gains, material gains, but this devotion she had developed for the Faith. And I think that being the daughter of Zamenhof was not paramount in her life. She was like you or I that speak of the Faith and forget our past.'

Aware of the growing persecution of the Jews in Europe, the Giacherys told Lidia she should not go back to Poland but should stay in America.

TWENTY-TWO

Sowing Seeds

Lidia soon found that, compared to Europe, America was indeed 'an entirely new world'. She was astonished by some aspects of life in the United States. 'One can eat ice cream here twice a day,' she wrote. 'It's almost the national dish and I'm sorry my nephew, who adores ice cream, is not here.' 'You can buy it in every drugstore,' she said in a letter to the European Esperantists, and added with surprise that 'in the American drugstores, medicines seem to play the least important role'. She told them of five-and-ten-cent stores where one could buy 'everything one needs for everyday life: in winter warm gloves, in summer a bathing suit, and in all seasons – ice cream'.

The skyscrapers of New York, Lidia was amused to find, had local and express elevators, like trains. And New York's rush hour: 'Herrings in a barrel enjoy comfort and luxury of space compared with New Yorkers in subway trains after the closing of stores and offices!'

She had never seen a used-car lot before. 'In some lands', she wrote, 'a poor man who can't buy new clothes goes to a second-hand store and buys an old coat. The American who can't afford a new automobile (such persons are many) but finds he needs his own car (such persons are even more) goes to a square where old cars . . . wait for someone to buy them.'

Because Lidia needed the income from her classes to pay her expenses, it was decided she would only visit large cities in the East and Midwest where there were established Bahá'í and Esperanto groups. She was disappointed, for she had hoped to travel around the United States, but experience had taught her to take things as they came. 'Sometimes it occurred to me to make plans which seemed to me very clever, wise, etc.' she said, 'and they were upset like a house of cards. And the Most Great Planner made other plans . . .'

In her public talks about the international language, Lidia still insisted on speaking Esperanto with a translator, but she now admitted she could 'try to speak English' with individuals such as journalists. While in New York she addressed an audience of five hundred at the Women's Press Association and spoke to the students of junior high schools in Brooklyn and East Orange, New Jersey.

One day in New York she gave an address at the Bahá'í Center on 'Language and World Unity,' sharing the program with Dave Hennen Morris, former US Ambassador to Belgium, and his wife. 'It went off well,' Della told Josephine. 'Mr and Mrs Morris spoke nicely, but without any particular spirit . . . Then Lidia showed up so, against them! Dr Khan [Ali-Kuli Khan] heard her for the first time that afternoon. His words to Mme Khan are the best description of Lidia on a Bahá'í platform. He said she has the fire of the spirit, faith and eloquence.'

In New York Lidia met Agnes Alexander, who had just made a pilgrimage to Haifa and was on her way home to the Hawaiian Islands after many years in Japan. Miss Alexander shared with Lidia her notes of conversations with Shoghi Effendi. The Guardian, she said, had told some Bahá'ís of Christian background that once they were Bahá'ís, they must resign from their Christian churches. Lidia wondered whether this instruction would apply to her as well.

Always concerned to do the right thing, she wrote to Shoghi Effendi for his advice. She was still officially and legally a Jew, but, she explained, in Poland belonging to the Jewish community had more of a legal than a religious meaning. Some Jews, she told him, left the community so as not to have an obstacle to their careers. She mentioned the persecution the Jews in Poland were suffering and added that to resign formally at such a time would mean weakening this minority. She did not want to do so, but, she told him, she was willing to do as he directed. Anxiously she waited for his answer.

Lidia was to move out of the house in the Bronx on December 1. But the person entrusted with making arrangements for her had not yet done so, so her departure was delayed. Lidia had continued to be ill with a cold most of the time she was there. Soon afterward, she moved to Allerton House on East Fifty-Seventh Street, where she stayed until she left New York. When asked, Lidia never spoke of the problems and gave no hint of the real reason she was moving, allowing only that it was the great distance – an hour's train ride from downtown.

After Lidia moved out of their home, her former host and his wife stopped attending her classes, and Samuel Eby dropped out as well. Her former host began to make, according to Della, 'very wild statements about her' – Della could not even bring herself to tell Josephine what they were. 'They are bad, the things he says,' she hinted darkly. 'And the remarks are legally actionable.'

At last, on January 2, Lidia left New York for Philadelphia, where she remained seven weeks, staying at the home of Mr and Mrs Joseph Dubin.

Things did not go as smoothly in Philadelphia as all had hoped. No radio speeches had been arranged, and although hundreds of announcements had been sent to schools and societies, they had little result. The press coverage was disappointing. The Polish papers and one Lithuanian periodical printed small announcements, and only two reporters from major newspapers came to interview Lidia. Only one paper, the *Philadelphia Record*, printed an article, with a large photograph of Lidia, her marcelled hair shining in the photographer's flash, and her strong chin jutting forward. The article was short, but the headline commanded attention: 'FELIĈAN NOVANJARON', EXCLAIMS THE BRIGHT YOUNG LADY; 'VERBOTEN', GROWLS HITLER . . . 'EUREKA', SAY 1,000,000.

The reporter found her 'a rather birdlike young woman', and was openly skeptical of the ease with which she assured him Esperanto could be learned. He wrote: 'Like the Hawaiian guitar or aeronautical engineering it can be mastered, she says, in twenty easy lessons.' The article called attention to Esperanto's suppression in Germany and the fact that Esperanto, 'Herr Goebbels found, was inconsistent with the aims of Nazi nationalism', as well as the fact that Esperanto's author was a Polish Jew.

Although the article may not have attracted much attention in Philadelphia, later events would show that publicity like it found interested readers in Berlin, especially at the Gestapo desk in charge of monitoring the activities of Jews abroad and the foreign press.

The Bahá'í meeting the day before the lesson was a catastrophe. Horace Holley introduced Lidia, but he had to catch a train and left as she began to speak. Later, Lidia was 'almost happy' that he wasn't there to hear what happened. Jessie Revell had suggested Lidia give her talk in English, but Lidia, wishing the audience to hear Esperanto spoken – and probably still hesitant about her own ability to speak in English – insisted on speaking with a translator. Afterward, she was sorry she hadn't taken Miss Revell's advice.

From the first phrases that the translator spoke, Lidia realized something was dreadfully wrong. The translator, a long-time Esperantist, was not interpreting her words properly. Rather than offend him by asking him to sit down, and begin to speak in English herself, Lidia struggled on. But it only grew worse. Several times she had to stop him and insist on a more correct translation: what he was saying was completely different from what she had said – almost the opposite! And she grew more annoyed at the lack of seriousness with which he was treating the matter. There was no excuse for his performance – she had given him the text of her remarks to study several days earlier.

Della expressed surprise about his conduct. 'He knows Esperanto well and certainly could translate correctly for you,' she told Lidia. 'I think perhaps he had difficulties with the Bahá'ís previously, and doesn't like them.'

The episode depressed Lidia, and the next day – the day of the introductory lesson – things went wrong all day until evening. But suddenly that evening, Lidia felt, 'the barometer changed'. At dinner, her host had been called away for a few minutes to attend to a visitor and the conversation 'gave me a chance to say some words about Bahá'u'lláh. Perhaps those words will be completely lost, I don't know,' she wrote Della, 'but I noted almost with astonishment that that short conversation completely restored and revived me.'

Although two hundred people attended the demonstration lesson, the course began with only twenty-five students. Lidia had insisted on holding the classes three times a week, but few people were willing to attend that often.

Della wrote to encourage her: 'Know that the friends surround you with their loving thoughts. At the Holleys Wednesday night when I said goodbye to Doris Holley, she said to me, "I think that Bahá'u'lláh loves Lidia Zamenhof very much."'

Even though things did not go smoothly for Lidia in Philadelphia, those who met her there were attracted to and impressed by her. Jessie and Ethel Revell entertained her overnight in their home several times. Later, Jessie Revell wrote Della Quinlan: 'Lidia is a very good Bahá'í teacher, her depth of Bahá'í knowledge is very wonderful . . . While here we took her to Cedarville, NJ, to visit a Baptist Minister, an Esperantist, and it was such a pleasure to us to hear her teach the Cause to this man. She also attracted a young couple . . . to the Cause . . . She is very dear to the hearts of all the friends here and also the Esperantists.'

Joseph Dubin, Lidia's host in Philadelphia, came to admire Lidia. He told Della that at first he had offered Lidia hospitality to help the Esperanto movement. But after her arrival, he 'saw and understood that she is a person who deserves to be given hospitality as a friend. She was no bother; she caused no inconvenience. She ate what we had, slept peacefully, came and went quietly.

'I enjoyed very much talking with her because she is highly intelligent. She understands deeply the problem of peace and of human life . . . One can only regret', he added, 'that she is so busy that she has little time for diversion, or to spend on social life. But that is the destiny of her ideal and of her work, and she does not complain about it. She wants only to help the movement.'

While staying in Philadelphia, Lidia also spoke in Baltimore (though it was a very stormy night and not many people came) and in Washington, DC, on 'The Return of Spiritual Heroism'. Doris Lohse, who met Lidia in Washington, later recalled that when Lidia came into a meeting, she was 'so very humble, very shy'. The people in the audience would look around the room for the speaker, not expecting it

47. *Della Quinlan*

48. *Cartoon from the September 1937 issue of* La
Praktiko: *'Miss Lidia Zamenhof (traveling to
America): Now I am flying from place to place!'*

49. *Part of the International Auxiliary Language Committee in 1941. From left: Della Quinlan, Mabelle Davis, Mabel Vicary, Louella Beecher, Lucy Marshall, Charles Witt, Roan Orloff, Josephine Kruka*

was the quiet little woman in glasses who sat among them. Then at the last minute, when she was introduced, Miss Lohse recalled, voices would whisper, '"Who is *she*?" "That is Lidia." And then this wonderful talk.'

'She was simple,' Doris Lohse remembered, 'and still you saw at first glance that she was an intelligent, fine girl. She was very mature. She wouldn't begin to talk; she would first wait until somebody spoke to her. She was so unassuming . . . and so satisfied with little. She was very selfless. Just a great light.'

Her talk that evening in Washington impressed the audience as 'very earnest and effective'. She had prepared the speech with care and seemed to have it nearly all memorized. Although she had brought the text with her, she laid the manuscript down on the table and scarcely glanced at it.

Now that Lidia had been in America for several months, she was finally getting used to the New World. She no longer felt the home-sickness she had suffered in her earlier years of traveling, although she still couldn't say she especially liked to travel: 'not at all,' she said. She loved her work, but, she admitted, if it hadn't been for the friends she had made in America, Bahá'ís and Esperantists, she would have felt 'somewhat strange at the beginning among the skyscrapers'. Her work in America had proved much more difficult than in France. 'One must sow a lot to reap but little,' she wrote a correspondent in Europe.

The diet in America also took some getting used to – she thought Americans used too much pepper on their food. The family she was staying with in Philadelphia were vegetarians, 'so also I have had to become somewhat of a vegetarian,' she wrote. 'Although I am used to eating meat, still it isn't very difficult for me.'

Even after Lidia left New York, the two men who had caused problems before continued to stir up trouble. The gossip spread to Washington, DC, poisoning people against her and dampening the enthusiasm of the Washington Esperantists, one of whom had returned from a visit to New York with 'quite a tale of woe about Lidia'. The Esperantists in the capital, wrote Josephine Kruka, were 'not enthusiastic' about inviting Lidia to give a course in their city. Some had been hesitant from the first, doubting that even a course given by the daughter of Zamenhof would be a success. Now they were even more discouraged, and were glad to let other cities go ahead of them in Lidia's itinerary. In the end, Lidia never did give a course in the capital city of the United States.

To make matters worse, the antipathy against Lidia had taken a new direction. 'Merry hell has broken loose again,' Della wrote Josephine. It was being said that a number of people had complained about Lidia, saying that outside her classes she was unapproachable and even rude.

They even accused her of acting superior because she was Zamenhof's daughter. Ernest Dodge, in Washington, to whom these stories had been reported, was much shaken by the accusations and suggested she might be suffering from ill health, overwork, or anxiety about her family in Poland. But, he wrote Della, if Lidia (whom he had not yet met personally) was really such a difficult personality, he questioned whether her visit to America was worthwhile after all. 'I think you will realize', he added, 'how these reports cannot help affecting the thoughts of some of us.'

Della retorted that the episode had been 'prearranged' by the antagonists. She believed that any misunderstandings that had come up were due to the fact that European and American manners were very different. Lidia didn't understand American ways, which often seemed rude and insulting to her. Some of her students were unhappy that she would not allow the open discussion of various points of grammar in her classes, but the Cseh method – according to which the entire class had to be in Esperanto – did not allow it.

At last the nature of the accusations that had been made against Lidia behind her back was revealed. The man in whose home Lidia had stayed, Della had been told, had called her a 'liar' and a 'thief'. These could be easily dismissed as irrational ravings, but there was something else which, while equally false, could have been seriously damaging to Lidia if it were spread around. In the presence of others he had claimed Lidia had come to America to spread 'communistic doctrines'. The extent of his confused mental state was clear, at least to Della, when she learned that 'in almost the next breath he proposed to them that they start a fund for her to travel throughout America'. When his listeners protested that they thought it unwise to contribute to a fund for someone teaching communism, 'he became badly mixed up in his endeavors to reconcile this proposal with his accusations'.

Knowing that the man was not responsible for his remarks, Della did not take his outbursts seriously. But others who did not know him well began repeating the stories and hurried to Della in alarm. 'Although these accusations are completely absurd,' she told Ernest Dodge, 'they do reflect quite accurately the depth of the malice that is felt toward her in a certain quarter.' What damage could be done to Lidia, Della worried, 'by judicious letters written here and there throughout the country?'

Josephine thought that Della tended to get 'a little too emotional' and advised her to 'let the whole matter rest'. She warned her: 'We cannot let a split come between the Bahá'ís and the Esperantists. It would be tragic.' Josephine felt that it was the Bahá'ís' fault for allowing the original confusion and misunderstanding to occur at the beginning of Lidia's visit.

Lidia gave no sign she knew about the goings-on in New York, and still showed friendly concern for her former hosts. She was puzzled as to why Della was getting so upset and had begged Lidia not to write to them.

Ernest Dodge's wary attitude changed when he finally met Lidia at her talk in Washington, DC. He told Della that his conversation with Lidia that evening left 'a very pleasant impression', and he felt that prospects for 'her future labors' were 'favorable'.

Although Lidia was teaching only one course in Philadelphia, correspondence took up all of her free time, as she made arrangements for her future courses and lectures – laboriously typing out copies of letters for Della – and wrote to friends and acquaintances. But somehow she found time to write articles for *World Order* and for *La Praktiko*.

Even while in the United States, she was teaching the Bahá'í Faith to correspondents in Poland and France. 'Esperanto correspondence about the Bahá'í Faith takes a lot of time,' she wrote, 'for which I am very happy.' After one of her correspondents wrote to her about his experiments with psychic phenomena, Lidia cautioned him about trying to make contact with other-worldly forces and revealed that on occasion she also had had psychic experiences. 'I must confess', she told him, 'that your relations with the other world rather disturb me. I also at one time used to feel some kind of influences, but I never was sure whether they were friendly or unfriendly. Here, on earth, we still do not have enough knowledge about the forces and ways of the other world. In submitting to the influences it is as if we blindly expose ourselves to the actions of forces unknown to us, and those forces may not always be favorable. The dark forces which are at present pushing the world into chaos can also act on the psychic plane. On the earth, enemies sometimes come to us as wolves in sheep's clothing, to outwit us. It can be the same also on the psychic plane.'

Lidia had begun to write to Harold Foulds, an Esperantist in Cleveland, encouraging him in his study of the Bahá'í Faith. 'It is more than a Faith,' she told him eagerly, 'because laying foundations and solving the perplexing world problems which now torment humanity so deeply, it is not merely a religion, but it is a new Order in the world. It is also like an abundantly laid table, upon which each can find something according to his pleasure: the believer – a high and noble faith; the philosopher – lofty philosophical thought; the sociologist – a solution to world problems; and everyone – new joy and courage.'

Lidia wrote many long letters to Mr Foulds revealing in detail her own thoughts and telling him of her own spiritual search. 'I remember', she wrote, 'that when I took my first steps in that new Faith, my interest, like the waves of the sea, rose and seemed to fall, but just like waves of the sea it flowed over my soul always more and more. Now I am like a person who, after great thirst and suffering, has reached the shores of a sea of sweet water, an ocean full of the water of life – and fears thirst no more.'

Mr Foulds once wrote Lidia that he had begun to correspond with 'Auntie' Victoria Bedikian. Lidia gently reminded him: 'She and I are only "crutches", so to speak, for you. When you truly attain the Source of spiritual health and courage you will be able to walk by yourself on the bright path, toward the Sun, and you won't need crutches any more. I ask you, continue courageously and steadfastly your study of the Bahá'í Teaching and turn to the Source itself, to the Writings of Bahá'u'lláh and of 'Abdu'l-Bahá. When the great Teacher speaks, the little teachers must be silent, or open their mouths only to repeat Their words of wisdom. When the Sun shines brightly, one puts out the candles, and when the Nightingale bursts into song, one doesn't listen to the chirping of sparrows.'

Most anxiously Lidia awaited the arrival of letters from Shoghi Effendi. 'The letters from the Guardian always bring new strength,' she told Della. Lidia had received her answer as to whether she must formally resign from the Jewish community of Warsaw: '. . . the Guardian feels', his secretary wrote, 'that in view of the fact that such membership, as you say, has a rather social and legal significance and does not involve necessarily any definite religious implication, it would not be necessary for you to formally resign from that body at present. He hopes later on conditions will develop to a point that would make it advisable for you to take further action in this matter.

'With the renewed assurances of his prayers for the confirmation of your labours on behalf of the Cause, and with his best wishes for your health and protection . . .'

In a postscript Shoghi Effendi had added: 'May the almighty hand of Bahá'u'lláh guide and sustain you in your marvellous and historic services to the Faith in America, and enable you to enhance the splendid record of your international unforgettable services. Your true and grateful brother, Shoghi.' Lidia was relieved. She would not be asked to forsake the beleaguered Jewish community.

Although for Lidia Shoghi Effendi's letters brought 'new strength', in January Horace Holley sent Lidia a copy of a letter from the Guardian which unsettled her. It was addressed to George Winthrop Lee, of Boston, who had been an Esperantist since 1906. For some time, Mr Lee had been trying to interest the Bahá'ís in Esperanto. Although he was not a Bahá'í, he occasionally wrote to Shoghi Effendi, he explained to Lidia, 'proposing that he for example, learn our dear language, but the answer through his secretary is always that he is too busy'.

The letter he had received from Haifa said: 'You complain that the believers in America do not attach sufficient importance to the study of the Esperanto; this may be true, and is partly due to the fact that they do no longer believe that it will *necessarily* develop into the international auxiliary language of the future. The interest which the Bahá'ís have and should have in this language is essentially because of the vital significance of the idea it represents rather than the belief in its *inherent* worth as a suitable and adequate international medium of expression.

'The Bahá'ís indeed welcome Esperanto as the first experiment of its kind in modern times. They are in full sympathy with the Esperantists in so far as they stress the absolute necessity for the creation of an international language to be studied by all the peoples of the world in addition to their respective national languages.

'The Guardian himself would have learned it, but his occupations are so manifold and overwhelming that he cannot possibly find the time to do so.

'It is his hope that Miss Lidia Zamenhof, the distinguished daughter of the creator of Esperanto, will through her contact with the friends in America help in stimulating afresh the spread of that language among various Bahá'í individuals and centers. You should certainly make every effort to meet her while she is in the States.'

Lidia was somewhat dismayed by a passage in the letter, but was unsure she understood the English correctly, and wrote Della asking her to clarify it. Did the Bahá'ís once believe Esperanto would become the international language, but *no longer* believed so? Why? she wondered.

Concealing her distress, she wrote Mr Lee: 'I met the Guardian of the Bahá'í Faith, beloved to all us Bahá'ís, eight years ago, when I visited Haifa. I saw myself that his obligations are so many, so diverse, and so pressing that he cannot devote his time to language study. But it is he himself who first suggested that I come to America, and by whose suggestion I was invited to this land by the National Spiritual Assembly, which made this journey possible. Without their help I certainly could not have come.'

In any case, it was clear from the Guardian's letter that Shoghi Effendi still felt that the Bahá'ís should learn and use Esperanto; he did not only hope that, while in America, Lidia would interest the Esperantists in the Bahá'í Faith, but that she would also interest the Bahá'ís in Esperanto.

Although Lidia was suffering her share of difficulties and disappointments in America, she wrote Harold Foulds not to become discouraged in his own spiritual quest, 'even if the Goal sometimes disappears from before your eyes and seems to retreat, even if earthly clouds sometimes hide from you the brilliance of the eternal sun, and those earthly clouds are now heavier than at any other time. All the forces of the night seem to exert their power to bar the way to the Sun. Those night powers can still triumph, but not for long. There is no darkness which the Sun cannot conquer.' And on another occasion: 'Dear *Samideano*, every seeker encounters difficulties along the way. If you also meet them, don't lose heart. Difficulties are our tests. They show us the strength or weakness of our spirit, the intensity and ardor of our search, and they temper us and make us stronger and stouter.'

By the end of her stay in Philadelphia, Lidia came to feel that the course was not such a failure after all. Although the number of students, thirty-four, was far below the number she usually had in France, for America perhaps it was not so bad. She felt encouraged because a talk and demonstration lesson she had given at the Drexel Technical Institute seemed to have generated great interest among students and teachers there. 'Sowing seeds', she wrote a friend, 'is never in vain.'

TWENTY-THREE

The Gray House and the Garden

At the end of February 1938 Lidia left Philadelphia for Detroit, Michigan. Although there were only two dozen active Esperantists in that city, they worked hard on publicity for Lidia's course, sending out thousands of leaflets and arranging interviews, broadcasts and lectures. A heavy speaking schedule had been planned for her and she addressed a variety of groups including the Bahá'ís, the Women Lawyers' Association, Zonta Club, the Vegetarian Society, two Masonic auxiliary organizations, and she gave a talk and demonstration lesson to 120 at the YMCA. While in Michigan she also traveled to address gatherings in Ann Arbor, Marysville, Flint and Roseville. The Bahá'ís of Maywood, Illinois, arranged for her to speak before an audience of 200 at Irving School, where the principal was an Esperantist and a number of teachers were studying the language. She gave a speech in English over WWJ, the *Detroit News'* radio station ('I hope my bad accent was itself propaganda for Esperanto', she said afterward), and two broadcasts in Polish over station WJBK, where her speaking ability drew very favorable comments from Polish radio station operators, and a Polish paper in Toledo picked up the broadcast and published an article about it. In all, in Detroit a remarkable thirty-two articles were published about her in nineteen periodicals in seven languages including Polish, Bulgarian, German, Ukrainian and Yiddish.

Lidia's hosts in Detroit were Robert and Mabelle Davis. The Davises were Bahá'í Esperantists and Mrs Davis frequently translated for Lidia at the many public talks she gave while in Detroit. Lidia had hoped to hold one of the Esperanto courses in the black YWCA, but all the classes were held in a store-front on the ground floor of the Convention Hall. She was disappointed that 'we have not one Negro in the courses'. She had also hoped to speak before the National Association for the Advancement of Colored People, but this never came about. She was told that their programs were 'too full'.

All the publicity had an effect: seventy-two students enrolled in her course, with fifty-seven completing the lessons. Afterward, the Esperanto Society of Detroit reported: 'Miss Zamenhof's work was preeminently satisfactory. Her pupils retained their interest during the course, made remarkable progress and at the end had a desire for more. Miss Zamenhof more than fulfilled all expectations. Her teaching ability has not been as yet fully appraised, much less has it been adequately announced to the American public. Moreover, Miss Zamenhof is more than a teacher, is more than a celebrity. To her, Esperanto is not a possibility to be demonstrated, but a triumphant reality to be exemplified. It is not a mere academic subject to be taught, but a part of life to be unfolded.'

At the close of the course in May, the Detroit Esperantists held a farewell picnic in Lidia's honor at Lake Orion. Dr Charles Simon of Cleveland recalled meeting Lidia that day. He had come to Detroit to talk to her about the upcoming EANA congress and was 'immediately impressed with her dynamic personality and with her unmistakable charm'.

The moment of her arrival, he recalled, was 'dramatic'. 'As Miss Zamenhof entered the hall where the picnic was being held, all present rose to their feet and quite spontaneously began to sing *La Espero*. She stood quietly during the singing, a slight but imposing figure, dressed in quiet good taste, with a black fur piece around her shoulders. Afterward she acknowledged the greeting in quite a dignified manner, and the picnic program continued, with singing of more Esperanto songs to the accompaniment of an accordion.'

'An intimate, vivid word picture of the "Majstro" as she knew him was her parting gift to us,' Robert Davis, secretary of the Esperanto Society, wrote in the official report. 'How enviable this opportunity of ours! How precious these hours with *nia kara lingvo* [our dear language] and the daughter of the "Majstro!"'

Even while she was in America Lidia was defending her father's legacy in Europe, where it was under attack from nationalists. In an article she hotly refuted a suggestion that the name of Esperanto should be changed to 'European'. In answer to allegations she had read of in an Esperanto journal claiming that the internationalism of Esperanto was not current, Lidia replied that the original name of Esperanto had been 'International Language'. 'When and where did the Majstro say that his language should serve only for Europeans?' she demanded. 'It is, to be sure, based on the European languages. But the reason for that was that its author was closest to the European cauldron of languages, to the European Babel. That doesn't mean that he wanted in any way to give privilege to the European languages. If they wish to look for deficiencies in Esperanto, they may find one in that very fact: that it is too European and does not sufficiently reflect oriental roots.' As the language evolved further, Lidia suggested, perhaps it would take on oriental influences in the degree to which Esperanto spread in Asia and the people of various Asian countries added their contributions to the language.

But the real question at hand, Lidia emphasized, was not linguistic. To try to use Esperanto, 'which had been created in order that all nations and all cultures should be equal on its foundation,' in order to proclaim the superiority of one part of mankind, would be 'completely contrary to the idea of Esperanto', she exclaimed. Zamenhof had not been willing to compromise about his ideas. He did not follow the trends of the times. Chiding the Esperantists not to 'follow the changeable winds of political opinion like weathervanes' or 'like chameleons obediently adapt to the ruling colors', she pointed out that had Ludwik Zamenhof been just 'one of the many sheep in the hopeless flock', he never would have created Esperanto.

As the year 1938 went on, the news from Europe was ever more ominous, the rhetoric of the dictators ever more hysterical and threatening. Discrimination, boycott and violence against the Jews were growing more widespread in Europe, not only in Germany and Poland, but in other countries as well. 'We are back in the Middle Ages,' one American Jewish leader observed after a visit to Europe.

On March 12 Lidia read in the morning paper that Austria had been taken over by Nazi Germany in what came to be known as the *Anschluss*. The Austrian government was dismantled and the nation ceased to exist, becoming a province of the Third Reich. With the *Anschluss* came a frenzy of violence against the Jews in Vienna more terrible than anything Germany had yet seen. 'Is it possible', Lidia wrote Della, 'that the great Drama is already beginning? More than ever one must turn to Bahá'u'lláh in these moments.'

She was glad that the National Spiritual Assembly had voted to have her give a course to train Esperanto teachers in the Cseh method at the Green Acre Bahá'í Summer School. Lidia knew that there was not much time left before war broke out in Europe, and she wanted to see the Cseh method spread as much as possible in America. When Europe was in chaos, she hoped that new ranks of American Esperantists might keep the movement alive – free of the divisions that had afflicted Esperanto in Europe. She wrote Della: 'The new war, which Europe will not escape, will silence the warring Esperantists in Europe. Then the American *samideanoj* will have to take up the call and begin to work for the Cause.'

Della also felt a sense of urgency. She confided her fears to Josephine Kruka: 'In view of the European situation, I feel more than ever how important it is that Lidia teach as many Esperantists as possible the Cseh method. When that volcano erupts, as it may any moment, it will be the end of Esperanto in the continent for many years to come. If there were only some other means by which one could do as much for Esperanto here, I would urge that also. But I do not see anything, anywhere that compares with it.'

Lidia shared that fear. 'Unfortunately', she wrote, 'I agree with you, that probably nothing will remain – not only of the Esperantist organizations but of Europe at all, in the near future. So we must exert our efforts here in America.'

When Lidia learned that Harold Foulds had begun teaching an Esperanto course to the Bahá'ís in Cleveland, she wrote him, 'I cannot tell you how happy that news made me . . . I hope that they will help you more and more on your new way of search . . . and on your part, you will help them get closer to Esperanto and to get to know that language which – I am profoundly convinced – was created directly under the influence of Bahá'u'lláh, although the author of the language was unaware of it.'

That the dark clouds which had spread over Europe were weighing heavily on Lidia was evident in a frightening dream she described in a letter to Harold Foulds. The dream would turn out to be chillingly prophetic.

'Coming back from a walk', she wrote, 'in the crowd I lost my little mother, who was not strong, and searching for her I found myself in a corridor. At the end of that corridor stood a large baptismal font. From there branched two roads, to the right and to the left. Crowds of people were going through that corridor, and, on reaching the baptismal font, they divided and without stopping they kept on going: part of them went to the right, the other part to the left. But wherever they went, whether to the right or to the left, they were making their way with the same effort, and I saw large beads of sweat on their foreheads . . .

'Searching for my mother, I found myself in a hospital ward. It was a strange hospital and strange patients: in the middle of the ward, on the floor, stood a large coffin with a silver cross. Some of the patients lay motionless on their beds, but others, completely wound in their bedsheets as if in shrouds, jumped and frolicked on their beds . . . I then understood that it was an insane asylum.

'I found myself later in another corridor, searching for the way out, which I could not see. Suddenly at the end of the corridor I saw a woman in a nurse's uniform, and her proud bearing gave me to understand that she was one of the heads of the hospital. I ran to her and asked for the way out. But she made an incomprehensible sound, looked at me with strange eyes – and in her eyes I saw also: madness. And I was afraid. Not for any personal danger to myself, but the thought terrified me that those who were in charge of that hospital were just as insane as the patients. And I awoke with terror, invoking the name of God.

'Later, during the day, when I thought about that dream, I understood its meaning and I understood why I had become so terrified. The hospital was the world. The patients wound in shrouds, and still insanely jumping on their beds, are the peoples of the world. And here is why the situation was terrifying: because those who are in charge of that great hospital, the world, are insane themselves. How could they find the way out? Suddenly I thought: too bad that I awoke. I could still go and see the Chief of Staff! And hardly had I thought that, when I remembered another dream, which I had dreamed when I went back to sleep after waking up:

'There was a garden, famous throughout the world. The most beautiful garden in the world, the garden every traveler greatly wishes to see and which is the object of many trips. I went out of an old gray house . . . and walked in that incomparable garden, where grapevines wound about marble columns, where the air was clean and sweet-smelling, and where the clear blue sky radiated peace and tranquillity. I came back into the old dark house and said to the people who were there: why don't you go into the garden? I am going back there! They answered: Not so quickly! The police are standing at the door and let the people in only one after another and for only one time! The police? I answered with surprise. I was in that garden, I walked freely, and no police forbade me to go in!'

Then Lidia offered her interpretation of the dream. 'Here is the future of the world, after the most bitter tests: the wondrous garden of mankind, the spiritual garden, the long-promised and long-awaited garden, the Kingdom of God to be founded upon earth! The police who stand guard at the entrance and stop the people from going in are our own prejudices, egotistical desires, limits, hatreds – everything that impedes entry into the Spiritual Realm. And yet the garden is waiting, the beautiful, promised garden! One after another the people go out of the old gray and dark house; one after another they go into the garden of the spirit.

'No guidebook, published by travel companies, contains a description of this most wonderful garden! No official of any of those companies will show you the way there. But, dear *samideano*, continue to read the books about the Bahá'í Faith. The way is shown there. Persist and have courage in your search. Cast off from your eyes the veils of custom and tradition. Search with a free, independent and unfettered mind, and with a free, warm heart. Sooner or later you will surely reach the goal!'

While staying in Detroit, Lidia made a two-day visit to Urbana, Illinois, during which she gave several public talks and a Cseh demonstration lesson. Margaret Kunz Ruhe, who at the time was a senior at the University of Illinois and chairman of the Bahá'í Youth Club there, was to meet Lidia at the railroad station. She wondered how she would recognize Lidia, but was assured that if she wore a green star on her coat, Lidia would recognize her.

'As the train from Chicago pulled to a standstill', Mrs Ruhe later recalled, 'the passengers poured off, and I watched them for some time with considerable apprehension and concern. At last a small, shy, blond, bespectacled lady stood beside me and softly introduced herself as Miss Zamenhof. She was warm, loving, sweet and rather retiring and modest in her manner and disposition. She was quiet with the signs of being more an introvert than an extrovert. She wore large glasses with strong lenses which gave her a rather scholarly and somewhat owlish look.

'She was a different person when she stood before us as our teacher. She was dynamic, and spoke in a vibrating, powerful voice. I recall that at one point she lifted a chair high in the air as she taught us the word in Esperanto . . . During her days in Urbana, she illumined the hearts and the minds with her knowledge, her sincerity and her inspiration.'

In May 1938 Lidia returned to Illinois at the invitation of the National Spiritual Assembly, to attend the Bahá'í Annual Convention, where delegates from all over the United States and, at that time, Canada, would elect the National Assembly for the following year. It was held in Chicago and Wilmette, the location of the Bahá'í House of Worship. There Lidia finally met Josephine Kruka. 'Have had several glorious days with Lidia,' Josephine wrote to Della afterwards. 'I love her dearly.' Josephine told Della that at the Convention, May Maxwell, whom Lidia had met several times in France, read from her notes of conversations with Shoghi Effendi in Haifa. Mrs Maxwell told the gathering 'that Shoghi Effendi had said that the Bahá'ís must adopt Esperanto as the International Language *for the present*. There was', Josephine added, 'a silence – '*

Lidia was deeply moved by the House of Worship in Wilmette. 'That Temple gave me very sweet feelings,' she wrote to Della. 'There I felt as if at home: in my spiritual home.' But two sad events had occurred at the Convention. News arrived from Palestine that Munírih Khánum, the wife of 'Abdu'l-Bahá, had passed away. The cable was read to the stunned audience on Saturday, May 1. Later that

* In her compilation of 'Haifa Notes of Shoghi Effendi's Words Taken at Pilgrim House Table during the Pilgrimage of Mrs May Maxwell and Miss Mary Maxwell, January, February, March 1937,' Mrs Maxwell recorded the statement thus: 'The Bahá'ís should adopt Esperanto at present as a universal language, even if only a temporary one.' Mrs Maxwell pointed out that these notes of her pilgrimage were 'free and spontaneous utterances' of the Guardian and not to be regarded as official statements, although 'he sanctions both their recording in his presence and subsequent sharing with fellow-Bahá'ís . . .'

same day, Mrs Grace Robarts Ober collapsed after delivering a report to the Convention and had to be assisted from the hall. Soon word came that she was gravely ill and the gathering began to say healing prayers for her. Mrs Ober's husband, Harlan, had been serving as the Convention chairman, but when his wife was stricken he hurried to be with her and a substitute chairman had to be found. The reports continued; there was another urgent request for healing prayers. But a few moments later, a member of the National Assembly came to the platform to announce that Mrs Ober had died.

The news of the two deaths, Lidia wrote, 'put a pall of great sorrow on the conference. But as you wrote, one cannot grieve overly, when one thinks what joy awaits those who passed away; for the Holy Mother – reunion with the beloved Master ['Abdu'l-Bahá], and for Grace Ober – well, I think that such a death, right after the inspiring talk, in the Temple, in the midst of the prayers of the friends, is something so beautiful, so joyous, that we can only wish a similar privilege for ourselves and at the same time realize that such a privilege must be well earned through a life of service.'

Lidia was asked to speak twice that day, 'once, a few minutes after Mrs Ober was carried out, before we knew she had died, and I spoke for a few moments although all my thoughts were concentrated on Mrs Ober, and I felt that her illness was very serious.' Later, the same evening, she spoke about Munírih Khánum, whom she had met in Haifa. Again, at one of the sessions in Chicago, she was asked to address the audience. 'I gave a very short talk,' she explained, 'because it is still difficult for me to speak in English without prior preparation.'

She was delighted when the Bahá'ís of Chicago, Wilmette and Maywood, Illinois, asked her if she would give Esperanto courses in their cities.

Sometime during that year, Martha Root, who was in India, wrote to the American Bahá'ís: 'I am so happy that Lidia Zamenhof is in our country. Every letter from the friends praises her splendid work – I always wish her loved ones in Warsaw could see these letters; they love her so deeply and appreciate what a great soul she is. I am so proud of our Lidia – I cannot be home to welcome her, help her, but every day I pray that you all will show her the love of your hearts.'

TWENTY-FOUR

Who Can Foresee?

Lidia's classes in America were not as large as she had hoped they would be, but the money she was receiving from them was sometimes even less than it should have been. The local groups deducted their expenses – for advertising the course and renting the classroom – from the tuition paid by the students, and although occasionally individuals offered contributions to help offset the expenses, sometimes by the end of the course less than a third of the tuition money was left for Lidia. Some groups deducted more of their expenses from the tuition than other groups did. Since Lidia did not do her own bookkeeping for the classes, she did not know, until it was too late, what was being deducted or whether the students were even being charged the correct amount for the course.

Lidia accepted what she was given without complaint, but Della was alarmed that she was receiving so little money. It seemed just one difficulty too many to bear, and Della began to think it might be better if Lidia returned to Europe. She suggested to Lidia that it was too great a sacrifice for her to remain in America since she wasn't earning much from her classes. Lidia replied that she 'did not come to the land of dollars to get rich' and that as long as she had no expense for food and lodging she did not mind that her earnings were not great. 'But even if I went back to Europe,' she pointed out, 'I could not count on great earnings with growing misery in the whole world . . .' Although things had not gone smoothly for her so far, Lidia hoped to extend her stay in America at least six months.

But Lidia was beginning to worry that when the time came for her to leave, she might not be able to go home. A law had been passed in Poland after the *Anschluss* of Austria when many Polish Jews who lived in Austria had tried to return to Poland. According to the new law, Polish citizens who had lived more than five years abroad could be stripped of their citizenship. The law was aimed at Jews: the Polish government feared that Germany would soon expel the thousands of Polish Jews who lived there, and it wanted to prevent them from entering Poland.

Lidia had only made three short visits home during the last five years, and she was worried that those three visits would not be enough to satisfy the requirements of the new law. If she lost her citizenship she would be unable to remain in America yet unable to return to Poland – a person without a country, in a world on the brink of war. The thought of Europe chilled her. 'One can hardly even dare think about that unhappy continent,' she wrote Della. 'I have my family and many friends there. My heart is oppressed when I think about them.'

Lidia's sister Zofia had written her from Warsaw that the new law did not apply to her, but Lidia was not so sure. She asked Della to telephone the Polish Consulate in New York to find out. But, she added, 'I beg . . . that *under no conditions* say for whom you need that information.' To do so might attract the danger, she feared, rather than ward it off.

While in Wilmette, Lidia had confided to Mrs Jeanne Bolles of New York City her fears about losing her citizenship. Mrs Bolles had suggested Lidia try to become an American citizen. 'And she said that President Roosevelt made some kind of call to the refugees, making it easier for them I don't know whether only to come to America or to become citizens. * This question of Mrs Bolles took up my thoughts,' Lidia told Della. 'An American passport would be much more convenient than a Polish one. Furthermore, who can foresee what will be the fate of the Jews in Poland in the near future?' She wrote to Shoghi Effendi for his advice.

Lidia left Detroit for Lima, Ohio, on May 21. She arrived in Lima ill from fatigue, and no doubt worried about the Green Acre course on which she placed so much hope. Because of financial problems, Della could not go to Green Acre to help Lidia, and she had asked Josephine Kruka to take over. But Josephine suddenly announced that she intended to go to Finland for the summer and would not be there to help. Della was frantic. Lidia, learning of Josephine's plans, cautioned her not to go to Europe without telegraphing Shoghi Effendi to ask his advice. Josephine dashed off a brief cable to him, but without mentioning the Esperanto responsibilities she would be giving up in order to undertake the trip.

Meanwhile, Della tried to talk Josephine into changing her mind. Lidia would need someone to help her at Green Acre: to enroll students, to distribute materials, but most important, to act as her *aparato*. Without the *aparato* to translate, Lidia could not give the Cseh course at all. 'If you do not go and I cannot go,' Della pleaded with Josephine, 'I do not see who is to help her.'

* After the *Anschluss* in March 1938, President Roosevelt had called an international conference, which was held in July in Evian-les-Bains, France, to seek resettlement of the Jewish refugees facing Nazi persecution. He pledged to open up to full use the United States immigration quotas for Germany and Austria (totaling only about 27,000), but he never planned to increase the numbers. At the Evian Conference, all of the thirty-two nations present excused themselves from accepting refugees, except for the Dominican Republic.

The course already seemed plagued by troubles. The publicity had not gotten out on time. And the announcement that had appeared in *Bahá'í News* was incorrect. Lidia wrote Josephine, 'If you also will not come, the outlook for the course, already dark because of the delay, looks darker and darker.'

Just as Lidia was preparing to leave Detroit, she learned that Josephine had received her answer. Shoghi Effendi had cabled her: 'APPROVE FINLAND. PRAYING.'

Lidia despaired. 'When I was coming to America,' she told Josephine sadly, 'I dreamed about that Cseh teachers' course which could be so important for the Esperanto movement in America, and I believed that it would be perhaps the most important service I could do for Esperanto in America. Well, apparently this plan and hope did not meet God's approval. There are moments when I am truly discouraged about Green Acre and would willingly give up that enterprise. But I won't do that and will persevere.'

Shortly after that, Shoghi Effendi's answer to Lidia's last letter arrived. The Guardian saw no objection to changing her citizenship and left the decision to her. Shoghi Effendi added: 'The friends, no less than myself, feel deeply indebted to you for your splendid and historic achievements. Persevere in your historic task, and never feel discouraged. My prayers accompany you wherever you go and serve.'

In Lima, Lidia stayed part of the time at the home of Frank and Charlene Warner, and part of the time at the home of Frank and Dorothy Baker at 615 West Elm Street. Louise Baker Matthias, who was seventeen at the time, recalled that summer of Lidia's visit. Lima was a city of about fifty thousand, but it was a metropolitan center for the area and a hub for petroleum distribution. The previous year, the pastors of the three largest churches had launched an attack on the Bahá'ís, and Frank Baker feared his business might go bankrupt when his bakery was boycotted. Local Bahá'ís were fired from their jobs or threatened with being fired. The attacks ended a short time later when Lima got its first radio station, and questions about the Bahá'í Faith were answered on the air.

Many people had been uneasy about the Esperanto course in Lima: unlike the other cities Lidia had visited, Lima had no Esperanto organization. It was the Bahá'ís who wanted Lidia to come, in particular Lima's one Esperantist, Dr Luella Beecher, Dorothy Baker's mother.

Dorothy Baker, a descendant, on her father's side, of Henry Ward Beecher and Harriet Beecher Stowe, was a member of the National Spiritual Assembly and a renowned Bahá'í speaker and teacher. Immediately, Lidia recognized a deep spirituality in her. 'She is truly an extraordinary person,' Lidia wrote Della. 'Sometimes when I look at her, I have the impression that I am looking at an angel. I love her very much and enjoy being with her. I would like to attain at least a little part of that spiritual greatness which is hers.' Because of other responsibilities, Dorothy Baker was not able to attend all the Esperanto lessons, but Lidia was astonished at how quickly Mrs Baker took to the Cseh method. 'Once,' she told Della, 'from another room I saw how Dorothy Baker was explaining the first lesson to a person who had missed it: she was giving a regular Cseh conversation! Dorothy is a brilliant person and can do anything!' Lidia asked Mrs Baker to ask the National Spiritual Assembly if it wished her to remain in America. She returned from the meeting with their answer: the National Assembly heartily approved Lidia to stay longer.

The Esperanto classes in Lima were held in a large room, 'a sort of game and party room' in Frank Baker's bread bakery. Many years later, Margot Miessler Malkin, though only a child when she met Lidia, recalled 'the enthusiasm, sincerity and loving manner in which Lidia presented the Esperanto language with a beautiful red rose in her hand to demonstrate the simplicity of the language while describing the rose, always with a smiling and radiant face.'

While in Lima, Lidia's speaking schedule was light, which gave her more time to make friendships. The young women of Lima sometimes found Lidia's Central European ways strange, and they immediately began to introduce her to American customs.

One day, Charlene Warner and Elcore Ebersole took Lidia to an ice cream parlor and bought her a strawberry soda. They had to show her how the straw worked and how to turn the straw around and suck out the strawberries as they became stuck in the straw. It took Lidia a long time, and she finally said: 'That was an awful lot of work!'

'She thought the Americans were a wasteful lot of folks,' recalled Mrs Ebersole. 'The first evening at the dinner table, Charlene had a beautiful linen tablecloth which hung down perhaps ten inches all around and was carefully ironed. Lidia said she was used to a tablecloth that just covered the top of the table. The ironed big bedsheets were another worry to her. "All of that extra material you just tuck under the mattress which is much thicker than it need be,"' Lidia said. '"All that is needed is a piece of cloth the size of a person. This is too much waste."'

Louise Baker Matthias recalled another episode that illustrated the cultural differences Lidia had to contend with in America. 'During the time Lidia was in Lima, one of the local Bahá'ís, Glen Sealts, who owned a dry-cleaning shop, offered to dry-clean all of her clothes free. Lidia was always absolutely clean herself, but apparently it was too expensive or it was not customary to dry-clean clothing as frequently as we have it done here. She thought it was not necessary. Mother

[Dorothy Baker] was shocked at her reaction, and of course did not express that, but told Lidia that it was too good an opportunity to pass up or some such tactful thing.' Finally, Lidia gave in and let him dry-clean her clothes.

When Lidia left Lima, Mrs Ebersole remembered, 'Our little group really sent her off in style. We bought her a complete formal outfit: pink taffeta formal, all the underpinnings, gold slippers, silk hose, jewelry and a new hairdo. The Bahá'ís gave her a handkerchief shower – that was popular then.' The members of her class held a farewell luncheon at a hotel and gave her a gift.

With the worsening situation in Europe, Lidia's new friends tried to persuade her that she must get her passport and papers in order. Meanwhile, the official at the Polish Consulate in New York had refused to give Della Quinlan any information about the new Polish law, insisting that the Polish citizen who wanted to know about it should come in and inquire in person. The response of the Polish official confirmed Lidia's suspicions: the law was intended to get rid of 'undesirable citizens' – in other words, Jews.

Still Lidia was confident things would work out: 'I know from my five years' experience', she wrote, 'that those official matters connected with visas, visitor's permits and so on, are always a source of difficulties for me – but that God smooths them. Once in France when there was a tendency against foreigners, they officially refused to extend my visitor's permit, and in spite of that everything was arranged: not by the support of ministers to whom my friends appealed, but by the intervention of an insignificant clerk. So I trust on; although I know that I certainly will not escape my usual share of difficulties and frayed nerves.'

Lidia still had Green Acre ahead of her and desperately needed someone to help her there. But it had to be someone who knew Esperanto well enough to be her *aparato*. Lidia wrote to Della suggesting Roan Orloff from Boston. 'I remember what Martha Root often used to say to me when I was distressed by various problems in my life: "do your part, and leave the rest to God" . . . But here's the thing: in the Green Acre matter our part has *not* been done.' Lidia was 'ready for failure'. But, she wrote to Roan: 'Fate seems to oppose us at every step. You know that I need an *aparato*, that is, a translator for the first lessons . . . I feel completely orphaned . . . could you possibly come and help me in my "misery"?'

Roan accepted.

'At first I was very embarrassed by the sudden departure of Miss Kruka,' Lidia responded, 'but I confided this matter to Bahá'u'lláh – and behold, he sends me the answer in your person!' 'So here is a new lesson,' she wrote with satisfaction, 'that God takes care of us and helps us.'

Josephine Kruka visited Lidia for an hour on her way across the country to embark for Finland. Lidia thought she looked 'very tired, and much less well than she was when I saw her in Wilmette. She looked somewhat depressed, and not at all enthusiastic about her trip to Finland, which she nevertheless regards as her duty. She said she should have gone last year and she considers this year's difficulties punishment for her lack of obedience to the Guardian's suggestion last year. But I agree with her completely that waiting until the coming year would not be good, because in the coming year Europe may be reduced to ruins.' Josephine also admitted to Lidia that she regretted she had not written to the Guardian to explain the circumstances under which she was leaving instead of sending a short cable. But now, Josephine felt, it was too late.

Lidia did not hold a grudge against Josephine and told Della: 'Yesterday I wrote to her to encourage her and tell her that she should consider her trip not as punishment, but as a privilege to be a pioneer of the New Faith in the land of her ancestors . . . We must always think that, as the Master ['Abdu'l-Bahá] said, the important things must give way to the most important. And although Miss Kruka greatly surprised and embarrassed us by her action, and even risked endangering the entire Green Acre matter, because she certainly did not do that out of ill will, although perhaps with insufficient forethought, we must be with her, and friendly to her in this important moment of her life as she goes forth to teach . . .'

In spite of the cultural differences and the strain of having to move her lodgings and stay at four different homes during her stay in Lima, Lidia had pleasant memories of the time she had spent there. 'How happy I was among the Bahá'ís of Lima!' she wrote. 'Truly, I feel wonderful with them, and they are so good and kind to me.' 'In fact', she confided to Della, 'they rather pampered me too much.'

When it came time to leave Lima, things looked somewhat better than when she arrived. The course had been a success: she had sixty-two students, more than in New York. Before Lidia had come, there had been only one Esperantist in Lima – Luella Beecher. After Lidia left, there were over sixty, two thirds of whom were Bahá'ís, and they formed an Esperanto organization with Luella Beecher as president. But the course had not been a financial success: Lidia was perplexed when she was given a much smaller sum of money than she had expected. It turned out that almost half of the students had only paid a dollar for the lessons.

In spite of the financial and other difficulties that had arisen for Lidia in America, Della was changing her mind about Lidia's returning to Europe. Even though the 'pernicious gossip' was 'still being propagated, especially the communist angle', she confided to Josephine, the prospect of Lidia's returning to Poland filled Della with fear for her. 'After her hard year here, to go back to that!'

The situation was indeed worsening in Europe as one international crisis succeeded another. In Germany, the summer of 1938 saw a 'tidal wave of terror' against Jews. Mass arrests had begun in the spring, and the concentration camps were being turned into forced labor camps. But if Lidia had lost hope that peace could triumph over war, she did not reveal it. In a radio speech over WBLY in Lima, she spoke of hearing a short-wave Esperanto broadcast from Brno, Czechoslovakia. 'The atmospheric conditions were very unfavorable on that day,' she said. 'A thunderstorm raged . . . but through that thunderstorm the words of the Esperanto language reached us clearly, words spoken about love between people and peace on earth.' It seemed, she said, 'like a symbol of the present world. Winds blow. Thunder rolls. The earth seems to tremble. But in spite of that, people of good will extend their hands to people of other lands. They wish to understand. They wish to love. They wish to live in peace.' It was a poignant symbol indeed. Political thunderstorms did deluge Czechoslovakia in the summer of 1938 and that country did not have long to live in peace.

Because Lidia was in America, she could not attend the Thirtieth Universal Congress of Esperanto which was held in London in 1938. But she sent a message to the Union of Esperantist Women to be read at the congress. Although war seemed inevitable, she urged them to work even harder for peace. 'At a time like this,' she told them, 'when the horizon of the world is covered by thick clouds, more than ever we women must exert all the peaceful efforts of our hearts. We must loudly proclaim that we want peace on earth. But so that our words are not only vain sounds, we must build. The foundation upon which we must build is the hearts . . .'

Lidia Zamenhof, above all, could not lose hope. After all, Esperanto, as she told an American reporter, 'means one who hopes'.

50. *The course in New York City*

51. *A group at the EANA Congress in Cleveland, July 1938, on the roof of the Hotel Allerton. (1) Ernest Dodge, (2) Roan Orloff, (3) James Morton, (4) Charles Simon, (5) Samuel Martin, (6) Lidia, (7) Louella Beecher*

53. *The cast in costume. Roan Orloff third from right, Lidia second from left*

52. *The Peace Pageant at Green Acre. Lidia as Zaynab*

TWENTY-FIVE

Green Acre

Although Lidia could not go to the London congress, her presence was the highlight of the Congress of the Esperanto Association of North America in July in Cleveland, Ohio. At the opening session, she greeted the congress-goers and told them: 'A great majority of the American people still does not feel the need of an international language. A great majority of mankind still does not understand the necessity of mutual understanding. To us belongs the lofty task of awakening in human hearts the consciousness of the solidarity of the human race, of the brotherhood of men wherever they are born, of whatever nation, race, faith.'

During the business sessions, Ernest Dodge reported, Lidia was called on several times 'to speak for instruction on some point or other'. She gave several talks including one at the Sunday morning nonsectarian service on the theme of human brotherhood, and at a special meeting on the subject of 'Esperanto in the Service of Religion', at which it was discussed how Catholics, Protestants, the Society of Friends and the Bahá'ís used Esperanto.

When Charles Simon first met Lidia in Detroit, he had learned that she was 'quite a determined and strong-willed individual, not inclined to deviate very much from her established practices'. In connection with the Cleveland congress, a public meeting had been planned at which the mayor of Cleveland was to speak, and Lidia was to give a demonstration Cseh lesson, which usually lasted an hour. Dr Simon thought this was a bit too long, since there were other speakers on the program, so he asked her if she couldn't shorten her lesson.

'I could, sir,' she answered, 'But I don't want to!'

The demonstration 'came off beautifully', he later recalled, 'and the audience reacted to it quite enthusiastically.'

Roan Orloff, who had been named to Lidia's organizing committee, served as her *aparato* for that lesson. Roan thought it was 'the most brilliant performance I have ever seen,' and Lidia's banquet speech, at which she recounted memories of her childhood and the last years of her father, 'spellbinding. Even when she was silent, her very presence electrified the air.'

The congress adopted a resolution expressing 'to Miss Lidia Zamenhof, talented daughter of the beloved founder of our language . . . our deepest gratitude for the inspiration of her presence and for her unselfish cooperation in the various congress activities,' and another conveying 'our feelings of appreciation' to the National Spiritual Assembly 'for the great part they have played in making it possible to have Miss Zamenhof in America to spread the Cause of Esperanto throughout this country.'

Lidia continued to believe that the difficulties she had encountered in America would be surmounted, and she was confident she would be given an extension of her visitor's permit so she could continue her Esperanto classes. Although her permit was to expire on September 30, she made plans to begin a six-week course in Cleveland beginning on September 25, followed by a course in Minneapolis.

After the Cleveland congress, Lidia took the train to Maine to rest a few days before the beginning of the Cseh course at Green Acre.

Green Acre was a rambling estate on the banks of the Piscataqua River in Maine. It had been established in 1894 by Sarah J. Farmer as a retreat for the study of religion and philosophy. From an institution representing a variety of views, by 1938 it had become a Bahá'í Summer School and could accommodate about a hundred guests at the Inn, a four-story frame building surrounded by a covered veranda.

That summer, the days at Green Acre began with morning devotions in the Bahá'í Hall. Besides Lidia's Esperanto classes, there were afternoon teas at the Ole Bull Cottage and study groups and conferences. In the evenings there might be supper parties, group discussions, musical recitals or lectures, readings from Bahá'í literature or the latest moving pictures of Haifa; and on Saturday evenings, dances to a radio victrola in the auditorium of the Inn.

As Lidia had foreseen, the number of students in her Cseh course was small, only ten, but 'enthusiastic', Roan reported. Six had come especially for the course from New York, Philadelphia and Delaware. Some were beginners; others were there to learn the Cseh teaching method. As before, not all who attended paid for the course. 'She has goodheartedly allowed the poorer people to take part gratis,' Roan told Della. One of those who had come to study the Cseh method was Samuel Martin from Emporia, Kansas. Although only fourteen, he was already an enthusiastic and competent Esperantist. He had gone alone to the Cleveland congress, and when the other Esperantists learned he wanted to attend the Green Acre course, they got together and contributed the money to send him there. Years later Samuel Martin remembered Lidia as 'being a very kind and generous soul, with a warm personality; an excellent teacher.'

During those weeks in Maine, Lidia and Roan became close friends. 'Once at Green Acre,' Roan remembered, 'we were walking together and somebody said to us, "You're always together!" And Lidia said, "Well, there's a double bond between us. We're both Bahá'ís and we're both Esperantists, so we like to be together."'

'From the picture of her father,' Roan Orloff Stone recalled many years later, 'Lidia was exactly his image.' She had, Roan remembered fondly, such a 'love for Bahá'u'lláh, a love for Esperanto – it was a double love – that you didn't look at her beauty or her lack of beauty, you just saw her personality; you just saw her soul in her eyes.' 'When the name of Bahá'u'lláh was mentioned, or the language of her father's invention,' Mrs Stone later wrote, 'as if through a miracle her whole personality changed . . . she forgot her own self as with shining eyes and vibrant voice she launched into discussion or recounted her experiences in her field of service. Especially did her face become illumined as she told of her pilgrimage to the Holy Land, her precious moments with the Greatest Holy Leaf, her talks with the beloved Guardian, her communion with God in the sacred shrines.'

The happy days at Green Acre passed quickly. At mealtimes they would sit around a large round table in a corner of the dining room. 'How heartily she laughed,' Roan recalled, 'when, at Sunday breakfast, I poured a river of maple syrup on my pancakes. "Roan, you're drowning!" she cried. On the other hand, she was very much displeased, and she made no secret of her displeasure, when I teased our co-eater, George Miller, more than I should have.'

Roan recalled that Lidia was 'always helping somebody. She was always there if anyone needed a word of comfort, or if anyone needed some advice as to what color to wear with something else, or if somebody had a spiritual problem to discuss. Finally she might say, "Well, why don't you write to Shoghi Effendi about it? He would help you."' But Lidia never talked about her own problems.

Even though there were only ten in the Esperanto class, Lidia gave it all her energy, teaching four hours a day. But, Roan confided to Della, 'She is pale and just all worn out! And I'm a little bit worried about her.'

At the close of the course, the class gave Lidia a gift of nineteen dollars and, in addition, someone else, not a member of the class, who 'fell head over heels in love with her', presented her with a check for fifty dollars.

Roan had to return to her job at the Boston State House until the Labor Day holiday. 'My eyes were filled with tears,' she wrote to Della, 'and there was a lump in my throat as I took leave of *mia amatino* [my sweetheart].'

Months earlier, Lidia had received an invitation to visit the mountain retreat of Roy Wilhelm in North Lovell, Maine, after the

Esperanto course. A long-time member of the National Spiritual Assembly, Roy Wilhelm ran an import business in New York City. For many years he had been a close friend of Martha Root, whom he had introduced to the Bahá'í Faith. Once the course at Green Acre was over, Lidia went to North Lovell to take up Mr Wilhelm's invitation. Elcore Ebersole from Lima, Ohio, was also there at the time. Many years later she recalled their sojourn: 'It was a fantastic home cut into the mountain high above the world. From a distance it looked like a huge cuckoo clock . . . Lidia and I were met by one of Roy Wilhelm's workers and driven to his mountaintop home.

'Lidia loved it there and just settled down as if she planned to stay a long time.' Apparently there was some misunderstanding as to just how long her invitation was for. Although Lidia planned to stay at least seventeen days, Elcore understood they were only invited for the weekend. 'After ten days,' Mrs Ebersole recalled, 'a cook asked me if I had any idea how long she expected to stay. I told her I would speak to Lidia and assured her that we couldn't stay much longer.

'At breakfast one morning, Roy passed a plate of bananas and said to Lidia, "Grab a banana and get to it." She asked me what he meant, and I said he meant that you should take a banana and peel it and cut it up on the cornflakes. At the close of a meal, Roy always said: "Now." Upon that command, each one at the table put his or her knee on the underside of the table where we put the folded napkin for the next meal. Lidia laughed at that command and waited each time for the table top to be raised by the pressure of knees.'

While staying at Roy Wilhelm's mountain home, Lidia had time to write to Harold Foulds, gently encouraging him in his spiritual search. 'In the world today there are many diverse "isms", schools, theories, philosophies, and we see people flocking to them,' she wrote. 'They grow rapidly, like wild weeds, and like weeds, rapidly die off. A tree which must stand for centuries grows slowly and slowly gives fruit. That is true of the rapidity with which superficial ideas spread and perish, while the great truths take root slowly in order to last a long, long time. The same is true also in relation to the individual in whose heart the roots of the tree of eternity only gradually become strengthened, while grasses of fantasy and man-made theories would quickly find a place in it. Therefore, may your heart be like rich ground, in which the roots of the tree of eternity become strong. Plow the soil of your heart and water it with Divine wisdom and inspiration which this great Teaching of today's Messenger of God brings . . .'

'Lidia wasn't too happy about leaving that paradise,' Elcore Ebersole recalled, but at last they took a bus back to Kittery, Maine.

During the first week of August, Lidia returned to Green Acre. She was busy translating again. Earlier that year, Mrs Amelia Collins had told her that Shoghi Effendi wanted to have *Bahá'u'lláh and the New Era* translated into Polish. Although Lidia had never translated anything into Polish before, she had written the Guardian: 'If there is no one else to do this, I should try it, if you wish me rather to do this work than other translations into Esperanto. Though my present work takes nearly all my time I shall nevertheless try to do what you direct me to do.'

Now at last she had some free time, but rather than rest she worked feverishly, spurred on by a letter from Shoghi Effendi asking her to finish the translation as soon as possible. She hadn't been taking part in the prayer sessions at Green Acre regularly, she admitted in a letter to Roan, 'because there are various forms of prayer and one of them is work. But in spite of all the effort I don't accomplish as much as I would like to.'

Many Bahá'ís visited Green Acre, and, staying there for almost the entire summer, Lidia was able to be with several people who had become very dear to her. Dorothy Baker, who was vacationing nearby, came to Green Acre and gave a talk on prayer and fasting. Afterward, Lidia wrote Roan, 'My dear, if I had come to America only to hear this talk and see the inspiration that spoke through her, even then the trip would have been worth ten times the effort. And when I compared myself to that inspired angel, I wept at my insignificance.'

May Maxwell, staying nearby in Portsmouth, had come to visit, she wrote Della. 'Yesterday I had two hours privately with her in my room – simply heavenly!'

One of those who had attended the Esperanto lessons at Green Acre was Louis Gregory, the outstanding black Bahá'í teacher. 'I learned to love and admire him very much . . .' Lidia wrote. 'If some of those people who have racial prejudice could know him, they surely would understand well that there are few white people that one could compare to Mr Gregory!'

Roan returned to Green Acre to find Lidia wrapped up in her translating. '"Shoghi Effendi," Lidia said, her face aglow, "has told me that I must hurry and finish this as soon as possible."'

The last Sunday evening of the Green Acre session, a 'Peace Pageant' called 'The Fountain of Light', written by Mrs Nancy Bowditch, was to be presented. Mrs Bowditch's pageants, living tableaux on Bahá'í subjects, were something of a tradition at Green Acre. People came from the surrounding towns to attend them, and this year 'the largest audience for many years was held spell-bound by the dramatic presentation' of scenes from *The Dawn-Breakers*, the story of the Báb, forerunner of the Bahá'í Faith, and his disciples who met a martyr's death at the hands of the Muslim clergy in nineteenth-century Iran. 'All the cast were in beautiful Oriental costumes with fine lighting effects,' an observer reported. 'The highest spiritual note was maintained throughout with increasing momentum, ending with the Call of the Báb to His Eighteen Letters of the Living as they were setting out all over the East to tell the Glorious Message. It was a masterpiece that will not be forgotten by any who heard it.'

Lidia and Roan had been recruited to act in the pageant. Lidia was cast as Zaynab, a peasant girl who disguised herself as a boy to fight with the besieged Bábís at Fort Zanján, where she was killed. Roan played the part of Mullá Ḥusayn, the first to believe in the Báb. Once, while being attacked by an armed mob of fanatical Muslims, Mullá Ḥusayn had pursued the killer of one of his companions to the place where his adversary was hiding behind a tree. With his sword he struck a blow of such extraordinary force that the sword cut through the tree, the man and his musket. The Bábís' enemies, observing that feat, fled in consternation.

The cast had only one rehearsal before the performance. For the part of Mullá Ḥusayn, Roan was to carry a big shield and sword, which she did not know how to use. Lidia came to her rescue. 'It was she who showed me how to "murder" the enemy with my sword,' Roan later recalled, 'she, the soft-hearted one, the peace-loving one!' Although Roan had practiced her part all month, during the presentation as she was concentrating on wielding the sword, she forgot her lines. 'Again it was Lidia who saved me. Standing near me on the "battle field", she whispered the first words, and all ended well.'

The idyllic days at Green Acre were coming to an end. After Lidia spoke at a Labor Day program on the theme of 'The Bahá'í Principles for Peace', it was time to leave for Boston and return to her work once more.

Lidia had already tried to apply to the Immigration and Naturalization Service to extend her permit to stay in America, but the Immigration Office refused to consider the matter until the end of August, when she petitioned again. Mountfort Mills, the lawyer, had examined her papers and pronounced them in order. At his recommendation, her letter stated: 'I wish to make it clear that I do not intend to stay permanently in this country.' She seems to have felt this was not the same as seeking citizenship. She went on: 'I wish to call your attention that in my work – teaching Esperanto – I am in no wise displacing any American teacher of this language . . .'

Her application to extend her stay by about eight months stated that she was 'not employed in the United States', but was 'engaged in business in the United States: teaching Esperanto in different cities . . .' and that her monthly income was fifty to sixty dollars per month.

Lidia had not entirely made up her mind about seeking American citizenship. She wrote Roan: 'I myself have not yet received the light about this step: I don't know if I should do it or not.' In any case, she believed that she could not even apply until she had been in America a year.

However, Ernest Dodge had learned from an official in the Immigration and Naturalization Service that if Lidia wanted to apply for citizenship, she would have to leave the United States and come in again on the quota for Poland, which was about sixty-five hundred per year. Mr Dodge advised Roan that if, for any reason, the government should proceed to deport Lidia, it would send her to the land of her citizenship – Poland. But no one thought such a thing would ever happen.

TWENTY-SIX

Denied

After leaving Green Acre, Lidia spent a week in Boston as a guest of the Bahá'í Spiritual Assembly, the Esperanto Society and the *Esperanto-Rondo Amika* (Friendly Esperanto Circle). 'Before and during her visit', Roan reported, 'the Bahá'ís and the Esperantists worked together in unity and harmony.' Lidia was busy from the moment she arrived in Boston, going from one speaking engagement to another, speaking to the Bahá'ís, the Esperantists and two Jewish youth groups; as well as attending luncheons and receptions given by the Esperantists, Bahá'ís and a group of Polish Jews. Apart from her formal engagements, Roan wrote, 'there were many others sandwiched in between these, when Miss Zamenhof talked to individuals on the Cause'.

Her talk before the Boston Esperantists, about memories of her childhood and her father, 'was full of pathos and interest to her listeners,' reported H. B. Hastings, a prominent Boston Esperantist. The next morning, after a radio interview, Lidia was 'formally' received by the mayor of Boston, Maurice J. Tobin. It was a hot day, Roan later recalled. 'He was in his shirtsleeves. He just said hi, welcome to Boston, had her sign the guest book and that was it.'

Roan had arranged for Lidia to give a short address at Temple Israel during the regular service. 'Rabbi Levi sat on one side of the platform, and she sat on the other side,' Roan recalled. 'When the service was over, the organist came running downstairs and said, "I liked what you said, but tell me, can't you say *o*?" Lidia said, "Sure I can say *o* but in Europe we don't say *ow*, we say *oh*." When she spoke English she always used the European *o*.'

Carl Alpert, a correspondent for the Jewish Telegraphic Agency, had taken an interest in Lidia and arranged two radio interviews and several appearances for her in Boston, including a talk before a group of young Jewish college graduates. Mr Alpert himself interviewed Lidia and his syndicated article, 'Esperanto – A Force for Peace', appeared in many Jewish periodicals all over America. When he asked if there were Esperanto groups in Palestine, Lidia answered, 'Many. Esperanto can really do much to help solve the Arab-Jewish problem in the Holy Land. The Jews don't want to learn Arabic and the Arabs won't learn Hebrew. Thus there is a good deal of misunderstanding of each other's aims. This is a perfect example of the usefulness of this simple language, which can easily be used by both groups as an auxiliary language to carry on their social and economic intercourse, while neither relinquish their national tongues.'

Roan had framed the first letter Lidia had written her and had hung it on the wall of the club room at the Hotel Gralyn where the Friendly Esperanto Circle held its meetings. When Roan took Lidia to see the club room, Lidia was startled to see her own letter hanging on the wall. 'She turned to me,' Roan recalled, 'and she said, "Roan, you're crazy!"' Lidia did not feel that she should be treated any differently just because she was the daughter of Dr Zamenhof. 'She didn't like that at all,' Roan reflected many years later. 'She wanted to be the same as everyone else.'

At the end of Lidia's stay in Boston, Roan wrote Della a letter that revealed the profound love, admiration and devotion Lidia had inspired in her. 'What a glorious week this has been!' Roan exclaimed. 'Just being with her, hearing her sweet voice, basking in the radiance of her love for Bahá'u'lláh, learning lessons in faith, patience, tact, gentility . . . enjoying her charming English, listening to her Esperanto pronunciation, watching her approach to others, observing her platform presence, thanking Heaven for her sweet smile – oh, just loving the ground she walks on – Della, my dear, I am powerless to put my feelings into words, powerless to express my deep and abiding love for her – but you know how I feel, for I am certain that everyone who knows her loves her the way I do.'

Lidia, genuinely humble, was disconcerted by the devotion she inspired in others. In a letter to Della she revealed: 'Roan writes to me often, always with great love which I really don't deserve, and seeing it, I am truly ashamed because I cannot get rid of the feeling that somehow I deceive my friends, who see me as much better than I am.'

Lidia was reluctant to leave Boston, but she had to go to Cleveland, where she had been invited to teach. The Esperantists of Cleveland were mostly young people. A group of high school and college students had worked hard to publicize the Cseh course: the foreign language papers gave Lidia generous coverage, and she was interviewed by the three principal newspapers of the city. At least one of these had an illustrated article ready to go to press, but it never ran; international conflict pushed it off the page. Hitler was threatening war if the Sudetenland in Czechoslovakia was not turned over to Germany. The world waited in fear as British and French diplomats, attempting to appease Hitler, agreed to his demands at the Munich Conference, naively believing the Führer's assertions that once the Sudetenland was part of the Third Reich he would have no more territorial claims in Europe. To Cleveland newspaper editors, Esperanto seemed far less deserving of newspaper space; many people thought that war in Europe was imminent.

In Cleveland, as she had done in other cities, Lidia spoke before a variety of church groups and school assemblies, which included Cleveland College, Schauffler College, Henry George School and Shaker Heights High School. As usual, she gave her lecture in Esperanto with a local Esperantist translating into English, and then, at the close of the talk, translating the questions into Esperanto for Lidia to answer. 'In spite of the rather cumbersome technique,' Dr Simon recalled, 'her talks excited considerable interest and curiosity about Esperanto.'

The Bahá'í Spiritual Assembly had offered its Center in the Hippodrome Building downtown for the classroom, but once when the Bahá'í Nineteen Day Feast occurred on an evening when there was an Esperanto lesson in the Bahá'í Center, the Esperanto class had to be moved to the local YWCA. Charles Simon and Lidia found themselves preparing for the lesson in the room where the cooking classes were held, with, he recalled, 'numerous stoves lined up in place of desks. Leading to this classroom was an anteroom which had a Dutch door between it and the classroom. I was immediately reminded of a shop counter and, leaning on the door, I pointed out the resemblance to a store, and Miss Zamenhof immediately saw the possibilities of the situation.

'"What do you wish to buy, sir?" she asked me, pretending to be the salesperson.

'"Give me a dozen eggs, please," I requested.

'"Certainly, sir, but can you wait until the hen lays them?" she replied.'

Lidia encouraged Charles Simon to become a Cseh teacher, and on several occasions when Lidia visited the Simon home for dinner, he later recalled, 'we would spend several hours during which I would demonstrate to her various aspects of the Cseh method and she would very assiduously correct every phase of my technique. Her penetrating analysis and helpful suggestions stood me in good stead, not only in later courses which I taught in Esperanto in London and at the Sorbonne in Paris, during my Army service, but also in my own courses in French, Spanish and German during my lengthy teaching career.'

One of the Bahá'ís who took the course, Mayme C. Jackson, wrote Della: 'I must say here that I would not have missed it for anything . . . I am quite sure that I voice the sentiment of the entire class . . . Miss

Zamenhof during the entire class included some hint of the teaching so near to our hearts and I am sure we shall see the maturing of the many seeds planted during her stay.'

By mid-September Lidia had received no word from the Immigration and Naturalization Service about her request for an extension of her stay. 'In the tense times we are living through now,' she wrote Della with a touch of apprehension, 'one cannot foresee anything. All mankind is now in a terrible situation, but Bahá'u'lláh has all power to protect and care for those who trust in Him and turn to Him. I also place my fate in His hands, because even if I remain in America during the terrible days that are coming, my situation may be very difficult here. But we must trust in Him, because we are powerless, and He is the All-powerful.'

Ten days passed, and still Lidia heard nothing – only four days remained before her visitor's permit would expire, but the two courses in Cleveland were just beginning. It seemed to her that, in spite of all the effort that had been expended, interest in the courses 'isn't very great'. 'I can hardly hope for anything,' she confided to Roan in a rare moment of pessimism. Later, however, she wrote one of the Esperantists that even though the Cleveland classes had only thirty-five students, 'if we consider that we had to do the major publicity, speeches, demonstration lessons, interviews in those tense last days of September, when the whole of mankind was getting ready to go to the terrible Armageddon . . . well, I think that under such circumstances, that modest number is really quite satisfactory.'

To her close friend Roan, she alluded to 'some other difficulties' not concerning her work, but she would not elaborate. 'And I realize', she wrote, 'that it is only the beginning of difficulties which will come more and more abundantly, when – But is there any remover of difficulties save God?'

The northeastern United States had just suffered the worst storm in its history, a hurricane that killed five hundred people. In Cleveland it was very hot. 'The barometer fell terribly,' Lidia wrote Roan. 'Meanwhile the sky is blue and clear, but it seems we will have a thunderstorm. Will the hurricane come here?

'I just heard a speech by Hitler on the radio . . .'

In New York, when Della inquired about Lidia's application, the officials told her simply not to worry. The day before Lidia's permit was to expire she still had heard nothing. Mountfort Mills was out of town, so Horace Holley asked Allen McDaniel, a civil engineer in Washington who was a member of the National Spiritual Assembly, to telephone the Immigration Department to find out the status of her petition 'and perhaps', Mr Holley added, 'put in a good word for her'.

'It would be a terrible thing for her to have to return to Poland.'

At last the Immigration Department's answer arrived. It was a form letter, dated September 30 – the very day Lidia's permit expired, and was signed by Byron H. Uhl, Director of the New York District of the Immigration and Naturalization Service at Ellis Island, New York. It said:

'Dear Madam:

'The Department of Labor has denied your application for an extension of your temporary admission to the United States, of seven months and three weeks.

'You are, therefore, advised that your departure should be effected not later than October 10, 1938.

'At least five days prior thereto, this office should be notified of the date, manner and place of departure. If you leave by steamer, please furnish the name thereof, date of sailing and numbers of your ticket, stateroom and berth, so that your departure may be checked to clear your record in our files for future reference.'

However, in 1981, under the Freedom of Information Act, several attempts were made to gain access to the Immigration and Naturalization's file on the case. At that time, the agency asserted it had no file on Lidia Zamenhof, and that the file probably had been destroyed.

Lidia was 'distressed and stricken' by the decision, so contrary to what she had hoped for and, indeed, expected. It came as an especially unpleasant shock since Della had just written her that the officials had advised them not to worry. Mrs Quinlan and the others immediately began to seek a reversal, contacting Esperantists who had acquaintances in Washington. Now that she was being forced to leave, Lidia suddenly realized just how much she wanted to stay in America; she did not want to go back to Europe at all.

Nevertheless, she began to make plans to sail on the Polish passenger liner *Piłsudski* at midnight on October 11 . She also cabled Shoghi Effendi: 'EXTENSION SOJOURN AMERICA REFUSED. FRIENDS TRYING TO CHANGE GOVERNMENT'S DECISION. OTHERWISE RETURNING POLAND. PLEASE CABLE IF SHOULD ACT OTHERWISE.'

Now all sorts of matters suddenly became critical. Lidia had been carrying around the check the National Assembly had given her on her arrival – she had been unable to cash it because she did not have a bank account. This was money she would need to pay her passage to Poland. But now the check was a year old and no bank would cash it. 'Knowing nothing about the banking and check customs' and being 'inexperienced about business affairs', she sought Roy Wilhelm's advice. Eventually she was given a new check.

During her year in America, Lidia had left some of her belongings at the homes of her various hosts. She never got her iron back, but luckily the fur coat she had left in a department store in Detroit to be mended had just been returned to her. She would need it in Poland.

On October 3 a telegram arrived from Ernest Dodge: 'OFFICIAL IN CHARGE CONSENTS TO RECOMMEND EXTENSION UNTIL DECEMBER 3RD. LETTER TONIGHT.' Mr Dodge had gone to the Immigration Department and had met with a Mr Whorrall to discuss Lidia's case. Now it was revealed that she had been denied an extension of her visitor's permit because by accepting money for the Esperanto classes, she had broken the law: the visitor's permit with which she entered the country did not allow her to work while in the United States. Mr Dodge described to Della his interview with the official: 'Mr Whorrall assured me that it had been a violation all along of the permit on which Miss Zamenhof entered, for her to have conducted classes as has been done, and as of course we all planned, all the time. Of course I stressed the uniqueness of the service, the invitation from two bodies of altruistic aim, and so on; also the fact that her teaching had not been a money-making proposition, since she had been entertained by personal friends of the cause in order to supplement the moderate receipts from classes. But he said a person on such a permit as visitor is not allowed by the law to work even for board and room.

'Finally he said: "What is the shortest time that would enable her to straighten out her affairs and leave the country voluntarily?" I said sixty days would be needed to finish the course already in progress in Cleveland. Then he said, "Well, I will give her sixty days, counting from today, December 3." And he added that he knew a good many people who came on visitor's permits did manage to work, but that it is against the law, and the department has the right and duty to arrest and deport them when they are aware of the facts. However, he left me to clearly understand that he has no wish to embarrass our movement or Miss Zamenhof personally, and he is ready to just pay no attention to that angle of the matter, provided she goes to some other country before the end of the time now allowed.'

Mr Dodge questioned him about 'future moves possible' and if there were not special rules for professors and educators. 'My understanding of the reply', he told Della, 'is this: that in some instances, in case of a regular professor or specialist, one having unique qualifications which cannot be duplicated in this country, they *do* grant a special form of entrance permit, without waiting for quota. But that such a permit can be given only on a request which clearly states and establishes the reason for the exception *when* the permit is *first requested*, and before entry to the country; and that they could not consider that sort of request at all from one who is already here on a permit which specifies a visit for pleasure, and who has not observed the limitations under which entry was granted.'

Mr Dodge's efforts had gained Lidia a reprieve of two months – time to finish the courses in Cleveland and to look for an alternative to returning to Poland. 'It is a strange thing,' Della told Roan, 'but every time something has gone wrong with Lidia's affairs, it has been Dodge who has pulled us out.'

Lidia was stunned by the news that by teaching Esperanto courses in America she had been breaking the law. 'I never imagined at all that for a year I have been defying Uncle Sam!' she wrote Della. 'What an unpleasant affair for me. And what would Shoghi Effendi say?

'It seems, thus, that under these circumstances it is useless to try to get permission to stay longer. So, the course in Minneapolis will not occur. These, the two courses in Cleveland, are the last which I will give in the United States, and, truly, writing that, I have tears in my eyes.'

How had things come to this unfortunate and embarrassing state? It seems that oversight and misunderstanding were responsible for the error that had led the United States government to order Lidia Zamenhof to leave the country. Lidia had always answered the officials' questions truthfully and had never tried to conceal the purpose of her trip or the fact that she received money for her classes. Certainly the American Consul in France was to blame for not making the matter clear to Lidia at the beginning. But the crisis probably would never have occurred if, before she had come to America, Mr Holley had obtained the 'Waiver from the Contract Labor Clause' which she had begged him 'not to postpone', or if the officials at the port in New York had caught the mistake when he signed the guarantee for Lidia, or if Della Quinlan had looked into the matter when Ernest Dodge reminded her about it, before Lidia had accepted money for her classes.

Lidia herself did not blame anyone. 'I feel very grateful indeed to the NSA', she wrote, 'for their right understanding of the situation as well as for the efforts still made for me in Washington.'

Now Lidia had to cancel all her plans to teach in other American cities. Sadly, she wrote to Minneapolis to explain why she could not come. But, unknown to her, because of 'lack of funds and the terrible inertia of Minneapolis people', the Minneapolis Esperantists had voted not to invite Lidia after all.

During her year in America Lidia had often been urged by friends to seek US citizenship. Now, one of the immigration officials suggested she go to Canada, or any other country – it did not have to be Poland – and try to come back to the United States on the Polish immigration quota. But Lidia doubted her chances to return to America would be good under the circumstances. She feared she might be on a 'blacklist'.

By now, she had received her answer from Shoghi Effendi. His cable read: 'APPROVE RETURN POLAND. DEEP LOVING APPRECIATION. SHOGHI.'

Although until now Lidia had not been eager to go back to Poland, she was beginning to feel that she had a reason to return home, and that she might have important work to do there. 'It may be rather important for the Cause,' she wrote Della, 'because there are now in the eastern part of Poland several people who are very much interested in the Bahá'í Faith.' One of these was a correspondent of Lidia's, Vasyl Doroshenko, a Ukrainian Esperantist whom Lidia had met at the Warsaw congress in 1937. Through him several of his Ukrainian friends, who did not know Polish, had also become interested. 'One thing is certain,' Lidia wrote, 'a break has been made in the clouds, and the light of the Sun of Baháʼuʼlláh is beginning to penetrate through that opening.'

She wrote Roy Wilhelm, who had suggested she apply for American citizenship, saying that the prospect now seemed 'a very doubtful matter though I would like it, because traveling with a Polish Passport implies many difficulties . . . There is another reason, too, and this is that the situation of the people of my race is more and more difficult in Europe. They are persecuted and chased from Germany, from Italy – and Poland may come next.'

Hoping to find a way Lidia could avoid returning to Poland, Della wrote to the Canadian Esperanto Association to ask them to invite Lidia to Canada. If they declined, Lidia would have no alternative but to return to Poland. Della also met with May Maxwell, who lived in Montreal, to discuss the possibility of Lidia's entering Canada. Mrs Maxwell, Della wrote to Ernest Dodge, had agreed 'to co-operate with us in helping Lidia enter Canada and entertaining her in Montreal . . .'

Everything hinged on the answer of the Canadian Esperanto Association. At last it came: they replied that the matter had so many complications that they had decided not to invite Lidia. It had been more than a year since they had first considered the possibility, they added, so they did not feel that they had come to a hasty conclusion in deciding against inviting her.

They did not know that their decision would ultimately mean for Lidia, although they certainly could not have been unaware that it meant, at the very least, sending her back to a continent on the edge of war.

Although Lidia had expected the worst, the Canadians' answer was a bitter disappointment. That letter 'settles the matter', she wrote Della. 'The Canadians aren't courageous enough,' she told Roan. 'They "see difficulties". Someone in Green Acre said: an optimist is a man who in every difficulty sees a possibility. A pessimist is a man who in every possibility sees difficulties.' It seemed to Lidia that 'our Canadian *samideanoj* belong to the second group'.

Thanking her for her efforts to get Lidia into Canada, Lidia wrote Della, 'I am very glad that you had the great spiritual joy which being with May Maxwell always gives . . . One feels closer to the Master ['Abdu'l-Bahá] when one is with her. And if the constant care of my affairs, often full of difficulties, gave cause for those heavenly moments you experienced, I am all the more pleased.'

On learning the Canadians would not invite her, Lidia cabled the Guardian to ask his permission to go to Haifa. She did not know when she would have another chance to make a pilgrimage, if ever. Even so, she 'strongly anticipated' that the answer would be no. 'First,' she explained, 'now I understand better than I did nine years ago, what it means to go to Haifa, what a privilege it is, that such a privilege is not often received and that certainly one must deserve it, and second – because of the war in Palestine . . . Shoghi Effendi will know best and whatever he decides will be good. Probably I will go straight to Poland. Still, I boldly made that request because it is a chance I may not soon have.'

Dr Charles Witt in Los Angeles had invited Lidia to go to California. She explained why she could not accept his invitation. 'Will I ever return?' she wondered. 'Only All-knowing God knows His own plans . . . And so, in spite of the feeling of unpleasant surprise, I try to serenely accept what has happened.' She would go first to Poland, she decided. Then perhaps to France. 'And perhaps', she added, 'some other plans will develop.'

The National Spiritual Assembly still wanted to try to keep Lidia in the United States, and Horace Holley wrote Lidia that they were trying to work out plans for her to take a teaching trip without conducting paid Esperanto classes. Allen McDaniel contacted Mr Dodge to find out if he could help extend her permit further, but Mr Dodge felt he had exhausted every means available to him in getting the extension of two months.

Then Shoghi Effendi's answer came: 'REGRET DANGEROUS SITUATION IN PALESTINE NECESSITATES POSTPONEMENT OF PILGRIMAGE.' The word 'postponement' gave Lidia hope. Perhaps there would be another time; but when? She booked passage on the *Piłsudski* sailing for Gdynia, Poland, on November 29.

Lidia had reacted first with shock and dismay – and fear – at the prospect of returning to Poland. But after a time she became resigned to the fact, and as she had done before, she placed her fate in the hands of God. In a letter to Roan she wrote of her submission to whatever destiny had in store. 'Isn't it marvelous for a believer to have in every difficulty and disappointment the knowledge and consolation that he (or she) is guided by the Supreme Hand? And so thanks be to God for everything that in His wisdom He sends to me!' It is clear from her letters that it was somewhat of a struggle to come to this attitude. To a Bahá'í Esperantist in Minneapolis Lidia wrote: 'It is a real disappointment for me, very painful, but we must accept serenely what comes, and trust that God guides us on the way that is most right for us.'

Lidia was able to conceal her disappointment and pain from those around her. Dr Charles Simon, who accompanied her to a lawyer's office early in her efforts to extend her visitor's permit, many years later reflected that she did not seem 'particularly preoccupied or disturbed by her failure to have her visa renewed, as I think she was by this time anxious to return to her family in Warsaw.'

There was something, however, that terrified Lidia. 'Tomorrow', she confided to Roan, 'I have an appointment with the dentist, which makes me very scared.'

TWENTY-SEVEN

Fragments

Just when everything seemed settled, a new crisis arose. On October 28 by chance Lidia read in a Cleveland newspaper that under the law passed in Poland earlier in 1938, all Polish citizens abroad who did not have their passports stamped by a Polish Consul would lose their Polish citizenship. The deadline for getting the stamp was October 29 – the next day! There was no Polish Consul in Cleveland, and Della had Lidia's passport in New York.

Lidia wired Della to take her passport to the Polish Consul in New York City, but she was 'in extreme fear' that the stamp would be denied her because she was Jewish. The next morning Lidia received news from her family in Poland that the granting of the stamp was generally 'left to the discretion and good-will of the consular official', but if he refused to give it to her, she would not be allowed to enter Poland.

Della rushed to the Polish Consul, but he seemed unconcerned about any deadline. Afterward Della sent the papers the Consul had given her to Lidia for her signature. Lidia returned them to Della with a letter. 'Perhaps you have read how much difficulty the Polish Jews in Germany have had because of that law', she wrote. Mass deportations of Polish Jews from Germany had begun on October 29, the deadline for obtaining the passport stamp. 'If it should happen to me, here is the situation: I must leave America before the third of December, but I *could* go nowhere, mainly not to Poland . . .

'In the section asking about religion,' she continued, 'I said the following: official confession: Jewish. Faith – Bahá'í. If anyone asks about that, you can easily explain the matter! You remember that I remained a member of the Jewish community with the permission of Shoghi Effendi. And I had to say that, all the more because the Bahá'í Faith is not recognized in Poland. Furthermore, it's a question here not of one's religious conviction, but of race!!!!!! Therefore, this is an important point against my favor.'

But Lidia's fears – in this case – were unfounded. Della took the passport to the Consul, who gave it the required stamp. Lidia would not be denied entry into Poland. But Della wrote afterward: 'O, Roan, when I received the papers from her, with enclosures of pictures that looked as though they had just been taken, my heart bled for her! Such a look on that face! . . . You can imagine how she feels that her own land is not closed to her.'

Thousands of Polish Jews who lived in Germany were not so lucky: they were expelled from Germany and transported to the border in boxcars. But because they had been stripped of their Polish citizenship, they were detained and kept in terrible conditions in a camp at the Polish border town of Zbąszyn. Finally international pressure forced Poland to admit them.

The crisis had brought about a change in Lidia's thinking. 'Truly', she wrote Della, 'a heavy weight fell from my heart and I thanked Bahá'u'lláh that He heard my prayers. Look how the circumstances change our attitude: some time ago I felt great regret because I had to leave America. Now I am *happy* that I *can* go to Poland.'

Lidia had decided to abandon efforts to seek American citizenship. It would require her to reside five years in the United States, and she believed she could never make her living teaching Esperanto in America for so long a time. In spite of the strong advice some of her friends had given her not to go back to Europe, this time her mind was completely made up. 'Certainly', she wrote, 'Europe is not a good place now. But Shoghi Effendi did approve that I return to Poland.' To go to Poland was, she now believed, her destiny.

A few days before, she had received a letter from Roan, who, knowing nothing of Lidia's passport problems, wrote that she had dreamed there were cockroaches and mice in Lidia's house. 'Your dream . . . was not completely untrue,' Lidia wrote to her. 'In the symbolism of dreams, as much as I understand it, those undesirable animals certainly represent something unpleasant, evil about my home.' To Della she further explained: 'undoubtedly the cockroaches and mice in my house symbolize the difficulties of my homeland.'

'Thanks be to Bahá'u'lláh!' she wrote Roan. 'Oh, I prayed so, so much to Him during those days, that He spare me the terrible fate of being expatriated. I know a man in that situation, so I know what it is like. And I had reasons for not being certain of the Consul's decision. The first reason – race!'

But Lidia's problems were still not over. Now she learned that, before she could leave the country, she had to show she had complied with United States income tax laws. The United States government was forcing her to leave the country because she had accepted money for her classes, and now it wanted her to pay tax on that money! She was presented with a 1040–C form and various tax schedules to fill out. The tax for aliens was ten percent with no exemption for a non-resident, who was not supposed to be earning money in any case.

When she opened the letter that contained the imposing official forms, she felt 'truly, a crocodile crawling out of the envelope couldn't have terrified me more than that densely printed sheet with so many sections, specialized terms, etc.' The total amount she had received from her classes was about 630 dollars.

Lidia's difficulties were coming at a time when the world situation was deteriorating in a frightening way, and the fear of war increasingly became a specter that overshadowed ordinary life. This atmosphere of anxiety led to a famous and bizarre event which happened that same week. On the night of October 30, 1938, the American public was seized by mass hysteria when a very realistic, though fictional, radio drama convinced many that New York and New Jersey had been invaded by spaceships from Mars. It was H. G. Wells's *The War of the Worlds*, narrated by Orson Welles. 'People across the country were in panic,' Dr Charles Simon recalled. 'The next evening I was explaining to Lidia Zamenhof the extent to which the public had been demoralized by the broadcast, and although she had not heard the program, she expressed amazement that Americans could become so nervous over a radio program.'

As she often did, Lidia saw a lesson in the incident and later wrote an article about it. She described the radio broadcast which had spread such terror across the country. When it was all over, she observed, 'no Martians had come to Earth to increase the confusion of our unhappy planet'. She contemplated the possibility: what would happen if beings from another planet landed on earth? Wouldn't they be more highly civilized than humans and long ago have risen above the primitive need to make war? And if not, wouldn't the peoples of the earth forget their differences and hatreds and unite to defend all mankind? 'It is strange and painful to think that unparalleled catastrophe is needed to awaken in men the awareness of human unity,' she wrote. 'But if that is the lesson mankind requires, can it escape it?

'Far from us,' she mused, 'the planet named for the god of war shines, a little red light. Let us not fear that planet. The danger that threatens does not come from it.' If Mars himself – not the planet but the war god Mars – were to fall upon the earth, reddening it with blood like the planet itself, Lidia wrote, 'even then, let us not despair. Let us work, endeavor and pray that it will be the last great test, that mankind will never again need another bloody lesson, that it will rise up chastened from the calamity and become what it should be' – one mankind in unity.

News of Lidia's journey to America had reached as far abroad as Johannesburg, South Africa, where an article appeared about her in the *Zionist Record*. 'The latest fashion amongst religion-mongers in

America is the Bahá'í sect,' said the article. 'This movement, which originated some eighty years ago in Persia, appears to be having a great vogue among seekers after new thought . . . I am reliably informed that many Jews are taking an interest in the cult. The most outstanding Jewish supporter is Lidia Zamenhof, daughter of that famous founder of Esperanto, the universal language.

'It is a long way from the Bialystok Jewish eye-specialist, who was a keen Zionist, to the Bahá'í Temple in Chicago. Yet Miss Zamenhof manages to make use of all her father's arguments in favor of a universal language for the purpose of the new "universal religion". Miss Zamenhof is a polished and a charming speaker and large audiences are being carried away by her eloquence.

'The Bahá'í Religion recognizes the Esperanto language,' the article continued, 'and hopes that it may become the universal medium of prayer . . .'

When Lidia saw a copy of the article, she wrote immediately to Roan objecting to an 'extremely incorrect and misleading piece of information in it'. Lidia's concern, her letter showed, was for absolute truthfulness and accuracy even when the matter was somewhat painful to her. 'I am afraid', she wrote, 'that all the readers surely will think that the Bahá'í Faith officially approves Esperanto . . . Can't you explain that the choice of the universal language must be, according to the instructions of Bahá'u'lláh, made by the Universal House of Justice, and that before that body makes the choice, no Bahá'í organization, neither the NSA, nor the Guardian himself, can identify the Bahá'í Faith with Esperanto? You can also say to him that Shoghi Effendi greatly encouraged the Bahá'ís (just as 'Abdu'l-Bahá did) to learn Esperanto considering that it is currently a tool of international understanding, but he cannot give any guarantee that it is the language which will be chosen . . . It is the duty of us Bahá'ís to avoid and try to avoid all inaccurate and misleading information concerning the Faith, even if that inaccuracy suggests something which we like, which we hope for, and of which we *personally* are certain.' The humble Lidia was embarrassed that the reporter had called her 'the most outstanding Jewish supporter' of the Faith. 'Can't he more modestly say "one of the supporters"?' she pleaded.

Roan wrote a letter to the *Zionist Record* explaining the Bahá'í position regarding Esperanto, which was duly published several months later. But some of the Esperantists were angry at her for writing it, not understanding the position of the Bahá'ís and unaware that it had been Lidia's request that the correction be made.

Personally, Lidia was convinced that Esperanto would become recognized universally as the international auxiliary language, and she was disappointed when some Bahá'ís dealt with the matter as if

Esperanto did not exist. Several articles on the topic of universal language had recently appeared in the Bahá'í magazine *World Order*, and Lidia told Della: 'it is certainly interesting to see that the magazine dedicates so much attention to the theme. But, whenever I see someone seriously discussing *which* language to favor, it makes me think of people who are discussing how to open a door that is already open . . .'

Lidia's classes in Cleveland ended on November 11, and on the following Monday she was to take the train to New York City, where she would spend her last two weeks in America. Her students gave her a farewell party at the home of one of the local Esperantists. She was particularly touched when one of them gave her a lovely corsage, to which was attached a card that said, 'You made me very happy!'

Dr Simon was among those at the railway station who saw Lidia off for New York. As she shook hands with them in the Pullman car, he later recalled, she urged them to continue to work for the spread of Esperanto throughout the world, and to be faithful to the ideals of the Esperanto movement.

Now, Lidia's thoughts were on returning to Europe, and she faced the prospect with determination but with the knowledge that the conflagration was not far off. In fact, war was already raging in the world: fascists were fighting republicans in Spain, the Japanese army was attacking China, and Italy had occupied Ethiopia. 'The tiger of war has broken out of its cage', Lidia wrote in an article. And like a tiger, once released, the beast of war could not be expected to respect the laws of civilized society. Lidia offered the scenario: a neutral ship, bombarded by a plane from one of the warring sides; the aviator ignores its identifying markings. 'The offended power energetically protests. The other side makes excuses for itself: fog, a regrettable error, the guilty ones will be punished . . .

'Abyssinia, Spain, China . . . here and elsewhere the victims cry out and bloody fountains spurt. A tiger that breaks out of its cage knows no restraints. The tiger of war also knows no restraints. For it, international laws do not exist, neutrality does not exist. Respect for civilian populations, for the Red Cross, for schools, for temples, does not exist.' Those who thought otherwise, she asserted were 'naive'. 'The tiger of war has no ears to listen, no brain to understand, no heart to feel compassion.' While the diplomats vainly tried to 'teach the tiger good conduct', Lidia urged women to build in their hearts, and the hearts of their children, 'the fortifications of Peace. Fortifications that will not be penetrated by the poison gases of interracial hatred and suspicion, that will not be demolished by the bombs of chauvinist fanaticism . . .'

Events soon showed that Lidia was right; the diplomats could not 'teach the tiger good conduct'. Just as Lidia was leaving Cleveland, news came that a massive pogrom had been unleashed against the Jews of Germany. In 'revenge' for the assassination of a German diplomat by a distraught seventeen-year-old Polish Jew, whose parents were among those whose Polish citizenship was cancelled and who had been expelled from Germany, a wave of 'spontaneous' violence swept over Germany and Austria. Led by Storm Troops at the direction of Josef Goebbels and Reinhard Heydrich, mobs burned Jewish homes, shops and synagogues. In the violence of that *Kristallnacht* or 'Night of Glass', which actually continued for a week, five million marks' worth of plate glass was shattered, seventy-five hundred Jewish businesses were destroyed, and nearly a hundred Jews were murdered. Some thirty thousand Jews were arrested and sent to concentration camps.

This was the Europe to which Lidia was returning.

Roan wanted to travel from Boston to New York to see Lidia off, but Lidia wrote her not to come. 'I must *not* encourage you to that expenditure of money, time and effort, however glad I too would be to see you again', she told her friend. Apparently Roan was also hesitant about going, but for reasons of humility. After receiving Roan's next letter, Lidia wrote: 'Now, I'm grumbling!!! You really have *crazy* motives for not coming to New York, if it is "because you are not worthy to shine my shoes" or something like that!!! (Parenthetically speaking, I shine them myself.) But watch out, Roan, because finally I'll really say: "she is crazy".

'But although I don't agree about the *motives*, I think that it is better for you not to come, as much for the expense of time and money, as for the fact that – and in this I have great experience – the personal separation is much harder than if you stay in Boston. You will not be happy when you see the ship pull away from the shore. I know those matters well. So, it is better for you to stay in Boston, but please remember that the reasons you gave completely differ from mine!'

As the day for her departure drew near, Lidia wrote farewell letters to her friends in America. Surely some of the most painful letters she had to write in those last dark days were letters like this one:

Dear Bahá'í Friend,
I received your kind letter a few days ago and am very grateful indeed for the kind invitation that the friends of Augusta [Georgia] are extending to me. I would be extremely happy to be able to accept it. Unfortunately, it is otherwise. I am compelled to leave America and am sailing for Poland in a week, on November 29th.

We never know what are God's plans for us. Maybe I shall come back one day – if it be His Will. Then, I hope, Mrs Quinlan would inform you and perhaps I could visit Augusta then. Meantime thank

217

you again for your kind letter. May the Blessing of Bahá'u'lláh be always upon the friends of Augusta.

With truest Bahá'í love, yours, Lidia Zamenhof.

Lidia's last days in New York were hectic and filled with meetings. Even before asking Lidia's approval, Della had arranged for her to give a Bahá'í talk in Brooklyn. 'Yes, you are right that I certainly would not refuse to speak,' Lidia had answered. 'That indeed will be the last service, I believe, which I will be able to render in America.' It was, Della wrote Roan, 'a fine meeting. Most of the people there were Esperantists. They were greatly attracted. I need not tell you how she spoke. A man said to me last Thursday night that over and over again he was saying to himself while she was speaking, "eloquent, eloquent". And don't we know it!'

The day before Lidia was to leave America was Thanksgiving. She had been invited to spend the holiday with Mr and Mrs Edward Kinney, and she stayed at their home until eleven that night at a meeting attended by both Esperantists and Bahá'ís. 'That night', Lidia wrote later, 'remained unforgettable in my memory. The whole atmosphere was profoundly penetrating and spiritual. I can still see the gray head of Mr Kinney behind the piano.' Mrs Kinney had mentioned that she knew of someone who might be able to help Lidia stay in America. 'But I thanked her,' Lidia told Roan. 'Shoghi Effendi approved my going to Poland, and I feel that I *must* do that.'

Lidia had made many partings in her life, but this was one of the hardest. Her letters revealed the sadness and melancholy she felt at having to say farewell to her American friends. 'I beg you', she wrote Roan, 'conquer your imagination and don't allow it to look at the departure of the ship if that must weigh on your heart. I absolutely *do not want* your heart to be depressed. Always be cheerful, always be happy!' Lidia admitted that she still owed Roan a few cents for some transaction or other. She joked in a letter: 'Ha, Roan, I really ought to send you the check for fourteen-and-a-half cents . . . But I am afraid that if I do that, I will no longer be able to pay for my ship passage. So I am running off to Europe without paying the debt (people in Europe who don't want to pay their debts run off to America). If you wish, send the police after me.'

She wrote her farewell to the National Spiritual Assembly the day before leaving. 'I feel sad to leave America where I have found so many friends, so many wonderful souls, deeply inspired with this Spirit which is the Destiny of the New Day. I consider it a great privilege to have come to this country and am hoping that what I have learned here will help me to become a little bit better instrument for the Cause of Bahá'u'lláh.'

On November 29 the *Piłsudski* sailed from the Sixth Street Pier in Hoboken, New Jersey. Helene and Martin Leonard were the only ones there to say good-bye to Lidia, Mrs Leonard recalled. Helene Leonard, who was Polish, had been a student in Lidia's first class in New York. Long afterward, she remembered that the day before the ship was to sail, Lidia called to tell her that she was leaving. Mrs Leonard telephoned many Esperantists to try to get a farewell committee together to see her off, but she was unsuccessful. She hoped that some people, at least, would come to the ship, but no one else did. 'So I stayed to the last minute,' she reminisced. 'Needless to say it was a tearful farewell.'

Mrs Leonard advised Lidia not to go back to Europe and invited her to stay at their home in New Jersey. But Lidia refused, saying, 'I have family there and they are frightened.' 'She had faith that she might escape,' Mrs Leonard said later, 'that maybe by some miracle she might be spared.'

The very day the ship sailed, Allen McDaniel, in Washington, tried to contact Lidia. He had been continuing his efforts to get the immigration officials to reopen her case. But her papers had been mislaid in the immigration office and only reached the desk of the official in charge as Lidia's ship was sailing. The official, McDaniel reported, was sympathetic but refused to make any change. However, the immigration official suggested Lidia not go to Poland but to France or even Cuba and apply to return to the US on a six-months' or a year's residence as a lecturer. As a lecturer she would be exempt from the law covering 'alien contract labor' and could receive compensation for her Esperanto classes. But it was too late. Lidia was on her way to Poland, and it is unlikely that she would have changed her mind.

When the *Piłsudski* stopped at Halifax, Nova Scotia, Lidia wrote Roan: 'Thank you, thank you for your love, much greater than I deserve.' She also posted a letter to Della: 'Again I want to thank you – ' she wrote, 'thank you for everything you did for me from the first to the last moment, for all your work, often so full of difficulties.' She asked Della to thank all those who had sent farewell telegrams to the ship, which touched Lidia very much. So far the voyage had been smooth, she told Della, the ocean calm. There were few travelers in the tourist class, and she had the entire cabin to herself. Not many people, it seemed, were eager to travel to Poland during those wintry days of 1938.

One reason for the ship's lack of passengers was probably because many of those who had come to the United States on visitors' visas were remaining there as refugees. After the *Kristallnacht* pogroms, in mid-November President Roosevelt had announced that refugees already in the United States on visitors' visas would not be forced to return to countries where they might face persecution. In spite of widespread anti-alien sentiment in the US at the time, some twenty thousand people were able to take advantage of this temporary relaxation in American immigration policy. But Lidia Zamenhof was not one of them.

While in America, Lidia had written a long essay entitled 'The Ways of God'. She left the typescript of it with Della Quinlan, asking her to translate it into English and submit it to *World Order*. Della apparently never did this, and the piece was never published. The essay was about the meaning of suffering. Clearly, in writing it, Lidia had drawn on her own experiences.

'The usual difficulties and sufferings of our everyday life are increased tenfold today by the circumstances of the unprecedented time in which we live,' Lidia began. 'In this day, the human hearts and minds turn to the Source of all and direct to that eternal Source a despairing question: why such suffering? Why didst Thou, Who art called Good and Compassionate, send pain to us? Why didst Thou fashion creation so that there is a place in it for suffering, Thou Who art called Perfect, Thou Who couldst have created everything in the state of constant and untouchable perfection?'

If it pleased God, she explained, He could have made creation in a state of static perfection. 'But He decided instead that eternal movement, as much physical as spiritual, should rule in the universe, that all should constantly evolve, progress and grow, that forms should decompose so that the liberated elements would fuse into ever new combinations and participate in ever higher realms of creation. In the existing order, man is born a small and weak infant, grows, matures, until he attains the fullness of his earthly destiny . . .

'God could have created man to be perfect from the beginning. But He made a choice which He knew to be better. He gave man potential perfections and endowed him with that attribute which belongs to Himself: free and conscious *will*, through which man raises himself upward on the path of his destiny. Bahá'u'lláh writes: "All that which ye potentially possess can, however, be manifested only as a result of your own volition."

'. . . Shall we claim, then,' Lidia continued, 'that it would have been more perfect if He had created us in the state of imposed perfection, perfection without will, without the tiniest effort, without any merit on our part?'

But why did suffering and pain have to be a part of man's development? 'Through oppositions and deficiencies we learn to judge the value of everything,' she explained. 'Adam Mickiewicz, the great Polish poet, began his *Pan Tadeusz* thus: "Lithuania, my fatherland, a

Lithuanian realizes, as with his health, thy great worth having lost thee." In fact, do we recognize and enjoy the value of health when we are well? Usually respect for health only comes with illness. We realize the value of sight when we are blinded . . . we learn the value of hearing when we can no longer enjoy music and conversation with our fellows. We realize the value of peace when war weighs over our heads. We realize the sweetness of home when ashes cover the home hearth or fate forces us to leave it . . . Even the nearness of our dear ones we usually only learn to value when separation comes.

'In existence arranged as it is, there is a place for pain. That seems incomprehensible to us, unjust; and again we reproach our Creator. But a short reflection is enough to make us aware that often pain is our guardian. It warns us against what is bad. A toothache is certainly unpleasant, but it makes us go to the dentist so he can take care of the sick tooth before it becomes incurable or poisons the entire body. If we put our hand into the fire, we feel the terrible pain of a burn. But that very pain warns us of danger and makes us pull back our hand . . . Yearning is hard to bear, but it makes us return to the object of our love and thus becomes the cause of happiness . . .

'Often we are the cause of our own suffering, but instead of bravely investigating and recognizing that fact, which would lead us to the improvement of our own behavior, we blame others. If we put our hand into fire, we ourselves are guilty for the burn. If we treat others badly, we reap the same feelings and behavior in return, which makes us suffer. If we act against the law, whether it be a law of nature or a judicial or spiritual law, we bring the reaction of that law upon ourselves . . . And the suffering makes us aware of our misdeed, which we otherwise would not have noticed.

'But our misdeeds have an effect not only upon us personally . . . Man is one small cell of a great organism. The functioning of that cell influences the other cells and is influenced by them. The illness of one member causes illness in the entire body and, likewise, that member, even though it be healthy itself, must suffer for the general illness, even if it is brought about by causes completely apart from itself.

'And such a relationship, such suffering because of others, makes us aware that those others are our fellows, our brothers, that we do not have the right to exclaim, like Cain, "Am I my brother's keeper?" and reject our responsibility for them. Because indeed we are our brothers' keepers, just as one cell in the organism is the keeper of another cell.'

For the believer, Lidia felt, suffering had a special function. 'Those who follow the real Truth are faithful to it to the last breath, whatever they may receive on earth in return for their faithfulness – criticism, mockery, hatred, persecution, death. "Trials and tribulations", writes Bahá'u'lláh, "have from time immemorial, been the lot of the chosen

Ones of God and His beloved, and such of His servants as are detached from all else but Him . . . Blessed are the steadfastly enduring, they that are patient under ills and hardships, who lament not over anything that befalls them, and who tread the path of resignation."

"'O my God," Bahá'u'lláh says again, "But for the tribulations which are sustained in Thy path, how could Thy true lovers be recognized . . .? The companions of all who adore Thee are the tears they shed, and the comforters of such as seek Thee are the groans they utter, and the food of them who haste to meet Thee is the fragments of their broken hearts.'"

TWENTY-EIGHT

Now Is Not Their Time

Lidia's voyage across the Atlantic, which had begun smoothly, began to get rougher. For several days the *Piłsudski* was tossed mercilessly by terrible storms. Two days before the ship was to arrive in Poland, Lidia began a letter to Shoghi Effendi. She explained to him what had happened in America and why she had been forced to leave. She told him that, whatever the future might bring, she had confidence she would be guided by Bahá'u'lláh.

Lidia had nearly completed her Polish translation of *Bahá'u'lláh and the New Era*; she asked Shoghi Effendi what to do with it as well as her other translations once the war began. Lidia also told the Guardian that she intended to remain in Poland for only a few weeks, then she would try to leave for France or some other country.

When the ship docked at the Polish port of Gdynia, around the ninth of December, Lidia was so fatigued that she had to take a hotel there for the night, instead of going on by train to Warsaw. When she finally arrived home, she was too weak to get out of bed for two days.

Warsaw seemed strange to Lidia after New York City, and it took her some time to get used to the conditions there again. To her surprise, Lidia found that some Warsaw streets even had new traffic lights, as in America, but they worked only until ten p.m., 'and on Sunday', she wrote a friend, 'they rest'. 'The highest skyscraper in Warsaw, of which the city is so proud, because it has seventeen stories, cannot impress me anymore. In America I was always "short" – here I am "medium height" again. And even the taxis seem somehow Lilliputian.'

Christmas was coming, but to Lidia it seemed 'a spiritually dead time when it is hard to do anything'. She explained to Della: 'Each is thinking only of his own parties, Christmas tree, gifts, etc., so only after the New Year will I begin to travel.' Lidia planned to visit several people in the southwest and southeast of Poland, who had shown some interest in the Bahá'í Faith.

That month, December 1938, *La Praktiko* carried a satirical story Lidia had evidently written while in the United States. It was called '*La suno revenas en Noktolandon*' ('The Sun Returns to Nightland'). In it

Lidia told of a country called Nightland, where the sun had not risen for so long that it had nearly been forgotten. In the absence of the real sun, lamps became very important objects and 'much attention was devoted to them. Special professions even developed, and the men who occupied themselves with lighting were generally called "Illuminationists". They had various ranks. There were High-Lampers, Lampers, Low-Lampers, Lanternists, and Candle-men. Sometimes various Illuminationists warred among themselves because some said to others: "Our lamps are the best, and yours give only soot."'

The story illustrated the Bahá'í principle that divine revelation was renewed from time to time through Manifestations of God who appeared at a time when religion had degenerated to empty forms. Although the story was phrased in allegorical fashion, it was Lidia's plea to the Esperantists to investigate the Bahá'í Faith. 'Dear Reader!' she concluded, 'If in the hour of black night you should hear that the sun has returned, do not turn away from those tidings. Raise yourself up to the heights, to the mountaintops, and look.'

Lidia's plans to remain in Poland a few weeks and then go to France were encountering difficulties. In Lyon, Emile Borel was trying to arrange for Lidia to teach in France; she was waiting to hear if a work contract he had drawn up would be approved by the French Ministry of Labor. Without it, she could not work there. It is not clear if this was a new requirement or if, after her unhappy experience in America, Lidia had become more aware of the need to find out about such regulations beforehand and had warned Mr Borel to make inquiries.

A correspondent in France had written Lidia expressing his opinion of why she had been forced to leave America so suddenly. Lidia answered: 'You say that it is, as it were, because of the rule of the Antichrist that I could not work longer in America. Well, God is stronger than the Antichrist, even when He allows the Antichrist to rule. If I left America, perhaps it was because God preferred that I work in another land. And in God's choice, the deciding factor is not my satisfaction, not my pleasure, not even my security – but the work which I can and must do.' To his objections to America, she answered with her impressions. 'I saw a nation different from the European ones,' she observed. 'A nation not rotting – young, strong, with hope in the future.'

The correspondent had said he thought that America was weakened by overindulgence in dancing and playing games. Lidia responded: 'No . . . play is not a sin, not evil. Man has the right to some pleasure, because he has been created to be happy, not unhappy, because there is a time to cry, but there is also a time to be joyful, and each is joyful in his own way. Furthermore, I don't agree with you that dancing is only play. Surely you know that to the ancient Greeks dance was an art not only lofty but sacred . . . I myself neither dance nor sing (especially the latter, I quite regret) but if only the matter is not taken to extreme, I really and sincerely do not see anything bad in it.'

Christmas trees were beginning to appear in Warsaw. Always thinking about what she saw around her, and finding a greater meaning in the ordinary things of life, Lidia set down her reflections on the season in an essay she called 'Kristnaskaj pripensoj' ('Thoughts on Christmas'). She typed copies of it and sent them to her correspondents. 'The Christmas tree is an old custom,' she wrote. 'Once the tiny candles that light its branches were made of wax. One after another they were lighted by the one who decorated the tree. He had to bend low, hiding among the lowest branches, or climb up to reach the highest ones. He had to push his hand through the branches and sometimes prick his fingers. And sometimes the candles refused to burn and he had to be patient until they caught fire. They did not burn long. Their life was short. They went out, leaving on the branch only a bit of wax in the empty candleholder and some smoke in the air.

'If we remember the words of Bahá'u'lláh, that all men are the leaves of one branch, then the Christmas tree becomes for us a symbol: it represents mankind. The needles are men. The twigs are the peoples. The branches are the nations. The tree is the whole of mankind. The hand that lights the tree is the Hand of God. And the candles with their flaming lights are the Light-bearers of God – his prophets.

'Each of the candles illumines a certain branch, a certain part of the tree. Each of the prophets spoke to a certain human group. Other branches of the human tree are not forgotten, however. Another candle was lighted in their midst, among the darkest branches – another prophet appeared to give light to another group of men, to a group which was at that time farthest from the spiritual light.

'Those prophets never appeared at the same time – one after the other the different candles were lighted; one after another various branches received the light. And when one had already been lighted, another branch was still in darkness. When one still burned, another candle had gone out: the temples were like empty candleholders without light: the light of the Spirit had gone; there remained nothing but the wax of external forms and the smoke of divisions, unrest and hypocrisy.

'But today the Christmas trees are lighted with electric bulbs. One no longer need bend over or climb up. A slight movement of the hand is enough to switch on the great light-giving power of electricity, and all the bulbs shine at the same time. The entire Christmas tree is illumined equally – and it is so today with the tree of mankind. Away with misunderstandings, divisions and hypocrisy; away with fear; let

the light shine forth: this light will not go out. It is the light of
Bahá'u'lláh, which will illumine the whole of mankind and the farthest
corners of the earth, the light which will burn for the whole time-cycle
of human progress on this planet, for a cycle of five hundred thousand
years . . .

'When the Word of God is revealed . . . what power can oppose it?
Whatever opposes it will perish and will come to nothing. Kings,
armies, nations may still oppose the Word of God – kings, armies and
nations will perish. The near future may still be one of opposition and
destruction. But the later, no longer very distant future, will see the
triumph of the Word of God, the glory of the day of God. And that is
why, my dear friends, whatever the near future brings – let us be firm.
The roofs under which we live may fall on our heads – let us yet be
firm. The air we breathe may be changed into poison – let us yet be
firm. And let us be happy and confident that behind the densest clouds
the sun is shining, that the Most Great Peace will come . . .'

In the dark days of the Great War, Ludwik Zamenhof had foreseen
that there would be no peace until the nations of the earth came
together in a world government. In his appeal to the diplomats who
would remake the map of Europe after the war, he had pleaded that
they secure the rights of all the peoples and that they 'abolish for ever
the *chief cause* of wars, the barbarous survival from the most remote
pre-civilized antiquity, *the dominance of one race over other races*'.

His predictions had come true. Now on the eve of another world-
wrenching conflict, his daughter Lidia once again was pleading for
justice, equality and unity among the peoples and the nations. Even
now, as world war was imminent, she was convinced that someday
peace would come. And while most people's attention was fixed on the
hatred and rivalry that divided the nations of the world, Lidia was able
to look ahead to a vision that went beyond even the unification of the
planet.

'There will come a time,' she wrote, 'when our planet will pass out
of its solitude, when the most courageous dreams of the courageous
will become reality and the inhabitants of earth will make contact with
the inhabitants of other planets. Then surely a new prophet will appear
to proclaim to all planets that they are the trees of one forest, the stars of
one heaven. But that is a distant day . . . hidden behind the veil of the
future. Our day is the day of mankind. This is the day of the birth of
mankind through the all-powerful and all-unifying potency of the
Word of God – this is a new Christmas.

'Christmas – the Word of God made flesh once more. The
Christmas tree – mankind – is lighted by the light of the One Who is the
Creator of all light. Shall we not be happy? Shall we not be joyful?'

The year 1939 began as a lonely one for Lidia; letters were not arriving from the United States, and she wondered if her friends in America had forgotten her. Lidia often reminisced about the time she had spent in America – she even dreamed about it. 'In my thoughts I often visit the Bahá'í Center,' she wrote Della, 'and remember it from my first visits there after my arrival to the last, unforgettable and holy night, when truly the Master was with us.' The difficulties Lidia had encountered in America had already begun to recede into forgetfulness; she looked back on her journey now only with fondness and nostalgia. In her letters she never mentioned the troubles and disappointments, only the friendships.

Although she had not heard from her friends in America, she had received a letter from Haifa. Shoghi Effendi's secretary wrote: 'The Guardian . . . is indeed glad to know that you feel quite satisfied over the results you have accomplished during the fourteen months of your stay in America. Although your efforts to obtain a permit for a further prolongation of your visit in the States did not prove successful, you should nevertheless be thankful for the opportunity you have had of undertaking such a long and fruitful journey. He hopes the experiences you have gathered during all these months of uninterrupted teaching will now help you to work more effectively for the spread of the Cause in the various European countries you visit, and particularly in your native country Poland, where the Faith is still practically unknown, and where there is considerable pioneer work still to be done . . .'

In his own hand the Guardian had added a postscript: 'Dear and valued co-worker: I am truly proud of what you have achieved in the States. The believers were delighted and encouraged. I trust the day is not far distant when I will meet you face to face in the Holy Land and assure you in person of my deep appreciation and gratitude. May the Beloved aid you to enrich in Europe the record of your past and notable services. Your true and grateful brother, Shoghi.'

'Those words are so kind,' Lidia wrote Della, 'that I feel simply ashamed! But also very thankful and happy.'

While she was still in America, Lidia had come to feel that she had important work to do in Poland: to raise up believers in Bahá'u'lláh. Years earlier, Martha Root had recognized how difficult it would be for Lidia to be a Bahá'í alone in her homeland. But now the situation was much worse than it was in the 1920s. Europe was on the edge of war; Poland was in a frenzy of anti-Semitism. Nevertheless, at this dark moment, Lidia turned her efforts to seeking out people to whom she could teach the Bahá'í Faith. During that winter, early in 1939, she traveled to several cities in Poland to visit people who were interested in the Faith. Some of those people became Bahá'ís. 'We sow and water,' she wrote, 'but only the rays of the Divine Sun can make the seeds sprout and the flowers develop. I pray that Bahá'u'lláh will lead me to those people who are willing to accept.'

One of the cities Lidia visited during that winter was Kremenets, where she stayed four days, giving four talks on the Bahá'í Faith before the Theosophical Society and Vasyl Doroshenko's group of seven 'seekers'. Mr Doroshenko was a retired teacher and school inspector living in the country near Kremenets, in what had been Ukrainian territory. In that city, he was 'the moving spirit' of a group of 'seekers' associated with the Theosophical group there. 'Figuratively speaking,' he explained, they 'lit their oil lamps and set out in search of the Coming of the Promised One. We study and examine different claims of different movements, and if any of us feels persuaded that he or she found what they have sought, they drop out and join that movement.' Ever since the Esperanto congress in Warsaw he had been corresponding with Lidia. Vasyl Doroshenko had found what he sought in the Bahá'í Faith and had become a believer, the first Ukrainian Bahá'í.

In March, confined in a hospital, Mr Doroshenko sent a penciled note to Anne Lynch at the International Bahá'í Bureau in Geneva. Mrs Lynch was also of Ukrainian descent and often corresponded with him.* 'I bless the Heavenly Father for this illness and for being in the common ward with the other sufferers,' he wrote. 'It is a preparation for another life for me, a fuller one than this . . . Just received a long letter from Lidia Zamenhof – full of encouragement and love, enclosing many prayers by Bahá'u'lláh.'

Lidia had finished the Polish translation of *Bahá'u'lláh and the New Era,* which she had begun in the United States, and now she was typing it on her brother's Polish typewriter, which she had 'confiscated' for the purpose. 'He is kind and allowed that,' she wrote, 'and because he isn't the grumbling type, he isn't grumbling. At least for that, I had to be in Poland!'

It did not look as though Lidia would be able to leave Poland soon. The French government had refused her permission to work in France. 'I'm not complaining or lamenting,' she wrote Della. 'I accept what Bahá'u'lláh decides. Perhaps I will have a chance to do something more in Poland.' She wrote to Shoghi Effendi: would it be possible to visit Haifa in the Spring?

Lidia missed teaching her classes, but she felt that she must devote her efforts, while there was still time, to teaching the Bahá'í Faith and translating scriptures. 'Oh, my unhappy animals are crying in their little valise,' she wrote Roan. 'They also want to come out, stand on a table, be shown, admired, cause laughter . . . They must be silent!

* While it might seem more appropriate to consider Anne Lynch the first Ukrainian Bahá'í, it was Mrs Lynch herself who gave the distinction to Vasyl Doroshenko.

Now is not their time.

In March 1939, the Polish travel companies were announcing special tours to the World's Fair in New York, which was to open in April. 'I will not go there,' Lidia wrote sadly, 'much as I would like to. On the whole, it is difficult to foresee what will happen before then, what state the world will be in.' Hitler had just taken over the rest of Czechoslovakia and was turning his attention toward Poland, demanding the Free City of Danzig and the strip of territory called the 'Polish Corridor'. The Nazis used the same excuse they had used before to justify invasion – claiming that the German minority in Poland was being persecuted and must be rescued.

Lidia finished typing her Polish translation of *Bahá'u'lláh and the New Era* and wrote Shoghi Effendi that it was ready for printing. Although she had hoped to publish it in Warsaw, it now seemed that printing costs would be too high. Mrs Lynch, in Geneva, had suggested it could be printed in France by a company they used for German books. If the books were printed there, they could be stored in Geneva. Lidia agreed; she feared for the safety of stored books in Poland in the days ahead.

But what of her own safety?

Lidia had received word of the death of a friend in France. In a letter of consolation, she expressed her own feelings about death. 'With immense sorrow I received the news of the passing of your dear, unforgettable mother from this world,' she wrote Mrs Faure. 'Personally I believe that . . . the destruction of the human body does not mean the death of the person. This body, composed of atoms, must disintegrate, because everything that is composed must decompose. But the higher part of man, his spirit, does not consist of atoms; it is not a combination of chemical elements and is not subject to the law of decomposition. I believe that our consciousness lives on in ways and conditions which we, still living in the body, cannot imagine, just as the little child in the womb of its mother is incapable of imagining the world it will be coming into and for which it is being prepared. Those thoughts are a great consolation for me, whenever physical death places a barrier between myself and those I love . . . Your mother has gone on to another path. But I deeply believe and trust that you, dear Madame, and all the French Esperantists, will never pause in the work for peace. That work is a noble service to mankind and the most beautiful monument for our beloved ones who have left us.'

Having finished the Polish translation of Esslemont's book, Lidia wrote Shoghi Effendi to ask which book he wished her to translate next. 'I supposed he would ask me to translate into Polish either *Some Answered Questions* or the *Kitáb-i-Íqán*,' she told Roan, 'and I was ready.' As she was waiting for his answer, Lidia felt an overwhelming inclination to translate into Polish *The Hidden Words*, and she began that work. She thought she could complete it before the Guardian's answer arrived, and in fact she was just finishing the final typing when Shoghi Effendi's letter came. 'Do you know what he told me to do?' she wrote Roan excitedly. 'To translate into Polish *The Hidden Words*! You can imagine, I got quite a start when I read that, and I felt very happy seeing that the words of the Guardian confirmed what was in my heart and what I recognized as divine guidance.'

In the same letter, Lidia enclosed a translation she had made of a passage from *The Dawn-Breakers*. At the time, Roan was working on her translation of that book into Esperanto. The passage Lidia had sent, the Báb's farewell address to His disciples, the Letters of the Living, arrived just as Roan needed to translate those very pages in the book. Lidia's translation of the Báb's address was published in the United States in 1944 as a leaflet.

Although some mail from abroad still did not get through to Lidia in Warsaw, she had heard from Agnes Alexander, who had returned to Hawaii, May Maxwell and Roan Orloff. In spite of Lidia's own difficult situation, she was concerned for her friends' welfare, even though they were all safe in America – glad to hear that Mr Kinney was better; worried that Della, who had been laid off her job, had not yet found another position; concerned that Roan was working too hard. Roan wrote Lidia that she would be teaching an Esperanto course at Green Acre in the summer. 'If you are in Ole Bull,' Lidia replied impishly, 'watch out that my spirit, crawling out from under the stairs or behind the window, doesn't frighten you suddenly.'

Lidia knew now that she would not leave Poland before 'the great Catastrophe'. And she knew that the Catastrophe was close at hand; war seemed ready to break out at any moment. Yet always the concern she expressed in her letters and her articles was not for her own safety, but for the consequences of the coming war for all of humanity.

In April 1939 she wrote Roan: 'The great Catastrophe seems extremely close, and here, where I am, thunder is inevitable. We are all in the hands of God. If it doesn't happen (which I don't believe) till autumn, perhaps I will try to arrange some course trips in Poland. But conditions are such that I doubt it will be possible.' She had begun teaching Esperanto courses in Warsaw. Conditions being what they were, she was happy that there were still people who wanted to learn Esperanto. 'What I will do after the summer vacation I still don't know,' she wrote Roan in May. Lidia's perception of the time Poland had left was quite accurate: until the end of summer.

Meanwhile, Joseph Dubin in Philadelphia was trying to get Lidia back into the United States through a university, and offered to collect money at the Esperanto Association of North America's Congress for her passage. Lidia felt his plans were unrealistic, and while she told him she would be glad to return to the United States, it would have to be as a salaried teacher; she could not risk going without a fixed plan for her income. She asked Mr Dubin not to collect money on her behalf at the congress. She did not want people to think it was her idea, or that she was asking for money, even to get out of Poland.

Now, there were three Bahá'ís in Poland: Lidia, Vasyl Doroshenko the Ukrainian, and a woman named Bianka Haas of German Jewish background who lived in Bielsko. This tiny community of believers demonstrated the practical utility of Esperanto: Mr Doroshenko's native language was Ukrainian, Lidia's was Polish, Mrs Haas spoke German and Yiddish. They could communicate among themselves only in Esperanto.

Lidia continued her efforts to tell people about the Bahá'í Faith. 'It is very difficult to interest the people here,' she wrote Roan. 'Some are completely unwilling to listen, others are willing to listen – and go off.' However, in Warsaw she had found three new people she hoped would someday 'accept the light of this great Faith'.

She wrote Roan that she had a lot of free time and wanted to use it in the service of Bahá'u'lláh. 'Now everyone here is taking special courses such as saving poison-gas victims in case of war, and I even thought of joining that course as well. But it would take too much time, because afterward one must take examinations, and study for them. I decided that there are enough people to specialize in those services, and very, very few in my land to serve the Bahá'í Faith.' She had begun to translate *Some Answered Questions* into Polish, using the typewriter that belonged to her brother, 'who is very good and kind and puts it at my disposal'. Her own Esperanto typewriter did not have the proper characters for the Polish language.

One day, on the way home from giving a talk on the Cseh method at the Esperanto Club, Lidia fell and injured her knee badly. It became painfully swollen and would not bend, so she had to cancel her Esperanto classes for several days and rest. 'But', she wrote Roan, 'one can translate very well lying down, and during those days I translated ten pages a day.'

She knew that her translation of *Some Answered Questions* would not be published soon, but she hoped it would be published sometime. She could not wait for that 'sometime' to come, so she was laboriously typing the text with six carbon copies. 'When I have enough typed copies', she wrote, 'they can serve those who are interested.'

While others in Warsaw were preparing for the war, Lidia quietly went on with the work she considered far more important. 'This morning I knew I would have a free afternoon, and I prayed Bahá'u'lláh would guide me how to spend it in a way somehow useful to His Cause,' she wrote Roan. 'At the beginning I wanted to visit an ill Esperantist with whom I had left a Bahá'í book, but when I telephoned, I learned that she was not well enough to receive my visit. Afterward I thought of going to see a lady I know, to whom I have already spoken of the Faith, but strangely I did not feel inclined to do that, so I gave up the idea.'

A letter had arrived from an Esperantist in Portugal with whom Lidia had been corresponding. 'Instead of going to see anyone, I felt a strong inclination to reply to her immediately, and I spent more than two hours at my typewriter writing a long letter to her – about the Faith. The rest I place in the hands of Bahá'u'lláh . . . Last week I made two new contacts for the Faith. Several people have become interested. One must "sow and sow", even if "a hundred seeds are lost, a thousand seeds are lost."'

Summer came to Warsaw, and Lidia's Esperanto classes were almost over. After the classes ended, she wrote Roan, 'I will be more free to go and see people. And I find also that the post is a very useful institution and helps the spiritual work in this Era very much.'

Lidia was quite touched to receive a cable from the Esperanto Congress in New York. It 'really made me very delighted because I did not suppose that the American *samideanoj* would remember me so,' she wrote modestly.

In July Lidia wrote Roan that there was a new Bahá'í in Poland, a woman in Bielsko whom Lidia had met during a visit to Mrs Haas. Lidia further told Roan of an Esperantist in Warsaw with whom Lidia walked in the park every Saturday and who had recently admitted to Lidia that she was beginning to believe in God. Lidia reported joyfully to Roan that at their last meeting, this woman had expressed her belief '"that Bahá'u'lláh is the latest Messenger of God". She is still not completely convinced,' wrote Lidia, 'but she seems very inclined to accept.'

A few weeks later, Lidia again wrote to Roan with happy news. 'I think I wrote you about an Esperantist in Warsaw with whom I spend time every Saturday and talk about the Faith. Yesterday she said to me, when I mentioned that I hoped to write soon to Shoghi Effendi: "Tell him that there is a new Bahá'í in Warsaw." But I said, "I would like you to write that to him yourself," and she did so. So now, counting the writer of this letter, there are in Poland five people who believe in the Bahá'í Revelation. Very few indeed, and because of that every new soul is such an important addition and a cause for joy.'

'One can never count very certainly on the post, especially

overseas,' Lidia told her friend, 'but I still trust that this letter will reach you in time, that means while you are still at Green Acre. I want it to carry to you in that beloved spot, blessed once by the presence of the Master, my dearest greetings and thoughts full of memories.

'I am astonished sometimes how quickly time passes. We were just together in Green Acre working together for the course, rehearsing the scene in the pageant for the last day, in Boston visiting the radio station and the hairdresser,' where she had a permanent wave. 'Not even a trace of his work remains.'

Lidia was hopeful that she could go to the Netherlands in October to teach classes for several months. It seems that the people at the Cseh Institute were trying to arrange this for her, but by mid-August Lidia had not yet received a permit to work there. In September she planned to go to the Polish Esperanto Congress in Lvov. 'They have already printed in thick letters on the congress program that I will give a speech!' She had finished translating *Some Answered Questions* into Polish, 'and instead of resting', she told Roan, 'I immediately began the *Kitáb-i-Íqán*.' She asked her friend to give her regards to those she had met last year. It was the last letter Roan ever received from Lidia.

August had come, and with it, as every year, the Universal Congress of Esperanto, which was to be held this fateful summer of 1939 in Bern, Switzerland. Lidia, unable to leave Poland, could not attend. The congress president, who had also presided at the Ninth Congress in Bern in 1913, noted in his speech that the 1913 congress had been the last one Dr Ludwik Zamenhof had ever attended, because the next year war had broken out. The 1939 congress in Bern would be the last until the end of the Second World War, because within weeks the Catastrophe came to Europe at last.

TWENTY-NINE

A Wave of Evil

On September 1, 1939, after SS troops in Polish uniforms staged a fake attack on a German radio station, the armies of the Third Reich invaded Poland, drawing Europe, and eventually the world, into a second global war. The besieged city of Warsaw held out for three weeks. When the bombardment was over, the civilian areas, especially the Jewish quarter, had suffered worst – the Germans had directed their fire especially at that part of the city. For the second time in her life, Lidia saw German troops march into Warsaw. The first time had been in 1915 when she was eleven. But in 1915 the German army had wanted to gain the support of the populace against Russia. This time they marched in to make the populace slaves.

Once again, Poland ceased to exist as an independent nation and was divided up, Germany incorporating a large part of territory into the Reich, and the Soviet Union seizing nearly half of the country in the early days of the war. The part of Poland that included Warsaw was designated the General-Government and was ruled by a German official.

Now, under the Nazis, as in the Middle Ages, Jews had to be distinguished from the rest of the population at all times. In Warsaw this meant having to wear a white arm band with a blue Star of David. Jewish businesses were confiscated, schools closed. Rations were cut. And the Nazis began to isolate the Jews of Warsaw from the rest of the population. First, the Jewish quarter was set apart as a quarantine area by fences and barbed wire.

The occupying German army roamed the city, subjecting Jews to the casual violence that Jews in Germany had learned to fear. Soon the Jewish quarter was full of refugees from other Polish cities and provinces, but the refugees found no safety in Warsaw. The Jews never knew what kind of terror they might meet when they stepped out of their door – whether they would be seized for forced labor, robbed by Polish ruffians, or killed by German soldiers for no reason at all.

After the invasion, news of Lidia's whereabouts came rarely and unreliably to her friends in Europe and America. In early November, several Jewish newspapers in the US reported that Lidia Zamenhof and

234

all of the family had been arrested on the charge that Lidia had gone to the United States to spread anti-Nazi propaganda. The same report appeared in the *Polish Daily News*. Lidia's friends in America were shocked to learn of her arrest. 'The American Bahá'ís . . .' Horace Holley wrote Shoghi Effendi, 'are deeply concerned about her fate in Warsaw, although we know that the purity and firmness of her faith in God raises her spirit above the darkness of human cruelty . . .

'We realize how much her fate is bound up with anti-Jewish and anti-international elements in certain nations, and we can only pray that she be protected by the divine power.'

Immediately, the Bahá'ís and the Esperantists in America and Europe tried to act to help her in the way they thought would be best. 'We and the Esperantists as well have a heavy responsibility to do everything we can,' Horace Holley wrote Allen McDaniel. Mr Holley intended to 'convey to the Nazis our formal denial of the truth of the charges and possibly also we should try and bring pressure through the German Embassy.' He and the others sadly overestimated their ability to 'bring pressure' on the Nazis by formal protests. Nevertheless, Mr McDaniel contacted Ernest Dodge to try to make use of Mr Dodge's contacts in the US State Department. Once again, the Bahá'ís and the Esperantists found themselves having to cooperate because of Lidia – this time to try to save her life. But Mr Dodge wisely pointed out that 'even to *write* to her now to express the grief and sympathy of Esperantists or Bahá'ís might work to her disadvantage; since it is precisely her prominence as an exponent of both Esperanto and Bahá'í principles which has caused those in control to hate and persecute her.'

Their efforts to exert influence through diplomatic channels failed. When contacted by the Bahá'ís, the First Secretary of the Polish Embassy pleaded helplessness and recommended sending a strong protest to Berlin. US State Department officials said they would take no official action as Lidia was not an American citizen. Unofficially they told Allen McDaniel they were willing to do what they could to offer advice in order to secure her release.

Mr McDaniel presented the case to the Swedish Legation in Washington, and the Counselor of the Legation agreed to transmit to Stockholm the Esperanto Association's and the National Spiritual Assembly's protests, along with evidence 'emphasizing the absence of any anti-Nazi propaganda during her stay in the US'. However, Mr McDaniel and perhaps even Mr Dodge did not realize that sending, as they intended, a packet of 'programs and newspaper publicity . . . which will indicate that the activities were confined largely to lecturing, conducting classes and other activities relating to the spread of Esperanto among the people of the United States and Canada' could only make things worse for Lidia if such material got into the hands of the Gestapo. Engaging in Esperanto activities had already been determined to be acting against the State in Germany. All the Gestapo chief in Warsaw needed would be a copy of one of the American newspaper articles mocking Adolf Hitler, such as the one that had appeared in the *Philadelphia Record* – if he did not already have a complete file.

The Swedish Foreign Office sent word that it was unable to take any steps in Lidia's favor, as the German government was not allowing Sweden to carry out the task of looking after the interests of Polish citizens in Germany, with which the Polish government had entrusted it.

Concern for the Zamenhofs grew when letters sent to 41 Królewska Street were returned with a stamp from the Warsaw Post Office saying that the family was no longer at that address, new address unknown. Rumors immediately began to circulate. It was reported that Lidia had been sent to a concentration camp in Germany. Then, in early 1940 it was announced that Lidia was living in France, and her friends breathed a sigh of relief.

But weeks passed, and no word came from France. Lidia was not there; the rumor was false. Its source was traced to a woman in southern France who had claimed to have received permission from the French government for Lidia to visit her – but this was all.

In February 1940 a cryptic letter from Lithuania reached officials at the Universal Esperanto Association in Geneva: 'My cousins about whom you asked are ill, in a very bad situation and I absolutely cannot at this moment give you their address because their former house is destroyed. If the parcel which came to your address might be useful to them, send it to one of their relatives, for example to Mrs Feliks Zamenhof . . .'

In March more news came from Stephen Zamenhof, Lidia's cousin. He was in New York; he had gone to the World's Fair and was there when the war broke out. From his brother Mieczyslaw, who was now in Russia, he had learned that the whole family had been arrested immediately after the occupation of Warsaw. No one was allowed to see them.

Although Esperanto had been forbidden in Germany for three years, and in Austria since the *Anschluss*, the SS and the Gestapo had continued to consider the movement a threat to the Reich. An eleven-page internal report in 1940 was said to show 'detailed knowledge' of Dr Zamenhof and his philosophy of Homaranismo. After the war, SS-Colonel Josef Meissinger, head of the Security Police in Warsaw, admitted he had received special orders from Berlin, probably from Reinhard Heydrich himself, directing him to imprison the Zamenhofs.

Adam was the first to be arrested. The Germans seized him at the Jewish Hospital, where he was Chief of Ophthalmology and had become Director of the Hospital after its previous director fled. On the same day, Adam's wife Wanda and sister Zofia were also arrested at the hospital. Henryk Minc, Wanda's brother-in-law, and Lidia were arrested at the Minc home. Henryk Minc was taken, it was believed, instead of Adam's son Ludwik, because the boy was ill and it was feared he might have typhus.

At last, through the International Red Cross, a message from Lidia got through to Mabelle Davis in Detroit. It was: 'All the family in prison. Our house burned.' During the bombardment of Warsaw, on September 25, an incendiary bomb had hit their house. Everything was destroyed: all their possessions, but most of all, the little shrine that was Ludwik Zamenhof's study – the great Esperanto library, the manuscripts and letters, the old typewriter on its oak table, the little broken paperweight in the shape of a dog.

According to Adam Zamenhof's son Ludwik, Lidia and Zofia were released after several months in the Pawiak Prison. But word that they had been freed did not reach abroad until March 1940. And there was no word about the fate of Adam in the Danilowiczowska Prison. A short postcard in German (as was required now) got through to the Isbrückers in the Netherlands. It revealed that Lidia and Zofia were living in Ogrodowa Street, in the Jewish quarter. The postcard said only: 'Dear Friends, Thanks for your card. How we are you probably know. Wanda and Ludwik live at 6–3 Foch [the Minc home], but we have no news of Adam. Heartfelt greetings from Zofia and Lidia.'

Now it was Hans Jakob, director of the old Universal Esperanto Association in Geneva, who was able to make contact with the Zamenhofs and to approach the head of the *Judenrat* (Jewish Council), the governing body of the Warsaw Ghetto, to offer help. The rival International Esperanto League, with its headquarters in England, now at war with Germany, could do nothing to intervene. The UEA planned to send food parcels to the Zamenhofs and hoped that Joseph Dubin in Philadelphia might secure a teaching position in America – and with it a visa – for Lidia. A fund was established to help the Zamenhof family if any of them were able to leave Poland. Some of the food parcels got through, but the efforts to get Lidia a visa failed.

One of those who was able to send food regularly to Lidia and her family was Mrs Gigi Harabagiu in Bucharest, Romania. She obtained permission from the Romanian government to send monthly parcels to the Zamenhofs in Poland, and in return she received postcards in German from them thanking her for the packages. Usually Mrs Harabagiu sent one kilogram each of sugar, fat, flour, dried fruit and sausage. Once she was puzzled when Lidia wrote her not to send bread anymore. Knowing that the parcels might take a long time to arrive, Mrs Harabagiu had never sent bread. Apparently a customs official had stolen the sausage in the parcel, replacing it with a kilogram of bread.

In May an inquiry reached Adam Czerniakow, head of Warsaw's Jewish Council, from 'the Esperanto Union' asking if the Esperantists could transmit money to the Zamenhof family. He noted again in his diary for May 8 that Esperantists from Geneva were offering to help the Zamenhofs. Czerniakow 'instructed Sztolcman [a member of the Jewish Council] to discuss this matter with Messing [a German official] in the *Districtchef*'s office,' but did not mention the matter again.

The two organizations, the UEA and the IEL, had difficulty coordinating their efforts to help the family. 'The schism in our movement', *Esperanto* commented bitterly, 'thus extends also to this area.' It begged the Esperantists not to let the division 'play its evil role' in this matter and hinder efforts to help the Zamenhof family. 'It is the sacred duty of the Esperantists to cooperate . . . Do not let the family of the Majstro perish!'

It was too late. Dr Adam Zamenhof had already been killed. At the end of January he was shot, along with a hundred other intellectuals and professional people who had been arrested and were being held as hostages. But it was not until July 30, 1940 that Adam Czerniakow noted in his diary: 'at the SS I was informed that Dr Zamenhof, his brothers-in-law, and Minc are dead.'* And only on 18 August did he note that his office was 'besieged' by the families of the dead hostages, 'who have just been notified' and were 'demanding further information; among others Mrs Zamenhof and Mrs Minc'. Nevertheless, Adam's family kept hoping that somehow he might still be alive.

On November 16, 1940 a section of the Jewish quarter was sealed off from the rest of Warsaw by walls and walled-up streets and windows. There, in the Warsaw Ghetto, within an area of about one hundred square city blocks, half a million people would be imprisoned, including Warsaw's Jews as well as refugees and deportees from elsewhere in Poland and some from other parts of Europe. After the sealing of the Ghetto, only those with special permits could pass the guards. Even doctors who worked in the Jewish Hospital, outside the Ghetto boundaries, had difficulty getting permits. During the days of the sealing of the Ghetto, over two hundred thousand people – Poles living inside the Ghetto boundaries, and Jews living outside them – were forced to leave their homes and belongings, and move.

Ogrodowa Street, where Lidia and Zofia were living with relatives,

---

* Adam's son later noted this was an error on Czerniakow's part. Dr Minc was Adam's brother-in-law.

was within the area that had been designated for the Ghetto. But Królewska Street was outside the walls, closed off to them forever. It did not matter anymore; nothing remained there but rubble.

Now, Lidia was unable to send her friends abroad more than a postcard written in German. Because of censorship, she could not give any details of the wretched conditions under which they were living. But several secret diaries that have survived, written by courageous Jews in order to record the grim events for posterity, give us a vivid picture of life in the Warsaw Ghetto. Historian Emmanuel Ringelblum, the archivist of the Warsaw Ghetto, recorded the day the Ghetto was sealed. 'The Saturday the Ghetto was introduced was terrible,' he wrote. 'People in the street didn't know it was to be a closed Ghetto, so it came like a thunderbolt. Details of German, Polish and Jewish guards stood at every street corner searching passers-by to decide whether or not they had the right to pass. Jewish women found the markets outside the Ghetto closed to them. There was an immediate shortage of bread and other produce. There's been a real orgy of high prices ever since. There are long queues in front of every food store, and everything is being bought up. Many items have suddenly disappeared from the shops . . . On the first day after the Ghetto was closed, many Christians brought bread for their Jewish acquaintances and friends . . .

'. . . Those who are slow to take their hats off to Germans are forced to do calisthenics using paving stones or tiles as weights. Elderly Jews, too, are ordered to do push-ups. They tear paper up small, scatter the pieces in the mud, and order people to pick them up, beating them as they stoop over. In the Polish quarter Jews are ordered to lie on the ground and [the Germans] walk over them . . . A wave of evil rolled over the whole city, as if in response to a nod from above.'

Because the Nazis erroneously considered the Jews a race, all those who had even one Jewish grandparent were treated as Jews, regardless of the religion they professed. Consequently, among those herded into the Ghetto to share the fate of the Jews were thousands of people who were actually Christians – and at least one Bahá'í, Lidia Zamenhof.

In the days before the sealing of the Ghetto, a Polish Esperantist of Italian ancestry named Józef Arszenik went to see Lidia. Mr Arszenik, a railway worker and a zealous Esperantist since 1925, apparently was one of the people to whom Lidia had been teaching the Bahá'í Faith. He bravely offered to hide Lidia in his home on the outskirts of Warsaw.

Ever since Lidia had returned to Poland in late 1938, all she had feared had come true, and events were turning out even worse than she could have imagined – the firebombing of her house, the brutal Nazi invasion, confinement under impossible conditions in the Ghetto. Until now, all her friends' efforts to get her out of Poland to safety had come to naught. When Józef Arszenik went to Lidia in those dark days of November 1940 to offer her a hiding place, she must have realized it might well be her last chance to escape.

But Lidia Zamenhof refused. After the war, Mr Arszenik wrote Ernfrid Malmgren, a prominent Swedish Esperantist: 'That noble woman refused my offer to save her, saying that I with my family could lose our lives, because whoever hides a Jew perishes along with the Jew who is discovered.' Indeed, this was true. Mr Arszenik was taking a great chance: any Pole caught concealing a Jew was subject to instant execution.

To Anne Lynch in Geneva, Mr Arszenik wrote that Lidia's last words to him were: 'Do not think of putting yourself in danger; I know that I must die, but I feel it my duty to stay with my people. God grant that out of our sufferings a better world may emerge. I believe in God. I am a Bahá'í and will die a Bahá'í. Everything is in His hands.'

After the war, Józef Arszenik became a Bahá'í. He died in 1978 at the age of eighty.

Accounts of another attempt to help Lidia escape are remembered by several German Bahá'ís, including Mrs Ursula Mühlschlegel, who heard the story from her husband Dr Adelbert Mühlschlegel, and Mrs Anna Grossmann and her son Dr Hartmut Grossmann, who learned of it from Dr Hermann Grossmann and from Mrs Karla Macco, a Bahá'í from Heidelberg. But in this case, Lidia's would-be rescuer was a German soldier named Fritz Macco.

Unlike the elite SS, the German Wehrmacht drafted men regardless of their moral views. To resist conscription meant death. Thus it happened that individual German citizens whose personal views were contrary to everything the Nazis stood for found themselves part of the German war machine, including some Esperantists and Bahá'ís.

After the Nazi occupation of the Netherlands, an Esperantist checking on the condition of the Esperanto House in Arnhem had been astonished to find on the locked door a piece of paper with a message, evidently placed there by a German soldier. It was in Esperanto and read: 'The house is deserted. A visitor cannot go in. Will the "mighty call" no longer "go through the world"? Take courage, soon another time shall come! Long live Esperanto! – A German Esperantist.'

In the late 1930s as it became clear that war was inevitable, the German Bahá'ís who were of draft age saw the dilemma that was approaching. As Bahá'ís, they were bound to obey their government; yet also as Bahá'ís, they did not want to fight. It was clear that the German army would tolerate no conscientious objection to bearing arms. According to Hartmut Grossmann, a letter was written to Shoghi Effendi on behalf of several young Bahá'ís, who were worried about what to do. The Guardian reportedly replied to the effect that if their desire not to take life were sincere, God would assist them to attain it. The young men went into the army, but all of them died during the first week of the war except for one, twenty-four-year-old Fritz Macco. 'He did not understand why he was spared,' Dr Hartmut Grossmann recalled. Fritz's letters to his mother were full of self-doubt: why had he alone survived? Had he done something wrong? Was he not sincere enough? One of the boys who had been killed was his brother.

As an ambulance driver in the German army, Fritz Macco was sent to Warsaw. It seems that fortunately he was able to get noncombatant duty. According to the Grossmanns and Mrs Mühlschlegel, Fritz Macco was able to find Lidia and visit her, possibly twice, to bring food and to try to persuade her to escape. Hartmut Grossmann was told by Fritz's mother, Karla Macco, that the young soldier had come to believe that he had been spared for just this: 'that this was his special task, to get in contact with Lidia . . .' But, he said, she refused to escape and said she 'wanted to stay with her people'. Fritz Macco survived until 1944, when he was able to intervene with the Gestapo on behalf of his mother, who had been imprisoned for her Bahá'í activities. His efforts kept her from being sent to a concentration camp. But in September 1944, Fritz Macco was killed on an island in the Vistula River, in Poland, presumably by Russian troops who overran northeastern Poland during the Red Army's summer offensives.

It seems that no one is still alive who heard this remarkable story from Fritz Macco himself. But the fact that a number of people knew the story of the German soldier's attempt to save Lidia Zamenhof, and have provided independent versions, is enough to make it worth recording.* Unless more information comes to light, it is not possible to know the full story. As Hartmut Grossmann has said, 'What really happened, we don't know.'

* However, Adam's son Ludwik, who was in close contact with Lidia until August 1942, never heard anything about the episode.

THIRTY

It Will Not Be Forgotten

The inhabitants of the Warsaw Ghetto knew that their only hope lay in an early victory by England. But as time dragged on and Allied liberators did not come, the situation in the Ghetto became worse. The Nazis intended to starve the Jews, and allowed them smaller food rations than they gave the Poles. In fact, the small amount of bread, potatoes and fat each person was permitted did not provide enough nourishment; but with food smuggled from the other side, the inmates of the Ghetto managed to cling to life. The penalty for smuggling was death; but, every day, people of all ages risked their lives to crawl through a hole in the wall or a sewer to bring back a loaf of bread. Many smugglers were children, for they were agile and could get through small openings in the wall. They were also more likely to inspire pity if caught by the police. As the Germans cut rations further, smuggling became virtually the only source of food in the Ghetto, and the cost of food rose drastically. Many people, especially the refugees, could no longer afford to eat. Charity soup kitchens could not feed all those who were hungry, and people began to starve.

'You see mobs of children in rags begging in the street nowadays,' recorded Emmanuel Ringelblum in early 1941. 'Walking down Leszno Street every few steps you come across people lying at the street corner, frozen, begging.' At a funeral for a number of small children from an orphanage, he had recounted earlier, the other children from the home placed a wreath on the monument inscribed: 'To the Children Who Have Died From Hunger From the Children Who Are Hungry.'

Since the occupation, people had been seized in increasing numbers for forced labor. The news from the work camps was becoming more and more alarming, as reports of the death of camp inmates reached the Ghetto. In his secret diary, Emmanuel Ringelblum recorded a heart-rending scene: one day, Jewish forced-laborers returning to the Ghetto were getting out of the wagon when their Christian watchman ordered them to sing. One among them, who was a cantor by profession, stood on the auto and began to sing. The street became filled with people listening to him. He was chanting in Hebrew a prayer from the memorial service, 'God, Full of Compassion'.

54. *On board the Piłsudski at the Sixth Street Pier, Hoboken, New Jersey, awaiting departure for Poland*

55. *Fritz Macco in* Wehrmacht *uniform. At extreme right, Karla Macco. Third from right: Dr Hermann Grossmann*

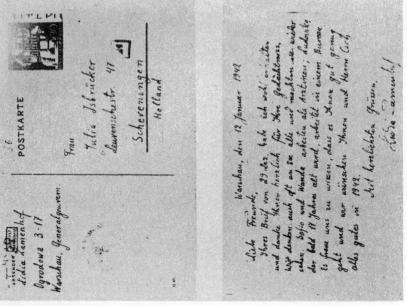

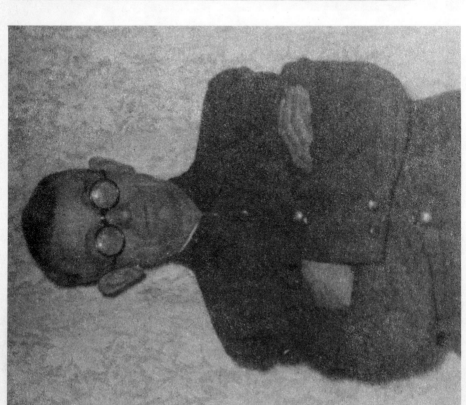

Warschau, den 19 Januar 1942

Liebe Freunde,
Ihres Brief vom 29.dez. habe ich wohl erhalten
und danke Ihnen herzlich für Ihre Gedaktnisse.
Wir denken auch oft an sie alle und machten wie weiter
sehen, Sofie und Wanda arbeiten als Artistinen; Dudonka
der bald 11 Jahres alt wird, arbeitet in einem Bureau.
Es freue uns zu wissen, dass es Anxe gut genug
geht und wir wünschen Ihnen und Herrn Cseh
alles gutes im 1942.
Mit herzlichste Grüssen,
Aneta Samuels

57. 'We wish you and Mr Cseh all good in 1942.'
Lidia's last postcard to the Isbrückers. In the upper
left corner it bears the stamp of the Warsaw Ghetto's
Judenrat (Jewish Council)

It had become clear to the people in the Ghetto that if the war did not end soon, they would all starve to death. 'The number of the dead in Warsaw is growing from day to day,' wrote Emmanuel Ringelblum in March 1941. 'In the house I lived in, a father, mother and son all died from hunger in the course of one day.' By April not even ration cards could get bread or potatoes. People were dying in the streets. Professional people like the Zamenhofs were in the worst situation. 'The professionals', Ringelblum wrote, 'are in desperate straits. By now everything they had has been lost or sold; their bodies are swelling from hunger.' In July: 'Ten houses are empty in 7 Wolynska Street. All the residents have died out. In general, this death of entire families in the course of one or two days is a very common occurrence.'

'Why are they all so quiet? Why does the father die, and the mother, and each of the children, without a single protest? Why haven't we done the things we threatened the world with a year ago? . . . There are a great many possible answers . . .' he wrote. 'One is that the [German] occupation forces have so terrorized the Jewish populace that people are afraid to raise their heads. The fear that mass reprisals would be the reply to any outbreak from the hungry masses has forced the more sensitive elements into a passivity designed not to provoke any commotion in the Ghetto.'

The Esperantists continued to send food parcels to the Zamenhofs, but not everything they sent reached them. In June 1941 Lidia got word to Hans Jakob in Geneva that she had received two parcels from Porto, Portugal, and one from Göteborg, Sweden. 'I thank you from my heart for your trouble,' she wrote. But in July she wrote to the Isbrückers in the Netherlands: 'Please forgive my long silence. I received your card and am happy to know you are well. However, I could not receive what you wanted to send me . . . I wish all good for you. About us I can tell you nothing new. About Adam there is no news at all. A long time ago I received a card from Ponti [Dick Ponti, in the Netherlands] but could not respond. Please give him my greetings . . .'

Her postcard could tell very little outwardly, for it had to pass the censor. She could not tell her friends that not all the mail reached the inmates of the Ghetto and that parcels were often confiscated. Nor could she reveal what she might have had to do without in order to send them a postcard: one had to bribe the postmen to send or receive mail, especially parcels. Perhaps she could not afford the price that was being demanded for the package they had tried to send.

The Zamenhof name had come to the attention of the Nazi authorities again. In February 1941 Zamenhof Street in Warsaw was changed back to Dzika.*

* It was changed back again to Zamenhof after the war.

243

Lidia's friends in America had not forgotten her, but their efforts were not enough to save her. The National Spiritual Assembly's letters of protest had had no effect; in 1941 the National Spiritual Assembly reported that American Bahá'ís had 'volunteered to finance the cost of transportation of Lidia Zamenhof and to guarantee her support in this country; but despite efforts put forth through every available official channel, Miss Zamenhof's whereabouts and condition are not accurately known nor has it yet been found possible to arrange for her travel to America through the authorities in charge of her country . . .'

The area of the Warsaw Ghetto was decreased, yet more and more refugees poured in. Now a tremendous number of people were crowded into the old buildings of the Ghetto, and the threat of disease grew. With it came another, more terrible threat. Rumors began to spread that the Jews, whom the Nazis blamed for the spread of typhus, were to be removed from Warsaw altogether.

'Next to hunger,' Emmanuel Ringelblum wrote, 'typhus . . . has become the burning question of the hour . . . The doctors calculate that every fifth Jew will be sick with typhus in the winter. Consequently, persistent rumors have spread about the possible resettlement of the Jews from Warsaw. This is said to be considered one possible way of removing the peril of typhus.' To some, resettlement in a camp, no matter how hard the conditions there, seemed infinitely preferable to another solution: 'The Pomiechowek affair, in which 800 people were exterminated because they were sick, caused the Jewish populace of the Ghetto to tremble,' Emmanuel Ringelblum wrote, 'because it demonstrates what can be expected to happen here if the attempt to arrest the spread of disease inside the Ghetto should fail.'

By November the first frosts had appeared and the people in the Ghetto were 'trembling at the prospect of cold weather. The most fearful sight is that of freezing children. Little children with bare feet, bare knees, and torn clothing, stand dumbly in the street, weeping.' That winter the Jews of the General-Government were ordered to surrender their fur coats to the Germans. Although the decree was 'a severe blow to the poorer people, who sometimes had nothing but an old tattered fur coat to wear,' some burned their coats rather than give them to the Nazis.

On January 12, 1942 Lidia managed to send a postcard to the Isbrückers in Holland. She thanked them for a letter and for their remembrance. 'We think often of you and would like to see you again. Zofia and Wanda work as doctors. Ludwik, who will be seventeen, works in an office. We are happy to know you are well and we wish you and Mr Cseh all good in 1942 . . .' Lidia called her sister and nephew 'Sofio' and 'Ludoviko', the Esperanto forms of their names.

This was something she had never dared to do before. In her postcard, Lidia said nothing of what work she herself was doing – teaching English. At first, under the occupation, schools and courses had been severely curtailed. Later with permission, some vocational courses were allowed. Other schools and classes existed secretly, at the *gymnazium* or even university level. But teaching English was unlikely to be sanctioned by the Germans – it was the language of the enemy. Nevertheless, many people in the Ghetto were eager to learn English. It gave them hope. 'Everyone is assiduously studying English,' Emmanuel Ringelblum recorded in his diary, 'in preparation for emigration after the war.'

The Spring of 1942 brought the terror of deportation. Word reached the inhabitants of the Warsaw Ghetto that other Jewish Ghettos in Poland were being liquidated. Thousands of people – at first the young and the old, but later everyone, regardless of age or ability to work – were sealed in freight trains and told they were being resettled in work camps in the east. But by now many knew that one did not go to a camp to work, but to die. 'Resettlement to the east' was the Nazis' euphemism for annihilation. Some people, swollen and apathetic from hunger, welcomed death, for it would bring the end of suffering. When the Germans offered rations of bread and marmalade to those who would volunteer for 'resettlement', this drew such large numbers that some days they exceeded their quota.

In July 1942 the dreaded order came to Warsaw. All the Jews of the Warsaw Ghetto were to be deported 'to the east'. Their destination was a camp called Treblinka. Adam Czerniakow, head of the Jewish Council, was told by the SS to provide a quota of five thousand people per day. The SS demanded that the quota be raised to seven thousand, and soon to ten thousand per day. He finally realized that the Nazis intended nothing less than the total extermination of Warsaw's Jews, and he committed suicide.

At the Umschlagplatz or 'trading place', the people were herded by the thousands into freight trains, as many as 150 people to a boxcar. When the day's quota was not met, people were seized randomly on the street. Neighborhoods were cordoned-off and all the inhabitants taken to the trains. Many thousands were killed outright during the operation: those not expected to survive the journey were simply shot. The Umschlagplatz was a nightmare. Yet, 'for believing Jews the conviction that their sacrifice was required as a testimony to Almighty God was more comforting than the supposition that He had abandoned them altogether,' Lucy Dawidowicz writes in *The War Against the Jews*. 'Morale was sustained by rabbis and pious Jews who, by their own resolute and exalted stance, provided a model of how

Jews should encounter death. On the Umschlagplatz that August an elderly pious Jew exhorted the despondent masses, sunk in the misery and squalor of their surroundings: "Jews, don't despair! Don't you realize we are going to meet the Messiah?"'

In August 1942 the Zamenhofs were taken to the Umschlagplatz. But, in doctor's smocks, Wanda and her sister Janina Minc escaped with Wanda's son, Ludwik. Changing their name to Zaleski, Adam's wife and son were able to survive outside the Ghetto until the war's end.

But Lidia's sister Zofia went deliberately on one of those grim trains, Adam's son Ludwik later recalled. She was 'convinced', he wrote, 'the deported people would need medical help she would provide them with. Lidia followed her several months later.' The train took them 120 kilometers from Warsaw to Treblinka.

In April 1943 the physical liquidation of the Warsaw Ghetto began, but the Nazis met armed resistance from a courageous band of young Jewish men and women. Although they were vastly outnumbered, the Warsaw Ghetto Fighters held off the well-equipped SS troops during April and May amid the rubble. At last they were overcome, but scattered remnants of the fighting organization persisted, in the tunnels and sewers of the Ghetto, until the end of the war. One of the last of those shot amid the ruins was historian Emmanuel Ringelblum, along with his wife and twelve-year-old son.

Near the hamlet of Treblinka, there was a small slave-labor camp with mostly Polish inmates, but by the summer of 1942 a new and different kind of camp had been constructed a few kilometers away in an area of woodland and sandy hills. It was not a concentration camp where some inmates survived as slave laborers, but an extermination camp where all went to their deaths.

The death camp Treblinka covered only about fifty acres and was surrounded by antitank barriers and barbed wire, with watch towers at each corner. In the lower camp were the sorting square and the living quarters for the SS and Ukrainian guards and the 'work-Jews' who sorted the goods seized from the victims. At the northeast end of the lower camp was a separate barbed wire enclosure. It contained a gray-white masonry building with at first three, then ten additional airtight chambers, connected to a room where a diesel engine generated lethal carbon monoxide fumes. The gas was piped into the chambers through false shower heads. Beyond the gas chambers were the burial pits, where the bodies of the dead were disposed of, originally by lime, later by burning on large iron racks. When the Nazis became worried that the mass grave might be discovered, the bodies that had been buried during the early days of the camp's operation were exhumed and burned.

In the countryside around Treblinka that summer, the villagers saw the crowded transports arrive from Warsaw. One of those who took special note was Franciszek Ząbecki, the traffic superintendent of the Treblinka railway station. He observed the entire operation of the death camp and passed reports on to the underground Polish Home Army, of which he was a member.

When the trains approached the station, he saw that the Lithuanian guards sitting on the roofs of the freight cars were holding guns. 'They looked as if they had killed; as if they had had their hands in blood and then washed before arriving,' he later told Gitta Sereny, author of *Into That Darkness*. 'The train was very full – incredibly full it seemed. It was a hot day but, bewildering to us, the difference in temperature between inside the cars and out was obviously such that a kind of fog came out and surrounded the train . . .'

Some Polish peasants from the village – and even some German railway workers – pitying the Jews who cried out to them, brought water to the trains, 'until', Mr Ząbecki recalled, 'the Germans began to shoot to keep them away . . .' Pity soon turned into 'sharp fear' that anyone who saw what was going on at Treblinka would be killed.

The quiet, pleasant pine woods had been transformed into a place of horror. The reek of death and the smoke of the ever-burning fires in the camp lay heavy over the district. The 'dark foggy clouds that hung over us, that covered the sky in that hot and beautiful summer, even on the most brilliant days,' Mr Ząbecki recalled, created 'an almost sulphuric darkness bringing with it this pestilential smell'. The constant hammering sound of the mechanical ditch-digger that excavated the burial pits reverberated through the countryside for miles, day and night. Escapees oriented themselves in the woods at night by its infernal, steady sound.

When the trains arrived at the camp, the people were brutally driven from the cars. Men and women were separated and sent to the undressing barracks. There they were ordered to strip, even of artificial limbs and eye-glasses, and told to turn in valuables at the window. Women and girls had their heads shaved; their hair was shipped to a factory in Germany to be used in upholstery.

Then, whipped along mercilessly by Ukrainian guards, the people were forced to run through a narrow corridor about a hundred meters long, with high barbed wire fences on either side. At the end of this corridor, which the SS guards jocularly called the *Himmelstrasse*, the 'Road to Heaven', the people, pushed by those in back, climbed little wooden stairs to enter the gray-white building. Inside, the chambers looked like those of a public bath, with white tiles halfway up the walls, sloping floors, and what appeared to be ordinary shower heads. But there were no drains, and the doorway was oddly narrow, so that the people could only pass through one by one.

Under the whip of an SS guard, they were crowded into the chambers, hundreds of people, pressed tightly together. The doors closed.

Franciszek Ząbecki counted the transports that came to his station, first from Warsaw, then from other Polish cities and nine other countries. By his calculations, 1,200,000 Jews died at Treblinka. Although in 1943 the SS demolished the camp and tried to obliterate the signs of what had been done there, it will never be forgotten. Among the ashes in the ground at Treblinka are those of Lidia Zamenhof.

EPILOGUE

Out of the Abyss

The fourteenth of April had always been a solemn day for the Esperantists as they gathered at the Jewish cemetery on Okopowa Street in Warsaw to mark the anniversary of the death of Ludwik Zamenhof. In 1946 that day came with ineffable sorrow. Miraculously, the Jewish cemetery had not been destroyed in the war. Like a symbol, the weathered granite monument on Zamenhof's tomb still stood; it had escaped the incendiary bombs and the liquidation of the Ghetto. The rest of the Jewish quarter was a vast, silent stretch of rubble.

How often, on other anniversaries of this date, the Esperantists had lamented the Majstro's death as premature. Now they called it a blessing that he had not lived through the Great War to see another world war even more devastating in its effect, to see the depths of savagery to which hatred between the races could goad human beings, to see the brutal murder of his own children. Had he lived, they realized, he himself might well have died in a Nazi gas chamber.

This year there were so many more to mourn. No longer would the oratory of Leo Belmont ring out through the April air, assuring the solemn gathering of *samideanoj* that Ludwik Zamenhof's legacy would triumph; Leo Belmont had died in 1941. Thousands of Jewish Esperantists had been murdered in Germany and the occupied countries; many other non-Jewish Esperantists had fallen in battle or been killed as subversives. Émile and Marie Borel's son Guy had been arrested by the Gestapo as a resistance fighter and died in 1944 during transport to Dachau concentration camp.

In the years after the war, the Esperanto movement rose out of the ashes of Europe, phoenix-like, as it had done before, but the war had dealt it a terrible blow.

After the war the neutral movement became reunited, the two estranged organizations, the UEA and IEL, merging under the name of the Universal Esperanto Association, which in 1954 achieved consultative status with UNESCO. The language problem continued to plague the new United Nations, which found itself burdened with large expenses for translation and a growing list of official and working languages. Yet efforts to encourage the United Nations to consider the matter of an international language, or to persuade it of the value of Esperanto, met a fate similar to that of earlier efforts at the League of Nations. A declaration bearing almost a million signatures, presented by UEA to UNESCO, resulted in a resolution recognizing the common ideals of Esperanto and UNESCO, but a second proposal submitted to the United Nations in the mid-1960s, with signatures of almost one million individuals from seventy-four countries as well as four thousand organizations representing almost seventy-three million members, never moved beyond the Secretariat.

The center of the Esperanto movement remained in Europe, but the movement continues to be tolerated in countries with opposite political orientations. In the United States, however, during the 'cold war' era, the secretary of the Esperanto Association of North America viewed the spread of Esperanto in communist countries with alarm and began a campaign of attacks against the UEA and the Esperanto League for North America (ELNA), which had been formed of EANA members dissatisfied with his leadership. Just as the EANA was about to be expelled from the UEA in 1956, it resigned from membership. It has since been superseded as the official Esperanto organization by ELNA, which is affiliated with the UEA. Elsewhere in the world, the Esperanto movement's significant membership in Japan and a recent upsurge of interest in the language in China – with the scheduling of the Seventy-First Universal Congress of Esperanto in 1986 in Shanghai – hold interest and promise for the future.

Incredibly, the world that emerged from the rubble of the Second World War still had not learned its deadly lesson. Many walls had fallen, but the walls between the divided peoples still stood strong. And with the ending of the war came a fresh terror: nuclear warfare. Even as humanity still stood 'soul-shaken, before the extent of the catastrophe,' *Heroldo* noted in its first edition after the war, on April, 14, 1946, 'an even more extensive calamity . . . threatens if the ways and means are not found to save our culture from full destruction in a third world war . . . The invention of the atom bomb stands over our planet like a dire warning . . .' Ten years earlier, Lidia had written of the terrible 'Concert' which the musician Death offered mankind after its 'Prelude', World War I. Mankind had stayed for the Concert, and had. paid a high price. Now, that same specter offers us another performance – a true 'Finale'.

Because Lidia, Adam and Zofia Zamenhof had disappeared without a trace, some still hoped, against all odds, that they might have survived and might someday return with the dazed, starving prisoners who had been liberated from concentration camps by Allied troops. Hope for

58. 'Those who follow the real Truth are faithful to it to the last breath, whatever they may receive on earth in return . . .'

59. *All that was left of the house on Dzika Street in 1945*

60. *'Let the memory of them last forever'*

Lidia was kindled when, at the beginning of 1946, Czechoslovakian radio repeatedly announced that she was still alive 'somewhere in Russia'.

But at last a modest plaque was set in place on Klara Zamenhof's grave with the names of Lidia and Zofia. It read: 'Murdered in the year 1942. Let the memory of them last forever.' Wanda Zamenhof never gave up hope for her husband Adam. She died in a traffic accident in Warsaw in 1954. Ludwik became an engineer and lives in France. Today no Zamenhofs live in Poland.

Other Bahá'ís had shared Lidia's fate. Those German and Austrian Bahá'ís whom the Nazis had labeled as Jewish, including most of the Bahá'ís of Vienna, were deported to the death camps never to be seen again. Of the little pre-war community of Bahá'ís in Poland no one seems to have survived. After eastern Poland was invaded by the Soviet Union early in the war, communication was cut off and no word was ever heard again from the ailing Ukrainian Bahá'í, Vasyl Doroshenko. Nothing is known of the fate of Bianka Haas; Bielsko saw brutal 'blitzpogroms' in the first days of the Nazi occupation.

Lidia's Esperanto and Polish translations, to which she had given so much effort and love, continued to work on, long after their translator's death. Before the outbreak of war, she had sent some of her manuscripts, including her Polish translation of *Bahá'u'lláh and the New Era*, to Geneva. On instructions from Shoghi Effendi, Mrs Lynch made an appeal for funds to the American Bahá'ís to publish it, but the money collected was not enough. Nevertheless, at Shoghi Effendi's direction, arrangements were made with a printer in France, just across the border from Geneva. The outbreak of war played havoc with the rate of exchange, and when the funds that had been collected were converted into French francs they amply covered the cost of the printing.

Mrs Lynch's Polish-born nephew was in an internment camp with his Polish army unit near Bern. At Mrs Lynch's request, Swiss military authorities allowed him to do the proofreading and indexing of the book. Parts of the manuscript and galley proofs made their way between Geneva, the internment camp and the printer in France, until in the winter of 1940 a thousand copies of the printed book were delivered to the International Bahá'í Bureau. Mrs Lynch distributed copies to seventy-three Polish internment camps in Switzerland. 'Touching letters of gratitude were received,' she wrote, 'but also a few with adverse criticism, from Polish army chaplains.'

After the war, Mrs Lynch mimeographed Lidia's Esperanto translations of *The Goal of a New World Order* and *The Unfoldment of World Civilization* by Shoghi Effendi, as well as twenty chapters of *Some Answered Questions*, and began to use them 'as a further means of teaching for countries where no Bahá'í literature existed, mainly those of Eastern Europe'.

In September 1947 the bulletin of the International Bahá'í Bureau reported 'lively interest in the Bahá'í Teachings is developing in Poland. Every week we receive new requests for Bahá'í literature', and in November *Bahá'í News* reported: 'There are nine people in Poland who are studying the Bahá'í Faith through correspondence; all but one are using Esperanto. One of these is he who offered to hide Lidia Zamenhof in his home . . .' – Józef Arszenik.

By October 1950 there were Bahá'ís in seven cities of Poland, but communication with them was 'no longer possible'. Mrs Lynch wrote that 'Almost all the Bahá'ís of Poland were attracted and confirmed in the Faith through the means of these teaching efforts in Esperanto'.

Lidia Zamenhof had been only thirty-eight when she died. Her death had stunned her friends, even those in Europe who had seen much of death. 'Oh, our poor, dear Lidia!' Father Cseh wrote to Roan Orloff. 'According to information received she had a terrible death. How will God ever punish the guilty ones? Their crime truly exceeds every heretofore known measure.' Martha Root had not lived to learn of the death of her 'spiritual daughter'. She died of cancer in Honolulu on September 28, 1939.

The National Spiritual Assembly of the United States and Canada wrote to Shoghi Effendi suggesting that a nationwide memorial service be held in honor of Lidia. Shoghi Effendi cabled back: 'HEARTILY APPROVE NATION-WIDE OBSERVANCE FOR DAUNTLESS LIDIA ZAMENHOF. HER NOTABLE SERVICES, TENACITY, MODESTY AND UNWAVERING DEVOTION FULLY MERIT HIGH TRIBUTE FROM AMERICAN BELIEVERS.' The memorial services were held the week of October 25, 1946.

The National Assembly had asked the Guardian if Lidia should be considered a Bahá'í martyr, like the thousands of Iranian Bahá'ís killed by the Muslims for their Faith. Shoghi Effendi replied, 'Do not advise . . . that you designate her a martyr.' Those who killed Lidia had not known she was a Bahá'í. They had killed her because of her 'race'. But Lidia Zamenhof had died, as she had lived, for what she believed. She might have avoided returning to Poland, but had gone because she felt it was her duty. She might have allowed others to hide her, but had refused to allow them to endanger themselves.

In April 1946 on behalf of Shoghi Effendi, his wife Amatu'l-Bahá Ruhíyyih Khánum (serving as his secretary) wrote to Roan Orloff asking her to write an obituary notice 'on our dear Bahá'í sister' for volume 10 of *The Bahá'í World*. 'She certainly deserves to be remembered by us all for her services to the Faith and her loyalty and devotion!' Ruḥíyyih Khánum wrote. 'Her death is a great loss, as she was so well able to serve and teach in different languages and different countries. It seems too terrible to contemplate what her end must have been!'

Shoghi Effendi's words: 'her notable services, tenacity, modesty and unwavering devotion . . .' well summarized the qualities that distinguished the life of Lidia Zamenhof. In a letter to the Bahá'ís of Persia in 1923 the Guardian had once written: 'How often the beloved Master was heard to say: Should each one of the friends take upon himself to carry out, in all its integrity and implications, only one of the teachings of the Faith, with devotion, detachment, constancy and perseverance and exemplify it in all his deeds and pursuits of life, the world would become another world and the face of the earth would mirror forth the splendors of the Abhá Paradise.' He might have been talking about Lidia Zamenhof.

Lidia had always sought the hidden significance in the ordinary, the meaning in what seemed meaningless – the blessing that was concealed in tragedy, the strengthening lesson in hardship, the providence in calamity. She believed that death was not really an ending, but a beginning; thus, the purpose of life was, in essence, to prepare for that moment. She believed that it did not matter what test one faced; it mattered only how one faced the test. The struggle was all.

Like the language to which she devoted her life, the message of her life was one of hope, of hope and faith – that one person can make a difference; that through the peaceful efforts of many, giving their 'widow's mite' to the cause of peace, the peoples of the earth would come together in brotherhood and would speak to each other in one universal language. That no matter what terrors and destruction the immediate future might hold, 'the later, no longer very distant future will see the triumph of the Word of God, the glory of the day of God . . . Let us be happy and confident,' she had said, 'that behind the densest clouds the sun is shining, that the Most Great Peace will come.' Faith, she had learned, might be only a gossamer thread, but it could triumph over all the forces of darkness. For, like the tiny spider on the threshold of the Shrine, 'whoever can still find in his heart a single ray of faith, as delicate and tiny as a spider's thread, will not perish in the abyss, but even if all the powers of this world rise to struggle against him to push him down, even in the fall itself he will stop, and by this ray, as by the biblical ladder, even out of the abyss will ascend to heaven.'

A Note on Sources

The following is offered as a general guide to the major sources that provided information for this biography. Those seeking an extensive, annotated bibliography of the international language movement in general, and Esperanto in particular, should consult Humphrey Tonkin's *Esperanto and International Language Problems: A Research Bibliography*, Washington, DC, 1977. An essential, comprehensive work about the Esperanto movement (in Esperanto) is *Esperanto en perspektivo* (London and Rotterdam, 1974), but readers of English will find much information in Peter Forster's *The Esperanto Movement* (The Hague, 1982).

Several archival collections contributed significant material for this book. Material from the International Auxiliary Language Committee Records, Julia Culver Correspondence, Della Quinlan Correspondence and Martha L. Root Papers, in the National Bahá'í Archives, Wilmette, Illinois, provided insight into the relationship of Lidia Zamenhof and Martha Root as well as details of Lidia's trip to the United States. Other material on various subjects was found in the National Bahá'í Archives of Switzerland; letters of Lidia Zamenhof to Shoghi Effendi in the International Bahá'í Archives, Haifa, Israel; those to Agnes Alexander, in the National Bahá'í Archives of Japan. Another group of Lidia's letters as well as some letters of Zofia Zamenhof are located in the International Esperanto Museum, Vienna; most of Lidia's letters in this collection have been published in facsimile in *Lidja Zamenhof: Vivo kaj agado* by Isaj Dratwer (Antwerp/La Laguna, 1980).

Personal letters, reminiscences and interviews given me by dozens of people who had known Lidia Zamenhof, and who are mentioned by name in the preface, covered their acquaintance with her over various periods in her lifetime. Many details of Lidia's childhood and later life were gleaned from her own articles and reminiscences published in *Heroldo de Esperanto, Ligilo por Vidantoj, Pola Esperantisto, L'Esperantiste Sisteronnais, Le Phare de l'Esperanto/ Lumturo de Esperanto* and *World Order*. Accounts in the Esperanto press, particularly *The British Esperantist, Heroldo de Esperanto, Esperanto, Pola Esperantisto*, and *Literatura Mondo* provided much information about the Esperanto congresses and various other events mentioned in the text, as well as contemporary attitudes and commentary on issues of the time. Local newspapers including *Der Bund* (Bern), *Berner Tagblatt, The Scotsman* (Edinburgh), *The Oxford Mail, Le Tribune de Genève, Le Petit Havre* and *Le Progrès de Lyon* provided another perspective of the congresses, interviews and sometimes even the weather.

Information about Bahá'í Esperantist activities including the meetings at the Esperanto congresses was found in *La Nova Tago, Sonne der Wahrheit, Bahá'í Nachrichten, The Bahá'í Magazine/Star of the West* and volumes of the series *The Bahá'í World*.

Details about Lidia's Cseh courses and lectures in Sweden, France and America were found in journals such as: *Svenska Esperanto-Tidningen, La Praktiko, Entre Nous* (Perpignan), *Normanda Esperanto Bulteno, Franca Esperantisto, Ĝis Mil* (Lyon), *Nia Gazeto* (Nice), *Amerika Esperantisto, Esperanto Internacia, Heroldo de Esperanto* and *Bahá'í News*, as well as in Dr André Védrine's book, *L'Esperanto et le mouvement espérantiste à Lyon des origines à 1950* (Lyon, 1983).

Sources for the life of Ludwik Zamenhof and the history of the Esperanto movement, as well as some details about Lidia herself, include the following:

Boulton, Marjorie. *Zamenhof, Creator of Esperanto*. London, 1960.
Courtinat, Leon. *Historio de Esperanto (movado kaj literaturo)*. 3 vols. Bellerive-sur-Allier, 1964–65.
Dratwer, Isaj. *Pri internacia lingvo dum jarcentoj*. Wembley, 1970.
— *Lidja Zamenhof: Vivo kaj agado*, Antwerp/La Laguna, 1980.
Forster, Peter G. *The Esperanto Movement*. The Hague, 1982.
Garis, Mabel. *Martha Root: Lioness at the Threshold*. Wilmette, Ill., 1983.
[Harris, Isidore]. 'Esperanto and Jewish Ideals.' *The Jewish Chronicle* (London), September 6, 1907.
Holzhaus, Adolf. *Doktoro kaj lingvo Esperanto*. Helsinki, 1969.
Lapenna, Ivo; Lins, Ulrich; and Carlevaro, Tazio. *Esperanto en perspektivo*. London and Rotterdam, 1974.
La lastaj tagoj de doktoro L. L. Zamenhof kaj la funebra ceremonio. Cologne, 1921.
Maimon, N. Z. *La kaŝita vivo de Zamenhof: originalaj studoj*. Tokyo, 1978.
Privat, Edmond. *Vivo de Zamenhof*. Rickmansworth, 1920.
— *Life of Zamenhof*. London, 1931.
—*Historio de la lingvo Esperanto*. 2 vols. Leipzig, 1923–27.
— *Aventuroj de pioniro*. La Laguna, 1963.
Waringhien, Gaston. *Lingvo kaj vivo*. La Laguna, 1959.
Wiesenfeld, Edvardo. *Galerio de Zamenhofoj*. Horrem/Cologne, 1925.
Zamenhof, L. L. *Leteroj de L. L. Zamenhof*. 2 vols. Ed. Gaston Waringhien. Paris, 1948.
— *Originala verkaro*. Ed. J. Dietterle. Leipzig, 1929.
— *Zamenhof Leteroj*. Ed. Adolf Holzhaus. Helsinki, 1975.

Among the many published sources consulted concerning the historical period covered in the book, the following provided specific details:

Ainsztein, Ruben. *The Warsaw Ghetto Revolt*. New York, 1979.
Der Bahá'í-Glaube in Deutschland: Ein Rüchblick. [Langenhain], 1980.
Churchill, Sir Winston S. *The Gathering Storm*, London, 1948.
Czerniakow, Adam. *The Warsaw Diary of Adam Czerniakow*. Eds. Raul Hilberg, Joseph Kermish and Stanislaw Staron. New York, 1979.
Dawidowicz, Lucy S. *The War Against the Jews: 1933–1945*. New York, 1975.
Dobroszycki, Lucjan, and Kirschenblatt-Gimblett, Barbara. *Image Before My*

Eyes: A Photographic History of Jewish Life in Poland, 1864–1939. New York, 1977.

Donat, Alexander, ed. *The Death Camp Treblinka: A Documentary.* New York, 1979.

Heller, Celia S. *On the Edge of Destruction: Jews of Poland Between the Two Wars.* New York, 1977.

Ringelblum, Emmanuel. *Notes from the Warsaw Ghetto.* Ed. and trans. Jacob Sloan. New York, 1958.

Sereny, Gitta. *Into that Darkness: An Examination of Conscience.* London, 1974.

Sharp, Samuel. *Poland: White Eagle on a Red Field.* Cambridge, Mass., 1953.

Shirer, William L. *The Rise and Fall of the Third Reich: a History of Nazi Germany.* New York, 1959.

Silver, Daniel J., and Martin, Bernard. *A History of Judaism.* 2 vols. New York, 1974.

Wyman, David S. *Paper Walls: America and the Refugee Crisis 1938–1941.* Massachusetts, 1968.

Index

'Adbu'l-Bahá, 36–7, 72, 86, 87, 155; ref. to
    Esperanto, 38–9
Afnan, Ruhi, 158
'After the Great War – Appeal to the Diplomats', 44
Alexander II, Tsar, 9
Alexander III, Tsar, 12
Alexander, Agnes, 38, 39, 83–4, 98, 172, 230
Alpert, Carl, 202
Amicale, 105
Anschluss of Austria, 183
Anti-Semitism, 5–6, 8–9, 18, 49–50, 52–3, 90,
    109–10, 132, 133, 158–9, 183, 194, 209, 212–13,
    217, 227
Antwerp, 77
aparato, 89
'*La araneo*', 95
Arnhem, 88, 108
Arszenik, Józef, 239–40, 252

Báb, the, 86, 87, 199–200, 230
Bad Nauheim, 22
Baghy, Julio, 58, 99
Bahá'í Faith, 65–6; Esperanto and, 36–9, 71, 97,
    134–35, 153–56; principle of universal language,
    37, 66, 154, 215–6; suppressed in Germany,
    153–4
Bahá'í National Convention, 186
Bahá'u'lláh, 36, 66, 86–7, 220–1; ref. to
    international language, 37
Bahá'u'lláh and the New Era, 81, 93, 95, 223, 228,
    229, 251
Baker, Dorothy, 190–2, 199
Baker, Frank, 190
Bakker, Hans, 130
Bakker-Smith, Mies, 108, 130
Baronnet, Felicien, 113
Bastien, Louis, 131, 141
Batory, M.S., 160, 162
Baxter, Evelyn, 90
Bedikian, Victoria, 114, 178
Beecher, Luella, 190, 193
Behrendt, Arnold, 74, 82–3, 110–11
Belmont, Leo, 2, 55, 249
Bergen-op-Zoom, 108
Bern, 33–40
Bialystok, 4–5, 21, 99, 159
Bielsko, 231, 232, 251
'*Birdo en kaĝo!*', 80

Bolles, Jeanne, 188
Borel, Emile, 105–7, 124, 126, 224, 249
Borel, Guy, 249
Borel, Marie, 105–7, 124, 125, 158, 249
Bordeaux, 114
Boston, 202–3
Boulogne, 13–14, 133
Boulton, Marjorie, 24, 26, 36
Bowditch, Nancy, 199
Budapest, 82
Budapest School, 58
Bujwid, Odo, 69, 95–6
Butin, Max, 91

Canadian Esperanto Association, 209
Cau, Georges, 113
Châteauroux, 113
China, 39, 63, 250
Christaller, Paul, 83, 90, 102
Cleveland, 203–5
Collins, Amelia, 198–9
Cologne, 108
Cooper, Ella, 66, 70
Couturat, Louis, 23–4
Cseh, Andrei, 88, 92, 96, 102, 252
Cseh method, 88–9
Culver, Julia, 81
Czechoslovakia, 194, 203
Czerniakow, Adam, 238, 245

Danilowiczowska Prison, 237
Danzig, 73–4
Davis, Mabelle, 181, 237
Davis, Robert, 181, 182
Dawidowicz, Lucy, 109, 245
Dawn-Breakers, The, 199, 230
de Beaufront, Louis, 20, 23–4
Dehan, Pierre, 125
Delafouilhouze, Paule Reynaud, 138
Delcourt, Marcel, 152
Delegation for the Choice of an International
    Language, 23
Detroit, 181–9 *passim*
Dodge, Ernest, 146, 157–8, 167–8, 176–7, 201, 207,
    210, 235
Doroshenko, Vasyl, 209, 228, 228n, 231, 251
Dratwer, Isaj, 60
Dubin, Joseph, 172, 174, 230, 237

257